MYUNG-JI KANG

A Legal Study on AI Inventorship Under Patent Law in Germany and the United States

Studien zum vergleichenden Privatrecht

Studies in Comparative Private Law

Band / Volume 33

A Legal Study on AI Inventorship Under Patent Law in Germany and the United States

Von

Myung-Ji Kang

Duncker & Humblot · Berlin

Die Juristische Fakultät der Georg-August-Universität Göttingen hat diese Arbeit im Jahre 2024 als Dissertation angenommen.

Bibliografische Information der Deutschen Nationalbibliothek

Die Deutsche Nationalbibliothek verzeichnet diese Publikation in der Deutschen Nationalbibliografie; detaillierte bibliografische Daten sind im Internet über http://dnb.d-nb.de abrufbar.

Satz: L101 Mediengestaltung, Fürstenwalde
Druck: Prime Rate Zrt., Budapest, Ungarn

ISSN 2567-5427
ISBN 978-3-428-19610-4 (Print)
ISBN 978-3-428-59610-2 (E-Book)

Gedruckt auf alterungsbeständigem (säurefreiem) Papier
entsprechend ISO 9706 ♾

Verlagsanschrift: Duncker & Humblot GmbH, Carl-Heinrich-Becker-Weg 9,
12165 Berlin, Germany | E-Mail: info@duncker-humblot.de
Internet: https://www.duncker-humblot.de

Acknowledgements

In the spring of 2016, back home in Korea, everyone was talking about artificial intelligence. The legendary Go player Lee Sedol was facing off against AlphaGo, an AI developed by Google, in a historic five-game match. I watched those games with awe – and somewhere in the middle of them, a seed was planted. I began to wonder: what does it mean for the law when machines begin to do things we once believed only humans could do? That question eventually led me here, to this dissertation.

When I began this journey, there weren't many papers exploring the intersection of AI and patent law. As a new PhD student, it felt intimidating. But the topic sparked something in me. It brought me joy, challenged me deeply, and became something I carried with me for years. I often say this dissertation is like a baby I carried in my belly for a long time. It was tough – but it was deeply meaningful. And I've been fortunate to have wonderful people by my side throughout the journey.

First and foremost, I owe my heartfelt thanks to my supervisor, Prof. Dr. Andreas Wiebe, LL.M. (Virginia). He has been a guiding light from the very beginning – through my LL.M. and into the PhD. His sharp insights, thoughtful guidance, and steady encouragement helped shape my thinking and pushed me to grow as a researcher. I could not have asked for a better mentor.

I also want to thank my *Doktorgeschwister* – my PhD siblings in Prof. Dr. Wiebe's team. Their passion for IT law and intellectual property law has always inspired me. Through their presentations, discussions, and friendship, I learned so much – not just academically, but personally. Thank you for sharing this path with me, and for the laughter, support, and kindness during the hardest moments. I am truly lucky to have you.

The University of Göttingen also holds a special place in my heart. Its incredible library – one of the largest in Germany – became my second home. Without such a rich academic environment and its abundant resources, this work would not have been possible.

I also wish to thank my dear friends in Göttingen – those who once called this place home, and those who still do. You filled my days with warmth, laughter, and comfort in countless small but meaningful ways. Whether we were cooking together, sharing a meal, walking through the city, or simply talking about our lives, those everyday moments grounded me and brought light to my days. Thank you for making Göttingen feel like more than just a place of study – for making it a home.

I am deeply grateful to my love, Chatch, who has always walked beside me. With you, my world continues to expand into a broader, richer landscape shaped by many cultures, languages, and ideas. You show me every day how beautiful it is when minds meet across borders, and remind me of the value of integrity in research – and the courage to stand by one's convictions.

Looking back, I remember a quiet moment from my childhood – reading a book and feeling, for the first time, the pure joy of learning. I told my parents how thrilled I was, and from that day on, I began to dream of becoming a scholar. My parents have supported me quietly and consistently, through every season of doubt, every detour, and every moment of fatigue. They have stood by me with unshakable faith and steadfast love.

My mother is both kind and strong. Her resilience has carried our family through many seasons, and her kindness shapes the way I see the world – with compassion, patience, and grace. My father, ever a source of energy and conviction, has taught me the value of a positive attitude. He has shown me that the most important thing in life is to hold on to positive thoughts, even when reality is harsh. He has always encouraged me to believe in myself, to stand tall with confidence, and to face challenges with courage. My sister has been my closest companion through it all. In moments when I felt lost or overwhelmed, it was she who lifted me up, cheered me on, and reminded me to keep going. Her unwavering support has been a powerful force – one I continue to rely on. Their love has accompanied me at every step. This journey was never mine alone.

This dissertation marks an end – but also a beginning. I carry the past with gratitude and step into the future with diligence and resolve.

Göttingen, June 2025 *Myung-Ji Kang*

Newton's science defined the future;
our science imagines it.

Table of Contents

Chapter 3

Comparative Studies of the Requirements for Inventorship Under Patent Law in Germany and the US 67

Chapter 6

Affirmation of AI Inventorship 162

Chapter 7

E-Person as Inventor 193

List of Figures and Tables

List of Abbreviations

ADS	Application Data Sheet
AI	Artificial Intelligence
AIA	America Invents Act
AIP	Artificial Inventor Project
ALI	American Law Institute
ANN	Artificial Neural Network
API	Application Program Interfaces
ArbnErfG	Gesetz über Arbeitnehmererfindungen (Employee Invention Act in Germany)
Art.	Article
BGB	Bürgerliches Gesetzbuch (in German)
C.C.D. Mass.	Circuit Court for the District of Massachusetts
CFR	The Code of Federal Regulations
CFREU	Charter of Fundamental Rights of the European Union
CNIPA	National Intellectual Property Administration of the People's Republic of China
CNN	Convolutional Neural Network
CPU	Central Processing Unit
DABUS	Device for the Autonomous Bootstrapping of Unified Sentience
DBNs	Deep Belief Networks
DL	Deep Learning
DPMA	Deutsches Patent- und Markenamt
ECHR	European Convention on Human Rights
e. g.	for example (from Latin: exempli gratia)
EPC	European Patent Convention
E-Person(s)	Electronic Person(s)
EPO	European Patent Office
EU	European Union
F. Cas.	Federal Cases
FITF	First Inventor to File
FTF	First-to-File
FTI	First-to-Invent
GA	Genetic Algorithm

GATT	General Agreement on Tariffs and Trade
GG	Grundgesetz (in German)
GP	Genetic Programming
GPU	Graphics Processing Unit
HI	Human Intelligence
HIV	Human Immunodeficiency Viruses
HTM	Hierarchical Temporal Memory
HW	Hardware
ICs	Integrated Circuits
i.e.	id est
ILSVRC	The ImageNet Large Scale Visual Recognition Challenge
Inc.	Incorporated
IoT	Internet of Things
IP5	The five largest intellectual property offices in the world
JPO	Japan Patent Office
KIPO	Korean Intellectual Property Office
KNN	K Nearest Neighbor
LAD	Language Acquisition Device
ML	Machine Learning
MPEP	Manual of Patent Examining Procedure
NIH	National Institutes of Health
NLG	Natural Language Generating
NLP	Natural Language Processing
NLU	Natural Language Understanding
NMF	Non-negative Matrix Factorization
OCR	Optical Character Recognition
OS	Offenlegungsschrift (in German)
PatG	Patentgesetz (in German)
PatV	Patentverordnung (in German)
PCA	Principal Component Analysis
PCPIP	Paris Convention for the Protection of Industrial Property
PCT	Patent Cooperation Treaty
PETA	People for the Ethical Treatment of Animals
PID controller	Proportional–integral–derivative controller
PLT	Patent Law Treaty
POSITA	Person of Ordinary Skill In The Art
R&D	Research and Development
ResNet	Residual Network

SMEs	Small and Medium-sized Enterprises
SPLT	Substantive Patent Law Treaty
SVD	Singular Value Decomposition
SVM	Support Vector Machine
SW	Software
TPU	Tensor Processing Unit
UCC	Uniform Commercial Code
U.S.C.	Title 35 of the United States Code
UKIPO	UK Intellectual Property Office
US or U.S.	United States
USPTO	United States Patent and Trademark Office
WIPO	World Intellectual Property Organization
XOR	Exclusive or

Chapter 1

Introduction

A. Background

In the last ten years there have been tremendous changes in the field of computer science, including the development of Artificial Intelligence (AI), an area that is still growing rapidly.

Marc Andreessen penned his famous essay, "Why Software Is Eating the World," in The Wall Street Journal in 2011,[1] aiming to highlight the explosive growth and rising importance of the software industry at that time. For example, many of the world's largest business success stories now center around software-driven services such as video, music streaming, and e-book sales, as exemplified by Netflix, iTunes, Spotify, and Amazon. In other words, software lies at the core of nearly every globally expanding business today.

Ten years after Andreessen's essay, we can observe that 'AI is eating software.' Sundar Pichai, CEO of Google, remarked, "We are now witnessing a new shift in computing: the move from a mobile-first to an AI-first world."[2]

AI has also been used as a tool to support the ongoing fight against the global viral pandemic that began in early 2020. It was AI that first warned of the potential for widespread human infection with COVID-19,[3] and it also played a role in vaccine development, clinical trials, and related manufacturing and quality assurance processes.

---

1 *Andreessen*, Why Software Is Eating The World, The Wall Street Journal, August 20, 2011. Marc Andreessen (born 9 July 1971) is an American software engineer and a venture capitalist. He developed Mosaic and Netscape and founded Andreessen Horowitz, a venture capital firm. He also invested in numerous ventures, including Facebook, Twitter, LinkedIn, Pinterest and so on.

2 *Pichai*, Making AI Work for Everyone, Google – Company News (blog), May 17, 2017, https://blog.google/technology/ai/making-ai-work-for-everyone/.

3 An algorithm from the Canadian company 'BlueDot' provided the first warning about the possibility of the mass transmission of Covid-19 among human populations. See also: Künstliche Intelligenz sagte Krankheitsausbruch in Wuhan voraus, Deutsches Ärzteblatt, January 31, 2020, https://www.aerzteblatt.de/nachrichten/109037/Kuenstliche-Intelligenz-sagte-Krankheitsausbruch-in-Wuhan-voraus.

Unlike previous technological revolutions which slowly built momentum, the current AI revolution is highly likely to be explosive. Furthermore, while it is ostensibly driven by the hope that it will significantly improve the quality of human life, many observers are more pessimistic and say it will destroy humanity. These perspectives bear a striking resemblance to those surrounding the use of nuclear energy.

A powerful AI can be likened to nuclear energy: highly beneficial when functioning as intended, but potentially catastrophic if something goes wrong. Opinions on nuclear energy include: (1) a position that warns of the dangers and outrightly rejects its use, (2) a position that emphasizes its economic feasibility and is unconditionally embracing and (3) numerous middle positions sitting between these extremes. Today, most countries have chosen a middle position, working towards peaceful uses while improving the economic benefits and safety. AI technology is similar. Neither extreme should dominate the debate, and we must find some compromise between them.

First, the push for technological development is a natural desire of human beings to improve human quality of life. It is not only impossible to suppress this instinct, but also it may lead to human rights infringements.

Second, unconditionally embracing technological advance exposes human society to multiple risks. For example, one needs only to think of nuclear weapons and the risks they pose while environmental pollution and resource over exploitation have been facilitated by technological development, not to mention the risk of being exposed to infectious diseases.[4] Therefore, I argue that mankind needs to pursue technological development in partnership with ethical responsibility.

We must actively realize the benefits of technological development while always considering the greater public interest, including ethics and social order.[5] Therefore, AI is essentially a convergence science. Various disciplines

---

4 Technological development contributes to the spread of new viruses as climate change occurs. For example, the Nipah virus, which occurred in Malaysia in 1998 and killed over 100 people, is a result of the migration of fruit bats. They were driven out of their habitats due to the El Nino-related drought and fires and went to pig farms in search of food Some pigs were infected with the virus and then spread it to humans. In other words, wild animals that have lost their habitat due to climate change can move to human-occupied areas, making people more likely to be infected with viruses. See the following paper for details: *Looi/Chua*, Lessons from the Nipah Virus Outbreak in Malaysia, The Malaysian Journal of Pathology 29, no. 2 (December 2007): 63–67.

5 Ethical AI development is not easy, because the question of 'what is ethical?' is philosophical and variable varies according to the times. For example, Microsoft introduced Tay, an AI chat robot that learns by talking to people, but it was deactivated after 16 hours because it indiscriminately learned and regurgitated the racist remarks, pro-Nazi praise and the political propaganda views it was taught by some users. *Wakefield*,

are combined with AI, such as computer science related to AI development, philosophy to consider what is ethical for its safe use and law for developing legal systems that can implement its ethical use. One of the key challenges that legal scientists must currently face in AI's development and deployment is, to understand this convergence-academic nature of AI and, in its overall flow, consider the legal procedures required to prevent the risks mentioned above, as well as other not mentioned, that AI can pose to humans.

This raises the obvious question of what risks can AI bring in the area of patent law?

First, unethical inventions, such as autonomous weapons, can be produced by using AI.[6] Autonomous weapons are used after machine algorithms makes life-and-death decisions, which is essentially a matter of ethics. These inventions with such algorithms are still viewed as detrimental to public order, good customs and/or harm public health, according to § 2(1) Patent Act (Patentgesetz, PatG) and the US patent court[7] and they may be subject to non-patentable items.

Second, AI can be used as a sort of 'patent troll', allowing companies to mass-produce patent rights but without actually selling products into markets, effectively hindering industrial development.

Legal scholars must consider what legal policies would be effective solutions to manage these foreseeable patent right problems. This research on AI inventorship will be a solution to control AI inventions effectively. AI inventions have already been developed and the inventor's name is 'erroneously' listed as a natural person in order to obtain a patent right. This dissertation argues that affirming AI inventorship is the most effective way to control the abovementioned problems. It will contribute to safe and ethical development

---

Microsoft Chatbot Is Taught to Swear on Twitter, BBC News, March 24, 2016, sec. Technology, https://www.bbc.com/news/technology-35890188.

[6] Autonomous weapons development and its associated legal discussions are already taking place. *Chesterman*, We, the Robots?: Regulating Artificial Intelligence and the Limits of the Law (Cambridge University Press, 2021), https://doi.org/10.1017/9781009047081. See also: *Bhuta et al.*, Autonomous Weapons Systems: Law, Ethics, Policy (Cambridge University Press, 2016); *Leveringhaus*, Ethics and Autonomous Weapons (Palgrave Macmillan UK, 2015); *Casey-Maslen et al.* (eds.), Drones and Other Unmanned Weapons Systems under International Law, International Humanitarian Law Series (Leiden/Boston: Brill Nijhoff, 2018); *Heintschel von Heinegg/Frau/Singer* (eds.), Dehumanization of Warfare: Legal Implications of New Weapon Technologies, 1st ed. (Springer Cham, 2018).

[7] *Lowell v. Lewis*, 15 F. Cas. 1018 (C.C.D. Mass. 1817). "All that the law requires is that the invention should not be frivolous or injurious to the well-being, good policy, or sound morals of society. The word 'useful,' therefore, is incorporated into the act in contradistinction to mischievous or immoral."

and responsible industrial activities by clearly writing the name of the actual inventor of AI inventions and which AI belongs to which company.

As a result of the convergent nature of AI, a variety of research areas have emerged – this dissertation being one of them. Within the context of AI and patent law, key areas of study include the patentability of AI software, the protection of input data used by AI, the patentability of AI-generated inventions, and, most notably, the issue of 'AI inventorship,' which forms the central focus of this doctoral dissertation.

Why is this research on AI inventorship necessary?

First, recent developments in AI have made it increasingly plausible for AI to contribute to or originate inventive ideas. This challenges traditional conceptions of inventorship, which are historically human-centered. For example, if AI develops computer software by engaging in code writing, it can cause controversy on the patent right side.[8]

Second, AI inventorship is directly related to industrial economies, and its affirmation boosts technology development. Governments worldwide now fully support the Fourth Industrial Revolution[9] as they recognize that those who quickly develop innovative technology gain a competitive edge on other countries; therefore, most countries are working hard to boost their R&D capacities and investment therein.

Third, the notion of 'ubiquitous computing'[10] is no longer novel; today, with the advent of the more advanced paradigm of 'ambient computing,' [1

8 Computer software may be protected by patents. For a detailed discussion of the legal protection of computer software: see *Wiebe*, Know-how-Schutz von Computersoftwares: eine rechtsvergleichende Untersuchung der wettbewerbsrechtlichen Schutzmöglichkeiten in Deutschland und den U.S.A., vol. 2, Schriftenreihe Recht der Computerpraxis 2 (München: Beck, 1993).

9 The Fourth Industrial Revolution refers to industrial changes in automation and connectivity maximized by AI. This term was first used by Klaus Schwab, one of the founders of the World Economic Forum, in his contribution to Foreign Affairs in 2015. "The First Industrial Revolution used water and steam power to mechanize production. The Second used electric power to create mass production. The Third used electronics and information technology to automate production. Now a Fourth Industrial Revolution is building on the Third, the digital revolution that has been occurring since the middle of the last century. It is characterized by a fusion of technologies that is blurring the lines between the physical, digital, and biological spheres". *Schwab*, The Fourth Industrial Revolution: What It Means and How to Respond, Foreign Affairs, December 12, 2015, https://www.foreignaffairs.com/world/fourth-industrial-revolution.

10 'Ubiquitous computing', which is derived from the Latin word "ubique," which means "anywhere and anytime," and first appeared in a 1991 paper by Dr. Mark Weiser's 1991 paper. It refers to a world where communicative computers exist everywhere. This Ubiquitousness has already been realized by carrying the proliferation of smart-

technologies such as smart factories and 3D printing are accelerating the large-scale production of AI-generated inventions. As AI systems increasingly contribute to innovation in ways that were once uniquely human, the question of how to legally define and attribute inventorship has become more urgent. Accordingly, the legal and policy implications of AI inventorship have become top priorities for legal scholars.

B. Previous Literature

Prior research on AI has been primarily undertaken by the following three groups.

First, there is the direct effort of engineers to develop AI inventors, a process that has been active since the 1990s and already had some success. Chapter 2 C. will cover existing AI inventors and their inventions registered as patents.

Second, there are studies in the branch of philosophy that speak about the dangers of AI and how to control it. Controlling AI within a legal framework is based on philosophical questions of morality as the actions AI should take in a specific situation should be the most socially appropriate, so the algorithm should be set in that direction. Therefore, the study of the seemingly inevitable rise of AI has no choice but to ask questions about ethics and philosophy. Those studies try to peer into the future, highlight the possible risks and provide guidance on how to prepare and proceed.[12]

Third, there is an effort by legal academia to deal with AI and law.

---

phones that can now, arguably, be found anywhere and anytime. *Weiser*, The Computer for the 21st Century, Scientific American 265, no. 3 (1991): 94–105.

[11] 'Ambient computing' means that technology is unobtrusively and seamlessly integrated into our daily lives rather than requiring us to interact directly with multiple computing devices. These computers now surround us and function quietly in the background, making human life easier.

[12] *Bostrom*, Superintelligence: Paths, Dangers, Strategies (Oxford University Press, 2014). The author is a professor of Philosophy at the University of Oxford and the founding director of the Future of Humanity Institute. His book explains the emergence of a superintelligence that far exceeds human capabilities and the dangers of the AI explosion. Thinking about how to control superintelligence, he describes two control methods: "ability control" and "motivation selection". Ability control is a way to prevent undesirable outcomes by limiting the activities that superintelligence can do while motivation selection is controlled by limiting the activities that superintelligence wants to do. Both methods require a moral judgment about which behaviour should be prohibited. See also: *Lin/Abney/Jenkins* (eds.), Robot Ethics 2.0: From Autonomous Cars to Artificial Intelligence, 1st ed. (New York: Oxford University Press, 2017), a collection of papers containing concerns about ethics and philosophy.

For example, since 1992 Springer has published a quarterly magazine called Artificial Intelligence and Law. In other words, the legal community has paid close attention to AI since the 1990s when AI inventors first appeared. In addition, the legal community is working hard to enact and amend laws to protect any "company that produces robots" and "people who purchase and use robots".[13] Meanwhile, research into the legal personhood of robots has been active since the 2010s.[14]

Within legal scholarship, ongoing efforts are being made in the field of IP law[15] to address the challenges posed by AI systems that have already generated patented inventions and copyrighted works.[16] Discussions on AI and IP law are actively underway, with WIPO playing a central role.[17] For example,

---

13 *Calo/Froomkin/Kerr* (eds.), Robot Law (Edward Elgar Publishing, 2016). It is a collection of papers about many legal concerns, including various issues such as liability and robotic weapons. *Corrales/Fenwick/Forgó* (eds.), Robotics, AI and the Future of Law (Springer, 2018). All three editors of this book are also jurists, dealing with many issues in AI and Law. *Weaver*, Robots Are People Too: How Siri, Google Car, and Artificial Intelligence Will Force Us to Change Our Laws, 1st edition (Santa Barbara, California: Praeger, 2013). This book handles general legal areas such as transportation, healthcare, law enforcement, childcare and real estate development. *Hallevy*, When Robots Kill: Artificial Intelligence under Criminal Law (Boston: Northeastern University Press, 2013); *Hallevy*, Liability for Crimes Involving Artificial Intelligence Systems (Springer Cham, 2014). These two books are studies from a criminal law aspect.

14 *Chopra/White*, A Legal Theory for Autonomous Artificial Agents (Ann Arbor: University of Michigan Press, 2011). Chapters 4 and 5 in this book explain the liability incurred when AI commits illegal acts while Chapter 5 also examines the possibility of AIs gaining legal personhood. *Gunkel*, Robot Rights (The MIT Press, 2018). In this book, the author categorizes perspectives on robot rights into four positions based on the axes of capacity ("can") and normative justification ("should"): (1) robots cannot and should not have rights; (2) robots can but should not have rights; (3) robots can and should have rights; and (4) robots cannot but should have rights.

15 *Barfield/Pagallo* (eds.), Research Handbook on the Law of Artificial Intelligence (Cheltenham, UK: Edward Elgar Publishing, 2018). This book presents a wide range of considerations in the areas of public and private law. In particular, Part IV focuses on IP and introduces five related papers. See also: *Samore*, Artificial Intelligence and the Patent System: Can a New Tool Render a Once Patentable Idea Obvious?, Syracuse Journal of Science & Technology Law 29, no. Fall (2013): 113; *Cubert/Bone*, The Law of Intellectual Property Created by Artificial Intelligence, Research Handbook on the Law of Artificial Intelligence, December 28, 2018, 411–27; *Buning*, Artificial Intelligence and the Creative Industry: New Challenges for the EU Paradigm for Art and Technology by Autonomous Creation, Research Handbook on the Law of Artificial Intelligence, December 28, 2018, 511–35.

16 Some examples of AI writers and AI painters are: GPT-3, *Wordsmith*, AI Dungeon, Hugging Face, DeepDream, Prisma, AICAN, and The Next Rembrandt.

17 WIPO has set aside a space related to AI on its official website: IP and Frontier Technologies – Artificial Intelligence and Intellectual Property, WIPO, accessed December 22, 2022, https://www.wipo.int/about-ip/en/frontier_technologies/ai_and_ip.

in 2019, WIPO circulated a set of 17 questions to relevant authorities in various countries to assess the impact of AI on their respective IP systems.[18]

A particularly contentious issue within IP law is the question of AI inventorship, which has not only prompted global legal discourse on whether nonhuman entities can be recognized as inventors under current patent regimes, but has also led to a steady stream of efforts in recent years by academics and international organizations to raise awareness and directly address the associated legal challenges.

In particular, since 2018 Ryan Abbott's research team at the University of Surrey has been applying worldwide for patents of two AI inventions[19] entering the AI's name in the inventor field. This project is named The Artificial Inventor Project (AIP)[20] and actively leads the discussion about AI inventorship. Their core argument is that the status of inventor belongs to the AI, and the applicant is the owner of the AI, Dr. Thaler.

The AIP team generally undertakes the following steps in each country's application:[21]

(1) The name of the applicant is recorded as Stephen L. Thaler, the developer and owner of the AI.

(2) The inventor's first name is given as DABUS, the name of the AI, and the family name is given as "Invention generated by artificial intelligence".

---

html. Since 2019, WIPO has been holding the "WIPO Conversation on Intellectual Property and Artificial Intelligence." As of 2022, six sessions have been held. WIPO, The WIPO Conversation on Intellectual Property and Artificial Intelligence, WIPO, accessed June 22, 2025, https://www.wipo.int/about-ip/en/artificial_intelligence/conversation.html.

[18] WIPO, AI and Intellectual Property: WIPO Call for Submissions (Impact of AI on IP Policy) (WIPO, 2019), https://www.wipo.int/export/sites/www/about-ip/en/artificial_intelligence/call_for_comments/wipo_ai_ip_call_for_submissions.pdf. The publication date is not provided, but I assume it to be 2019, as the first session of the WIPO Conversation on IP and AI took place in that year.

[19] See Chapter 2 C. I. regarding these two inventions. One of these inventions is called a Neural Flame, a light beacon that flashes to effectively attract attention. The other is called a Fractal Container, a beverage container based on fractal geometry. Both inventions were invented by the AI named DABUS.

[20] *Abbott*, The Artificial Inventor Project, accessed September 20, 2022, https://artificialinventor.com/.

[21] Decision on Petition (In re Application of Application No.: 16/524,350) (United States Patent and Trademark Office (USPTO) 2020). As each country's patent procedure is different, the steps which the AIP team takes to lodge the application in each country also varies slightly. Their US application has been selected and dealt with in this dissertation, however, numerous other countries applications are substantially similar. The key point in each application is that the AIP team cites the inventor's name as DABUS.

(3) Since the AI cannot write, a substitute statement – such as one submitted under 37 CFR 1.64[22] in the US – is provided in place of the inventor's declaration or oath. Furthermore, 'assignment documentation' enabling the replacement declaration is also attached, this document assigns all the inventor's rights to Dr. Thaler.

(4) The applicants also prepare and submit an additional "Statement of Inventorship" describing the specific circumstance about AI inventor.

Denials for the applications have been received from most countries because the inventor is not a natural person. However, the application had notable successes with South Africa's Patent Office[23] and in Australia after domestic courts affirmed the validity of the AI inventorship. Chapter 3 E. will specifically deal with the German and US situations regarding how they refuse to accept AI inventorship. Subsequent to this, Chapter 6 B. I. 3. will cover the contents of the Australian court's rulings in detail and how they ruled positively concerning AI inventorship.

It seem reasonable to assume that if the AIP team had put the inventor's name as "Stephen L. Thaler" instead of "DABUS", they would have obtained patents from most, if not all, of their applications without any problems. This begs the obvious question then of why does the AIP team repeatedly use the name of the AI as the inventor? Any patent lawyer can predict that designating an AI as the inventor has a high chance of being rejected. The actual reasons

---

22 The Code of Federal Regulations (CFR) is a collection of administrative orders issued by the federal administration. Each volume of the regulations is updated once a year, and is published quarterly in groups thematically. The CFR consists of 50 titles, each of which comprises multiple chapters, and each chapter contains regulatory domains. 37 CFR specifically refers to Title 37 of the CFR, which contains regulations related to patents, trademarks, and copyrights. It covers topics such as patentability, examination procedures, maintenance fees, and appeals.

23 There are two main reasons why this application was able to pass in South Africa: (1) There is no definition of "inventor" in the South African Patent Act and (2) there is no substantive examination in the South African Patent Act. Therefore, only the formalities examination based on the PCT (Patent Cooperation Treaty) was passed without much difficulty. South Africa's decision is the world's first case affirming AI inventorship, however, some criticisms reduce its meaning in that it has only gone through a formalities examination. However, the AIP team was delighted at that time with South Africa's decision to pass the formal examination, pointing out that substantive examinations had been passed in the UK and EPO. DABUS Gets Its First Patent in South Africa Under Formalities Examination, IPWatchdog.com | Patents & Intellectual Property Law, July 29, 2021, https://www.ipwatchdog.com/2021/07/29/dabus-gets-first-patent-south-africa-formalities-examination/id=136116/. "Kirk Hartung of McKee, Voorhees & Sease […] explained that South Africa patent laws do not define 'inventor'. The country also does not have substantive examination, so 'as long as the paperwork is filled out correctly, the patent office pretty much rubber stamps for approval,' Hartung said."

can only be speculated on, however, the present author suspects: (1) The AIP team purposely intend to spark a practical debate about AI inventorship and (2) the team recognizes that it is consistent with the substantive truth to designate the AI as the inventor.

Driven by the AIP project, WIPO published a report in 2022 that analyzes whether AI can be recognized as an inventor, with particular focus on the incentive structure within the patent system. The report concludes that, at present, it is inappropriate to grant legal personhood to AI.[24]

Furthermore, a report on AI inventorship published by AIPPI provides valuable insight, as the 19 survey responses it received formed the basis for focused discussions on the legal implications of AI inventorship.[25]

As noted above, a wide range of discussions surrounding AI is currently underway. Building on the aforementioned body of prior research, this dissertation aims to take a step forward in contributing to the argument in favor of recognizing AI inventorship.

C. Gaps in Existing Literature and Contribution of This Study

Prior research on AI inventorship exhibits several limitations, which this dissertation seeks to overcome.

First, prior legal scholarship presumes that inventorship must involve human mental activity. Most domestic laws require inventors to be natural persons, and no regulation explicitly affirming AI inventorship yet exists. However, with the rapid emergence of AI during the upheavals of the Fourth Industrial Revolution, a new and complex set of legal conundrums has arisen – ones that demand a different approach from traditional legal frameworks. In light of these limitations, this dissertation contributes to the existing scholarship by arguing that the longstanding human-centered presumption of inventorship must be critically reexamined in view of autonomous or semi-autonomous AI systems capable of generating patentable inventions.

Second, prior research tends to rely on literal interpretation, which holds that only human beings can be recognized as inventors. However, this narrow approach overlooks the potential of purposive and historical methods of inter-

24 WIPO, Incentive Structure and Inventorship for AI, WIPO Conversation on Intellectual Property and Artificial Intelligence, 2021, https://www.wipo.int/export/sites/www/about-ip/en/artificial_intelligence/call_for_comments/pdf/ind_borges.pdf.

25 Report of the Swiss Group, Inventorship of Inventions Made Using Artificial Intelligence [Q 272] (AIPPI, 2020), https://aippi.soutron.net/Portal/Default/en-GB/RecordView/Index/3832.

pretation. Effectively addressing AI-related challenges in this context requires examining the background and legislative history of the relevant regulations, rather than focusing solely on the wording of existing legal texts. This dissertation adopts such a flexible point of view.

Third, existing research often focuses on single jurisdictions in isolation. Comparative or harmonized analysis across legal systems is still limited, leaving gaps in understanding how international patent frameworks may converge or conflict over AI inventorship. This dissertation undertakes a comparison of German and US patent law. These countries' laws represent the two extremes in terms of the history and form of patent law (see, Chapter 1 E. III.); therefore, other countries with a mixed form of civil law and common law could naturally find direction. Through this comparative framework, the dissertation seeks to evaluate the applicability of AI inventorship from a global perspective.

Fourth, this dissertation – particularly Chapter 2 – aims to provide sufficient engagement with the technological realities relevant to AI inventorship. Many legal studies rely on generalized or abstract descriptions of AI, without engaging deeply with how AI systems actually work in inventive processes. As a result, a disconnect often emerges between legal theory and the technical realities of machine learning and algorithmic invention.

Fifth, prior legal research has largely overlooked philosophical frameworks, resulting in limited exploration of foundational questions: Can machines hold rights? What is the nature of creativity? This dissertation – particularly Chapter 6 – seeks to address these questions in depth.

D. Overview of the Structure

This paper consists of four main chapters.

Chapter 2 begins with understanding the structure of AI and compares AI and HI (Human Intelligence). How does AI's 'brain' software work and does AI lead the inventive process? This question is necessary to give the status of an inventor to an AI. The status as an inventor is determined by law, and it is currently given exclusively to natural persons, while juridical persons may not acquire it, as the inventive process has, to date, been considered a uniquely human activity that requires human creative thinking. Thus, naturally, any incorporated organizations that lack human creative thinking could not acquire the status of inventors. Then, what if AI proves that its 'brain' software actually performs the inventive process just like natural persons? In this case, there will be no problem recognizing the inventorship of AI along with natural persons. Therefore, Chapter 2 handles what exactly is happening in AI's 'brain' software, and how AI's software runs and clarifies how similar or different it is from HI's brain.

In addition, Chapter 2 introduces AI inventors that have already produced patentable inventions. When it comes to affirming AI inventorship, the first questions that can come to mind are, "Is it not too early? Is this still an issue for the future?" The answer to both is that it is not. AI inventorship is a growing problem that is already happening.

Chapter 3 handles how the law decides inventorship, especially based on a comparative study of German and US patent law. It is necessary to understand how the law defines creative thinking and decides who is the inventor. A patent right is legally granted only after it goes through an 'Invention Process' and a subsequent 'Application Process'. The inventorship regulations in Germany and the US will be compared by examining each country's version of these two processes. Before dealing with the two processes, three preliminary research questions will be handled: (1) what are the relevant constitutional provisions related to inventors, (2) is there a definition of inventors in the regulations in both countries and (3) how the current regulations are worded to allow only natural persons to be inventors. Furthermore, the official positions of the German and US patent offices, as well as domestic courts, towards AI inventorship will be examined.

By the time Chapter 4 begins, the reader has already noticed that: there are already inventions invented by AI (or 'simply used by AI' according to the negative view of AI inventorship) on the market; and what legal requirements determine inventorship, especially in Germany and the US. The key question of this paper is, "Does AI have inventorship?" The answer to this question will be yes or no. Chapter 4 puts a hypothetical condition that AI has no inventorship and asks continuously who did creative thinking, if not AI. In other words, it examines a group of natural persons who are candidates to be inventors if AI inventorship is not legally recognized. The problem is that a legal standard is needed to identify these individuals. Based on the comparative German and US law study in Chapter 3, a '2/7 questions process' was used here to address this. At the beginning of Chapter 4, these 2 and 7 questions are introduced and the process is applied to each candidate to clarify whether he/she is a suitable candidate as an inventor.

Chapter 5 briefly addresses the implications of leaving the inventor designation blank.

Chapter 6 argues that AI inventorship should be legally affirmed based on the following five reasons:

(1) If AI inventorship can be affirmed under current law. The '2/7 question process' will be applied to AI like the natural person candidates above.

Furthermore, positive decisions about AI inventorship made in South Africa and Australia based on their current laws will be introduced.

(2) From the point of view of patent theories including incentive theory, personhood theory, Lockean theory of labour and utilitarian theory, the possibility of AI inventorship being recognized in law will be discussed.

(3) From a legal and historical perspective, AI inventorship will be dealt with. Why has the inventorship of corporations been historically denied? What was the legal status of enslaved people and domestic animals in the past and does their circumstances have any bearing on modern AI inventorship?

(4) From a practical point of view, the reasons for giving AI legal personality and inventorship will be dealt with. Considering the current market situation, the affirmation of AI inventorship will be a solid basis for solving problems.

(5) From a philosophical point of view, whether or not the nature of non-human entities and that of humans are fundamentally different will be explored. If they are the same, it will become a solid basis for the affirmation of AI inventorship.

Chapter 7 explores the concept of 'Electronic Persons' ('E-Person')[26] as a potential legal framework to address the growing disconnect between the "formal expression of the inventor" and the "substantive truth". The chapter examines the current legal difficulties arising from this mismatch and considers possible solutions. It argues for the creation of a new category of legal personality – distinct from natural and legal persons – accompanied by a clear definition of its legal character. Assuming the recognition of E-Persons, the chapter further investigates how their rights might be structured under patent law. In this context, inventorship and entitlement to patent rights are analysed across four distinct scenarios, with particular attention given to the parallels between employee inventions and those generated by AI systems.

---

26 The term 'Electronic Persons' was proposed by the European Parliament's Legal Committee in the report of the Civil Law Rules on Robotics. *Nevejans*, European Civil Law Rules In Robotics (European Parliament, Policy Department C: Citizens' Rights and Constitutional Affairs, October 2016), https://www.europarl.europa.eu/RegData/etudes/STUD/2016/571379/IPOL_STU(2016)571379_EN.pdf. "The motion for a resolution proposes creating a new category of individual, specifically for robots: electronic persons".

E. Scope of the Research

I. Inventorship v. Patent Ownership

Inventorship and patent ownership are different concepts under patent law. Inventorship refers to individuals' "status as an inventor," while patent ownership refers to the "status as an owner of a patent right". In other words, inventorship belongs to the person who invented the new item or process; this is the origin of the patent right and the inventor's right to reputation. On the other hand, patent ownership can be obtained as the original inventor or his assignee, and it is a property right rather than a right to reputation.[27]

In most legal systems, including that of Germany and the US, only two types of persons enjoy legal subjectivity: natural and legal persons. However, inventorship is limited exclusively to natural persons while both natural and legal persons can obtain patent ownership.

This paper focuses on inventorship, however, since both are closely related concepts within the same patent law, patent ownership will also be handled as a supplementary aspect.

II. Patentability of SW v. Patentability of SW-generated Inventions v. Inventorship of SW

The core of AI is, after all, software, a product that has been dealt with for a long time by patent law. The "patentability of SW itself," "patentability of SW-generated-inventions," and "inventorship of SW" are all completely different topics from each other, even though the word SW is common to all. All three are briefly detailed below.

AI inventors run in three steps as shown in Figure 1[28]: (1) Input data related to an invention is entered; (2) the SW works with the input data; and (3) an invention is derived as the output.

---

[27] "Apple has a total of 95500 patents globally" (Apple Patents – Insights & Stats (Updated 2023), Insights by Greyb, accessed June 1, 2023, https://insights.greyb.com/apple-patents/), but the inventors' names are not Apple Inc, but Steve Jobs and co-inventors. For example, the inventorship of "Highly portable media device" (US patent number: US20200150785A1) belongs to Steve Jobs, but the patent ownership belongs to Apple Inc.

[28] [Figure 1] was generated with the assistance of ChatGPT, developed by OpenAI (2025).

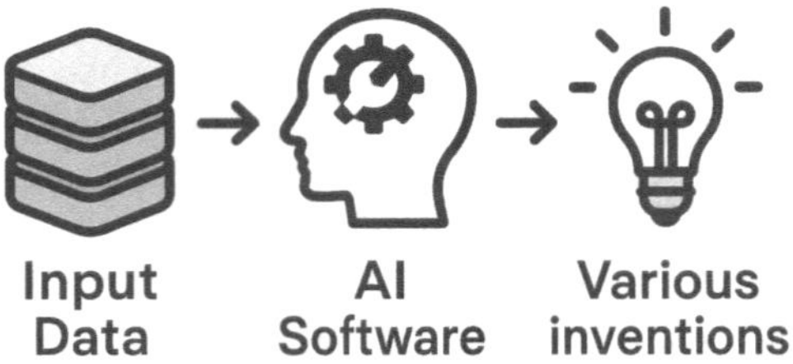

Figure 1: Three Steps to Run an AI-Inventor

The "patentability of the SW itself" is linked to the SW mentioned in the second step. It has been debated for a long time whether SW can be protected by patents along with copyrights.[29] In other words, the "patentability of SW itself" has a bearing on whether a particular AI can be protected as an object of patent rights.

The "patentability of SW-generated inventions" relates to the inventions resulting from the third step. It focuses on AI inventions and whether they satisfy patent requirements, such as novelty and inventiveness. In particular, the "inventiveness or non-obvious" requirement is controversial in relation to AI inventions. A new invention will not be able to get patent rights because AI raises the obviousness standard from the POSITA (Person of Ordinary Skill in the Art)'s point of view. Using AI as a tool may violate the non-obviousness requirement of patent rights and result in the rejection of patentability. For example, an opinion is that the invention is obvious and, therefore, the invention is not patentable if the use of AI software – particularly Genetic Programming – becomes widespread in the future.[30]

What this paper deals with is "the inventorship of SW". It includes all three steps mentioned in [Figure 1] above in seeking to answer who is the inventor of AI inventions. In the overall process that results in AI inventions, many natural and legal persons are typically involved. The candidacy for inventorship of each involved party will be analyzed in detailed in Chapter 4 before Chapter 6 provides clarification that ultimately, the AI is the true inventor.

III. Comparative Study between Germany and the US

As noted above, this paper's legal research on AI inventorship will be analyzed based on a comparative legal study of German and US law. The reasons

29 *Wiebe*, Know-how-Schutz von Computersoftware.

30 See *Samore*, Artificial Intelligence and the Patent System: Can a New Tool Render a Once Patentable Idea Obvious?.

why German and US law were chosen above other legal systems will be explained in detail in Chapter 3 A. III. In short: (1) The two systems offer a clear comparison between civil and common law approaches; (2) as the US had a unique patent system centered on inventorship, called First-to-Invent (FTI) that contained a more detailed consideration of inventorship than other legal systems; and (3) both were selected from IP5 countries.

IV. Weak AI v. Strong AI v. Super AI

AI is classified into three types according to how much it compares to and imitates human intelligence (HI): AI typically starts as weak, which is superior to HI in at least one specific field; it can then develop to the stage of strong AI, which is deemed to have the similar intelligence as humans in all fields;[31] its ultimate development sees it become a super AI that surpasses HI in all fields.[32]

Weak AI (or narrow AI) is a technology that imitates a part of HI to solve problems in a specific area, such as foreign language translations or playing chess. This form of AI is widely used today and examples can be found in Google's AlphaGo, IBM's Watson, Amazon's Alexa, Apple's Siri and Facebook's automatic face recognition. Strong AI and super AI have not yet been developed. However, However, Strong AI is expected to be able to learn and apply knowledge across various domains, similar to HI; furthermore, it will likely lead to Super AI that transcends humans in all aspects. The development of these Strong AI and Super AI is analogous to the previously cited example of nuclear power, a very efficient means of doing what it is designed to do but the harm caused if something goes wrong can be catastrophic. It is a double-edged sword. The development of Super AI may ultimately allow humans to enjoy eternal life,[33] or there is a warning that it will cause human extinction.

---

31 Nils Nilsson, one of the veterans in the field of AI, defines weak AI in his book as "the variety devoted to providing aids to human thought". At the same time, strong AI does "the variety that attempts to mechanize human-level intelligence". *Nilsson*, Quest for Artificial Intelligence: A History of Ideas and Achievements (New York: Cambridge University Press, 2009); *Bostrom*, Superintelligence. Weak AI and Strong AI are first used in 1980 by Professor John R. Searle, proposing the famous Chinese room argument.

32 Bostrom defines super AI in his book as "any intellect that greatly exceeds the cognitive performance of humans in virtually all domains of interest". *Bostrom*, Superintelligence.

33 According to Ray Kurzweil, a former Google engineer and Futurist, he predicted that by the year 2029, humans would attain immortality. This would be made possible through the use of minuscule nanobots that have the capability to repair aging cells and tissues, thus making us resistant to diseases such as cancer. *Kurzweil*, The Age of Spi-

Of the abovementioned three categories, this paper focuses primarily on weak AI. This is for several reasons, not the least of which is that it is meaningless to differentiate between weak, strong and super AI when dealing with AI inventorship for the following reasons:

First, super AI are already 'beyond-human beings' because they will have the higher intelligence as humans as well as emotions and self-consciousness comparable to humans. Therefore, if such AIs are created at some future point, it will be easy to recognize their inventorship, as far as the legal attribution of AI's inventorship is socially necessary, and humans can effectively control the risks associated with AI.

Second, strong AI and super AI have yet to be developed and it is difficult to predict how or even if they will be controlled and used. Therefore, it is too early to discuss specific legal aspects of a future that is still so unclear. Since legal research is not prophecy, but scientific research, it must be conducted based on objectively verifiable data.

Third, weak AI is already producing patentable inventions and is causing legal problems. As such, there is a need to address these problems as soon as possible and trying to find solutions that have provisions for forms of AI that do not currently exist will only complicate and slow this process.

V. Computer v. Robot v. AI

Many papers equate AI with computers and robots, which are used interchangeably.[34] However, these three words have different historical etymologies and meanings.

---

ritual Machines: When Computers Exceed Human Intelligence (New York: Penguin Books, 2000).

34 (1) For example, some papers use the word "computers": *Abbott*, I Think, Therefore I Invent: Creative Computers and the Future of Patent Law, Boston College Law Review 57, no. 4 (2016): 1079, https://doi.org/10.2139/ssrn.2727884; *Clifford*, Intellectual Property in the Era of the Creative Computer Program: Will the True Creator Please Stand Up, Tulane Law Review 71 (1996): 1675; *Fraser*, Computers as Inventors – Legal and Policy Implications of Artificial Intelligence on Patent Law, SCRIPTed 13, no. 3 (December 2016): 305, https://doi.org/10.2966/scrip.130316.305; (2) also some "AI": *Barfield/Pagallo*, Research Handbook on the Law of Artificial Intelligence; *Blok*, The Inventor's New Tool: Artificial Intelligence – How Does It Fit in the European Patent System?, European Intellectual Property Review 39, no. 2 (2017): 69–73; and (3) some "robots": *Calo/Froomkin/Kerr*, Robot Law; *Chesterman*, We, the Robots?; *Nevejans*, European Civil Law Rules In Robotics.

The word "computer" has been used since the 17th century. It means until the 1950s, "humans who perform calculations."[35] These people were hired for simple calculations and were literally called "computers," meaning 'those who calculate.' The word "computer" is a combination of "compute" and "-er" and is derived from the Latin word "computare,"[36] which means to calculate. In the 1950s, with the development of science and technology, digital electronic computers developed. As a result, 'human computers' disappeared, and 'digital electronic computers' succeeded them.

The word "robot" was first used in 1920 in Rossum's Universal Robots by the Czech writer Karel Čapek. It is known that the etymology of robot comes from the Czech word 'robota,' meaning 'labor.' In Rossum's Universal Robots, Čapek introduces robots that are equal to or superior to humans in all work abilities but do not have human feelings or souls. In other words, a robot is a mechanical device that automatically performs complicated tasks according to specific SW instructions and has the most efficient HW structure to achieve its purpose. In general, it refers to industrial robots. For example, a robot that carries goods from one point to another in a factory is implemented as an automatically rotating 'belt', and a welding robot works on a part to be welded in the form of a needle-like tip.

The word "AI" was first used in the summer of 1956 at the Workshop in Dartmouth. Corresponding to the 'natural intelligence' of humans and animals, the term 'artificial intelligence' is what machines have. AI comprises three main elements: SW capable of self-learning, HW, and data necessary for implementing the software. The three elements of AI and their specific types will be covered in detail in Chapters 2 B. and 2 C.

In everyday life, the images presented by computers, robots, and AI can evoke thoughts of entirely different objects. For instance, computers may bring to mind laptops and desktops utilized by individuals, robots may bring to mind humanoid machines depicted in science fiction movies, and AI may bring to mind cutting-edge software developed by today's leading conglomerates.[37] However, examining the historical etymologies of computers, robots,

---

[35] *Bruderer*, Computers Were Originally Humans, Communications of the ACM (blog), October 7, 2021, https://cacm.acm.org/blogs/blog-cacm/256056-computers-were-originally-humans/fulltext; *Grier*, When Computers Were Human (Princeton University Press, 2005): It cites the Oxford Dictionary's explicit reference to the computer as "a person."

[36] Derived from "computo" (meaning 'to calculate'), which is made by combining the Latin words "com-" (together) and "putare" (to think). "Compute," in Online Etymology Dictionary, accessed June 25, 2025, https://www.etymonline.com/word/compute.

[37] In addition, the meaning of these three terms in the Oxford dictionary is defined as follows: "computer" is "an electronic machine that can store, organize and find in-

and AI mentioned earlier; we can observe that these three entities can be broadly equated.

The term "computer" has a history that dates back to the 17th century and has evolved from "human computers" to "digital electric computers." With the progress of science and technology, computers have become smaller, lighter,[38] and gradually transformed into high-performance devices. On the other hand, the term "robot" first appeared in plays during the 1920s and has predominantly been used in science fiction stories. However, the human desire to create machines resembling humans has been realized through the development of AI since the 1950s. As a result, robots and AI are integral parts of the computer's history and are actively pursued in the academic field of computer science by leading scientists and technologists.

Therefore, many papers interchangeably equate AI with computers and robots, and this paper also follows the same approach.

---

formation, do processes with numbers and other data, and control other machines"; "robot" is defined with two meanings, (1) "a machine that can perform a complicated series of tasks by itself" (2) "(especially in stories) a machine that is made to look like a human and that can do some things that a human can do"; and "AI" is defined as "the study and development of computer systems that can copy intelligent human behavior." Therefore, these three concepts have in common that they are machines designed to perform tasks that humans require. The development of AI aims to create machines that emulate humans to assist in human life.

[38] Computers were once used only in government agencies, the military, and large corporations. There was a time when one could not even think computers would be used at home. For example, in 1943, Thomas Watson (Chairman of IBM) said, "I think there is a world market for maybe five computers." As ENIAC computers weighed about 30 tons at that time, one naturally supposed there would be only a handful of places to use such a super-large machine. In 1977, Ken Olsen (founder of Digital Equipment Corporation, who invented the magnetic core memory) commented, "There is no reason for any individual to have a computer in his home." In other words, it is pretty amazing that computers are everywhere today.

Chapter 2

Understanding AI in the Patent Field

A. Three Key Components Defining AI and the Significance of Understanding Software

What is AI? It is surprisingly difficult to define AI as a concept. The term 'artificial intelligence' was coined in the summer of 1956 at the Workshop in Dartmouth, eastern United States of America. John McCarthy, Marvin Minsky, Nathaniel Rochester, and Claude Shannon, who were at Dartmouth College at the time, jointly proposed it.[1] However, the basic idea of AI had begun with Alan Turing. In his famous paper Computing Machinery and Intelligence where he raised the question, "Can machines think"?[2] This question prompted related research in various fields of study, including philosophy, psychology, logic, neurosurgery and computer science.

'Artificial' can arguably be easily defined as the opposite of 'natural', however, the real problem is the definition of 'intelligence' in a software context. Since the 'intelligence' aspect is difficult to define, the meaning of the term 'artificial intelligence' has varied slightly over time and according to who is defining it and which research area is involved.[3] However, in this paper, AI is

---

[1] Artificial Intelligence Coined at Dartmouth, Dartmouth, accessed September 28, 2023, https://home.dartmouth.edu/about/artificial-intelligence-ai-coined-dartmouth.

[2] *Turing*, Computing Machinery and Intelligence, Mind 59, no. 236 (October 1950): 433–60. Alan Turing (1912–1954) is widely considered to be the father of theoretical computer science and artificial intelligence. He introduced the concept of artificial intelligence with his paper asking "Can Machines Think?" and sought to answer it using the Turing Test, which can determine whether a machine is intelligent. In the Turing Test, there are one human evaluator and two players, that consist of one human and one computer. The evaluator determines which one is the computer while talking with the two players on the keyboard. The computer passes the Turing test if the evaluator cannot determine it. In other words, if a computer can talk like a human, then the computer is assumed to be able to think like a human. Alan Turing worked during the Second World War to decipher the 'Enigma', the military codes used by Germany and its allies. Winston Churchill said Turing's breaking of German codes shortened the war by two years. The Bank of England decided to celebrate Alan Turing by using his image on the new £50 note issued in late 2021.

[3] For example, Ravid and Liu identified eight crucial features of AI systems: they are (1) creative; (2) unpredictable; (3) independent and autonomous; (4) rational;

defined as "a machine that uses self-learning software, based on a large amount of relevant data and advanced hardware". Computers operate using three essential components: Hardware, software and data, which to use a human analogy, are like the body, brain and knowledge. AI is a type of computer that better consists of three components: higher-performance hardware than previous computers, greater amounts of processing data, and even self-learning software.

First, high-quality hardware is needed for AI to run. Such hardware can be run by (1) a combination of a Central Processing Unit (CPU) and a Graphics Processing Unit (GPU)[4], or (2) a recently developed Tensor Processing Unit (TPU)[5].[6]

Second, an enormous amount of data that fits the purpose of the AI's activity needs to be entered, which in this paper is referred to as 'Input Data' or 'Training Data.' It is often mistakenly referred to as 'Big Data,' however, this latter term refers to extremely large and complex sets of data that cannot be effectively analyzed using traditional data processing techniques,[7] while 'Input Data' or 'Training Data' means a specific subset of data entered into an AI for a given purpose. For example, knowledge of various road conditions is

(5) evolving; (6) capable of data collection and communication; (7) efficient and accurate; and (8) freely able to choose among alternative options. *Ravid/Liu*, When Artificial Intelligence Systems Produce Inventions: An Alternative Model for Patent Law at the 3A Era, Cardozo Law Review 39 (2017): 2215.

4 The CPU and GPU are two crucial components of modern computer systems. The CPU is often considered the brain of a computer and performs complex calculations and tasks. On the other hand, the GPU can handle simple calculations and tasks and is primarily used for graphical tasks as an auxiliary function to the CPU. In recent years, GPUs have gained significant attention and popularity due to their effectiveness in accelerating AI algorithms, particularly deep learning. Deep learning, a subfield of AI, heavily relies on neural networks with many layers, requiring substantial computational power for training and inference. GPUs are well-suited for this task due to their parallel processing capabilities.

5 Hardware has so far primarily consisted of CPUs and GPUs. However, there has been a shift towards utilizing Application-Specific Integrated Circuits (ASICs) for specific applications. One such example is the TPU, which is an ASIC developed by Google. TPU plays a role in quicker data processing and reducing memory read times. It is also noteworthy that energy efficiency has also been improved.

6 Meanwhile, patent acquisition of CPUs, GPUs, and TPUs has no particular problem as long as each chip meets the legal requirements of novelty and inventiveness. The largest CPU manufacturing company is Intel, Nvidia for GPUs and Google for TPUs. They have acquired patents under their own strategies, or protect the related technologies as trade secrets.

7 The '3Vs' refer to the three key characteristics of Big Data, namely, Volume, Velocity, and Variety: (1) Volume refers to the vast quantity of data gathered from diverse sources; (2) velocity refers to the speed at which data is produced; and (3) variety refers to the different types and structures of data.

needed for self-driving cars while the results for numerous move combinations are required for chess AI. Today companies working with AI are trying to obtain more accurate data, as the more data they have, the greater the accuracy and the better performance of their AI.

Third, special software must be run to process the already massive amount of data being input.[8] In the definition of AI used in this paper, the software under consideration is capable of machine learning (ML), which let the machine learn on its own to 'digest' the data it is fed.

It is argued here that the software is the most important of the three components for this paper's purposes, although each one makes an indispensable contribution to the inventive process. Software is the critical issue regarding AI's inventive process because it is the brain that is using and guiding the other components.

Answering the first question, "Does AI have creative thinking?" requires an in-depth understanding of software, such as the 'brain activity' of AI. If there is a comparable process in the brain of AI to the creative thinking undertaken by natural people, AI's inventorship would be more likely to be acknowledged. In addressing this issue, this text will: (1) review the concept of ML (by AI software) and its sub-algorithms by type, including Artificial Neural Network, Deep Learning, Genetic Algorithm and Genetic Programming; while also (2) comparing how much the process that occurs in AI software resemble and differ from the activities of a human brain. This knowledge of the functioning of AI software will be linked to logic that affirms the validity of AI inventorship and that will be detailed in Chapter 6.

B. Understanding AI Software

I. Traditional Machine Learning

In general, computers process information in two ways: (1) Passive exposure to input-output values pre-populated by humans; (2) ML that allows the machine to learn by itself. In this paper, these processes are referred to as 'non-self-learning' and 'self-learning' for the sake of clarity.

---

[8] In the US, 'computer software' is defined by 48 CFR 2.101 to mean (i) computer programs that comprise a series of instructions, rules, routines, or statements, regardless of the media in which recorded, that allow or cause a computer to perform a specific operation or series of operations; and (ii) recorded information comprising source code listings, design details, algorithms, processes, flow charts, formulas, and related material that would enable the computer program to be produced, created, or compiled.

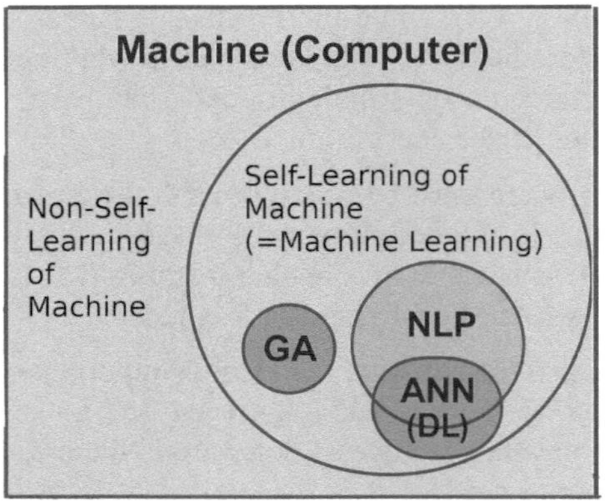

Figure 2: Venn Diagram of Computer Software

To begin this discussion, non-self-learning simply means, unsurprisingly, that a machine cannot learn on its own. For example, in response to inputting "love", such a machine will respond with "a very strong feeling of living and caring for someone/something, especially a member of your family or a friend"[9]. However, both the input and the output must be pre-populated by humans and the machine simply provides the output pre-determined by humans to match the input. A model of an early chatbot had a simple structure that conducted a chat conversation via text or recorded voice according to a set rule. With the advent of chatbots, humans were able to remove themselves from the labor of engaging in highly repetitive conversations.[10] Figure 3[11] is the representative black box explaining the function f(x)=y. In this non-autonomous learning where all (x, y) values must be entered by humans.

[9] "Love," in Oxford Learner's Dictionaries (Oxford University Press, 2023), https://www.oxfordlearnersdictionaries.com/definition/english/love_1.

[10] With the development of AI, the functions of chatbots have also evolved. Chatbot models and solutions can largely be divided into 'Natural Language Understanding' (NLU) and 'Natural Language Generating' (NLG). The latter is much more complicated than the former and required significant technological developments to take place. However, both are important in practice. Many companies are more interested in NLU than NLG as they only have to have an AI capable of providing a set answer in a customer consultation setting. However, NLG is required to have a more truly interactive conversation experience. Since the late 2010s, there have been continuous attempts to provide more in-depth conversational abilities and reinforcement the learning capacities of chatbots.

[11] [Figure 3] was generated using ChatGPT (OpenAI, 2025).

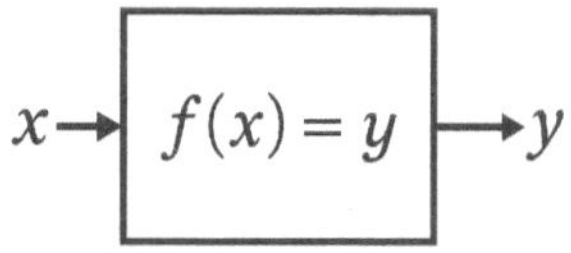

Figure 3: Black-Box Function

In contrast, a self-learning machine is capable of learning by itself through experience. Experiencing many (x, y) values, manually input by humans, the machine predicts the values of f(x) by itself, which has not been input by humans. In 1959, Arthur Samuel[12] defined ML as a field of study that gives computers the ability to learn without being explicitly programmed.[13] Machine learning can be understood as computational methods that use prediction and/or deduction based on input data. Therefore, Tom M. Mitchell defines ML as follows: "A computer program is said to learn from experience *E* with respect to some class of tasks *T* and performance measure *P*, if its performance at tasks in *T*, as measured by *P*, improves with experience *E*".[14] As this definition suggests, the most important thing in ML is the data (experience *E*) as having a lot of good-quality data can lead to higher performance. The expression "machines learn on their own" makes it sound like a machine has almost human-like qualities or that ML is a complicated new technology. However, ML has been used for a long time, sharing many similarities with statistical inference, including the extraction of insights and making predictions from data.

For example, the Iris flower data set contains 150 data sub-sets, including the length and the width of the sepals and petals, for three species of iris (se-

[12] Arthur Samuel (1901–1990), an American computer scientist and AI pioneer, is renowned for his contributions to the development of ML. His most notable achievement was the creation of the Samuel Checkers-playing Program, which stood as one of the earliest successful instances of a self-learning program. See: *Samuel*, Some Studies in Machine Learning Using the Game of Checkers, IBM Journal of Research and Development 3, no. 3 (July 1959): 210–29, https://doi.org/10.1147/rd.33.0210.

[13] This is not an original quote but a paraphrased version of Samuel's sentence: "Programming computers to learn from experience should eventually eliminate the need for much of this detailed programming effort". *Samuel*, 210.

[14] *Mitchell*, Machine Learning (McGraw-Hill, 1997), 2. Tom M. Mitchell is a computer scientist and professor specializing in ML and AI. He co-founded the Machine Learning Department at Carnegie Mellon University, where he served as the department's Chair. Mitchell has played a pivotal role in advancing the field of ML by making substantial contributions to the development and progression of ML techniques and their practical applications.

tosa, vermicolor, and virginica).[15] Based on this data set, if one inputs data of an iris found on the street, the machine will show which species of iris it is likely to be. As such, ML has long been used for various purposes, albeit with relatively little data having been input for the assigned tasks.

In summary then, in the case of non-self-learning, machines merely provide the predesignated results after humans entered all the required (x, y) datasets one by one. In contrast, a self-learning machine can, with sufficient experience, identify the overall trend and accurately process newly introduced input to provide appropriate output that has not necessarily been pre-populated by humans.

At this point, it is worth briefly explaining the algorithms[16] that are used for ML. Since so many already exist and new ML algorithms continue to be written and studied, it is difficult to clearly classify each one. Moreover, each algorithm is an independent and complex field of research, therefore, it is impossible to understand all algorithms in-depth, especially for a law-centric paper. As mentioned in the previous chapter 2 A., this text will only examine the extent to which the groundwork can already be laid for acknowledging inventorship by providing an overview of the operating principles of AI software.

Machine learning is classified into three primary categories: (1) Supervised learning algorithms; (2) unsupervised learning algorithms; and (3) reinforcement learning algorithms. Supervised learning is applied when there are intended results, while unsupervised learning has no intended results and reinforcement learning with making decisions.

[15] The Iris flower data set is commonly used as a dataset to introduce ML and was introduced by Ronald Fisher. *Fisher*, The Use of Multiple Measurements in Taxonomic Problems, Annals of Eugenics 7, no. 2 (1936): 179–88, https://doi.org/10.1111/j.1469-1809.1936.tb02137.x.

[16] An algorithm is a procedure for solving frequently repeating problems, in other words, it allows a step-by-step process to solve a problem or accomplish some end ("Algorithm," in Merriam-Webster Online Dictionary (Merriam-Webster, 2023), https://www.merriam-webster.com/dictionary/algorithm.). A computer program can be considered as a set of sophisticated algorithms where software development began with the designing of a single algorithm that is then added to by others. There has been a tendency to mistakenly believe that algorithms are a recent phenomena, however, algorithms existed long before the advent of computers. For example, if a person solves a problem with a pencil and piece of paper using a certain procedure, they have employed an algorithm. However, it is true that algorithms have developed rapidly with the advent of computers. See also Math Vault, The Definitive Glossary of Higher Math Jargon, August 1, 2019, https://mathvault.ca/math-glossary/: "In mathematics and computer science, an algorithm is a finite series of well-defined, computer-implementable instructions to solve a specific set of computable problems".

In short, supervised learning is akin to a teacher providing questions and then helping the student with the answer. This leads to computers being able to predict correct answers to future and previously unknown problems after learning multiple questions and answers under supervision. For example, imagine an AI is being taught to distinguish between dogs and cats by using pictures of both. In this case, a data set that contains pictures of dogs and cats must be selected and input with each image labeled as 'dog' or 'cat' to teach the AI.

Types of supervised learning algorithms include classification models and prediction models. The category of the classification model is again divided into sub-categories depending on the algorithm used, such as K Nearest Neighbor (KNN), Support Vector Machine (SVM) and Decision Trees. In the prediction algorithm category, the Regression Model is a prime example. Both classification and prediction algorithms are supervised learning models, so their input data must come with labels. The output from classification models comes with one of the labels being designated as the best fit while prediction models pick the most probable fit from a functional formula derived from the learning data. Humans must put directly label each piece of learning data, so it is a double-edged sword: The data is highly accurate as a result of human involvement, however, labor cost problems arise and the amount of data is proportionally limited, because it has to be entered manually by individuals.

A classification model is used when the values of label y are finite, such as in a given numeric set. It is one of the most accessible, studied and interesting algorithm usages employed in our everyday life. For example, license plate recognition computers in parking lots typically run a classification model, however, while it is understandable to think recognizing license plates is easy given their limited forms and displayed information, it is actually somewhat problematic for an algorithm due to weather, dirt, damage and stains. As such, even for such relatively mundane tasks increasing accuracy remains the main challenge. In addition, cursive optical character recognition (OCR) programs, face recognition on Facebook and voice recognition on Apple Siri are all classification models.

The representative algorithm of a prediction model involves regression analysis, which distributes labeled learning data and then creates a function graph that best depicts the data. This model can be used to help predict the future based on past and current data; for example, to predict sales for next year based on sales of this year and the previous year, or to analyze and predict movements in stock prices and exchange rates.

Each piece of input data fed to a supervised learning algorithm has a fixed answer, so-called 'labels' while this is not the case for an unsupervised learning algorithm. The latter allows a machine to process a lot of unlabeled data and find patterns or structures in what is called the data mining process.[17] For example, company A wants to open a new branch in New York and to know the prospects for that branch. An AI can predict the locational assessment score of the new branch through unsupervised learning based on the input data, which contains all the scores gathered from all the other branches of company A. This unsupervised learning model would typically include a clustering algorithm that classifies the entire dataset into similar types of groups and analyzes each group to find a unique pattern or structure as well as a dimension reduction algorithm to help produce its output.

Unsupervised learning is beneficial for generating personalized recommendations of products and target marketing. For example, it is useful when company A wants to show its customers' preferred products on its website to increase sales. Personal information, including customers' age, gender, place of residence, purchase history and product search history are stored in the company's database and organized into informational clusters. This grouping of information can take place in various formats, for example, by gender, place of residence, time and day of purchase, price range, category of goods purchased and so forth. Various patterns can be found by such clustering. For example, if customers A, B, C, D and E are women in their 40s, searching primarily for women's clothing, on sale and at the beginning of the month, a company can seek to increase its sales by highlighting more women's clothing on its website when these individuals are browsing and sending them a sale notification email at the beginning of the month.

A dimension reduction algorithm[18] reduces high-dimensional data with many features to low-dimensional data that has perhaps only one or two features. This is done by eliminating features that are deemed irrelevant or redundant to the task at hand from among the often numerous variables contained in the learning data. Using dimensional reduction it is easier to represent data visually by compressing it and the processing procedures required for learning are reduced as the size and complexity of the learning data has been reduced.

The third operating principle of AI software cited above is reinforcement learning, a method designed to maximize rewards and minimize punishment.

---

[17] Data mining is the process of extracting valuable insights and hidden patterns from large datasets. It involves using various techniques such as clustering or classification. The term "data mining" is commonly used and has been developed and applied by many researchers and practitioners over the years.

[18] Dimension reduction algorithms include models such as Principal Component Analysis (PCA), Singular Value Decomposition (SVD) and Non-negative Matrix Factorization (NMF).

Game AI is typically used for strategy games such as chess and Go[19]. This algorithm has basically two elements: (1) an 'agent' that makes judgments; and (2) an 'environment' that is in-game situation of the agent. Every time the 'agent' makes a judgment and acts, the state of the 'environment' changes and appropriate rewards are received. In a chess game, for example, 'state values' fluctuate depending on how close the agent is to winning. Depending on how the agent moves, it can be advantageous or unfavorable for winning. The agent receives either rewards or punishments depending on the 'state values'. Over time, the game AI learns which actions maximize the reward. In other words, reinforcement learning aims to teach 'agents' to maximize the rewards they receive in a given environment. By setting function values, 'state' values that indicate the current situation and 'reward' values associated with agent action, the 'agent' is trained to choose the most rewarding behavior, which is not short-term rewards but the best cumulative results in the long term.

As such, various algorithms are employed in ML. The next section will look at what is arguably the most famous algorithm, the Artificial Neural Network (commonly referred to as Deep Learning). Deep Learning is an algorithm that can be executed in supervised learning, unsupervised learning and reinforcement learning and has contributed to advancing machines to the next level beyond humans in image recognition tasks.[20]

II. The Artificial Neural Network and the Deep Learning Algorithm

The Artificial Neural Network (ANN) is an algorithm that mimics the functionality of a biological neuron.[21] Cells in the human nervous system store information and communicate with each other in electrical signals, with much of this information being processed by the more than 100 billion neurons in the human brain. These neurons are complexly interconnected, and when stimulated, they send electrical signals to other neurons. It is beyond the scope

---

19 In March 2016, AlphaGo, an AI system, achieved victory over Lee Sedol, the world's top Go player. Go is a strategic game that demands intuition and creativity due to its incredibly large number of possible positions, which exceeds the quantity of atoms in the universe. See also: AlphaGo – The Challenge Match, Google DeepMind, accessed June 22, 2023, https://www.deepmind.com/research/highlighted-research/alphago/the-challenge-match.

20 See Chapter 2 B. II. in this paper about 2015 ILSVRC.

21 The concept of 'neural network' first appeared in the famous paper published in 1943 by Warren McCulloch and Walter Pitts called "A Logical Calculus of the Ideas Immanent in Nervous Activity". *McCulloch/Pitts*, A Logical Calculus of the Ideas Immanent in Nervous Activity, Bulletin of Mathematical Biology 52 (1990): 99–115, Reprinted from the Bulletin of Mathematical Biophysics, Vol. 5 (1943): 115–33.

of this paper to detail this process, however, neurons reacting to information received from our nervous system and then reacting to that information allows us to distinguish a chicken from a duck, for example. By modeling these human learning methods, numerous photographs of chickens and ducks are given as input to a machine until it can recognize what is a chicken and what is a duck.

In 1958, Frank Rosenblatt published his 'Perceptron study' that developed the neural network model previously presented by McCulloch and Pitts.[22] It received public attention for its remarkable achievements in discerning English letters, numbers and even simple images. The 'Perceptron study' placed a 'weight'[23] on each artificial neuron, setting it to rise if the result ended well and to fall if it ended badly. If the 'weight' falls below a certain level, if the 'weight' falls below a certain level, it generally signifies a diminished significance or contribution of the associated input feature to the ultimate output prediction.

However, Marvin Minsky, the principal pioneer of both the symbolic and connectionist schools of AI, criticized the 'Perceptron study',[24] claiming it is only capable of solving linearly separable patterns and cannot solve most problems, especially those including non-linear patterns and an XOR function.[25] This presented a substantial challenge to perceptron research, leading to the widely recognized period of stagnation known as the "(first) AI winter". This term refers to the late 1960s to the 1970s, during which there was a decline in funding and diminished interest in the field of AI.

---

[22] *Rosenblatt*, The Perceptron: A Probabilistic Model for Information Storage and Organization in the Brain, Psychological Review 65, no. 6 (1958): 386–408, https:// doi.org/10.1037/h0042519.

[23] A perceptron is an artificial neuron that mimics the operations of a biological neuron found in the human brain. In perceptron study, the concept of "weights" pertains to the numeric values assigned to the input features of a perceptron. The core of perceptron study is the function of weight, as it governs the significance and influence of each input feature on the ultimate output prediction. For more detailed information, refer to: *Goodfellow/Bengio/Courville*, Deep Learning (MIT Press, 2016), https://www.deeplearningbook.org/. Chapter 7 of this book explains the utilization of 'weights'.

[24] Minsky's main criticism originated from his book, "Perceptrons," which he co-authored with Seymour Papert in 1969. *Minsky/Papert*, Perceptrons; an Introduction to Computational Geometry (MIT Press, 1969). In their book, Minsky and Papert emphasized the limitation of the Perceptron in solving problems that were not linearly separable.

[25] The XOR function, which stands for "exclusive or", is a logical operation that produces a true output only when its two inputs are different. It was utilized to criticize the Perceptron Study because the Perceptron algorithm was incapable of solving the XOR problem.

In 1986, a piece dealing with the 'Multilayer Perceptron' was published by Geoffrey Hinton,[26] who added 'hidden layers' to the Rosenblatt's Perceptron that enabled it to solve more complex problems, including XOR. The 'Multilayer Perceptron' is a method of controlling 'weights' and 'connections' through a backpropagation algorithm to follow the neural network and then, after viewing the results, retrace its steps and adjust 'weights' and 'connections'. This proved to be a slow process but ultimately it offers stable results.

In 1989, Yaan LeCun developed a program that recognizes handwritten zip codes and categorizes them automatically.[27] It was able to recognize handwriting with approximately 90% accuracy. Later in 1998, LeCun and his colleagues published the Convolutional Neural Network algorithm (CNN) that also employed backpropagation and has proven to be one of the most popular deep learning architectures in image processing to this day.[28]

Despite the relative success of CNN, Artificial Neural Networks were not suitable for many practical applications. This was because the more the neural network learned, the slower the learning speed became and the more often the learning process returned incorrect output. Thus, Artificial Neural Network studies faced their second AI winter until the middle of the first decade of the 21st century.

In the first few years of the new millennium, hardware performance increased dramatically and increased internet speed meant data flowed more readily around the world.[29] Therefore, Geoffrey Hinton challenged the ANN study once again, and published his concept of the 'Deep Belief Networks'

---

[26] *Rumelhart/Hinton/Williams*, Learning Representations by Back-Propagating Errors, Nature 323, no. 6088 (October 1986): 533–36, https://doi.org/10.1038/323533a0.

[27] *LeCun et al.*, Backpropagation Applied to Handwritten Zip Code Recognition, Neural Computation 1, no. 4 (December 1989): 541–51, https://doi.org/10.1162/neco.1989.1.4.541.

[28] *LeCun et al.*, Gradient-Based Learning Applied to Document Recognition, IEEE 86, no. 11 (November 1998): 2278–2324, https://doi.org/10.1109/5.726791.

[29] Moore's Law is an observation and forecast made by Gordon Moore, co-founder of Intel Corporation, in 1965. The law asserts the doubling of transistor count on integrated circuits (ICs) approximately every two years, alongside a decrease in cost per transistor. This principle, which has been influential in the semiconductor industry for many years, has had a significant and far-reaching impact on technological progress. In the early 2000s, computational speed was growing incredibly fast, as Moore had predicted. For example, the performance of semiconductors doubled every two years. In addition, high-speed internet (for the time) was also available during this period and data was readily flowing worldwide. This data provided a lot of learning material for AI. In short, the extraordinary advances HW, SW and data flow provided significant stimulus to the AI industry.

(DBNs).[30] This paper is generally seen as the start of the Deep Learning era as it introduced the possibility of training a deep neural network by layerwise training. This term refers to the layers of complex neural networks that were now possible because of the newly developed computing power and the ability to input significant amounts of data. This greatly improved deep neural network training as it was possible to adjust initial values properly on each of the layers. These layer-based adjustments are called 'layerwise pre-training' and enable solving real-life problems, such as recognizing objects, speaking and translating from one language to another.

Geoffrey Hinton participated in the 2012 ILSVRC, hosted by ImageNet.[31] The competition identified numerous images, with the first-place holder in 2011 having a 74.23% recognition rate, and a goal in 2012 was the achievement of 75%. However, Hinton surprised the AI world when his Alex Net system, which utilized Deep Learning, returned an outstanding success rate of 84.69%. Since then, Deep Learning methods have become commonplace and derivative learning methods have appeared simultaneously. Furthermore, the recognition rate in ILSVRC competitions began surpassing that of humans in 2015.[32]

---

[30] *Hinton/Osindero/Teh*, A Fast Learning Algorithm for Deep Belief Nets, Neural Computation 18, no. 7 (July 2006): 1527–54, https://doi.org/10.1162/neco.2006.18.7.1527. The increased hardware performance and internet speed have significantly contributed to the realization of DBNs. DBNs rely on substantial computational power and quicker internet connections to effectively access data, particularly when working with extensive datasets. These advancements have made it possible to significantly decrease training durations from weeks or months to mere days or even hours.

[31] The ILSVRC, an annual competition organized by ImageNet, held considerable importance for the progress and growth of AI computers, specifically within the realm of computer vision. From its initiation in 2010 to its conclusion in 2017, the challenge played a crucial role in advancing the capabilities of AI systems by focusing on large-scale visual recognition tasks. ImageNet Large Scale Visual Recognition Challenge (ILSVRC), ImageNet, accessed June 23, 2023, https://image-net.org/challenges/LSVRC/index.php.

[32] In the 2015 ILSVRC, the winner was "ResNet" (Residual Network), developed by Kaiming He, Xiangyu Zhang, Shaoqing Ren, and Jian Sun. The error rate of ResNet in the 2015 ILSVRC was reported to be 3%. Worth mentioning is the reported human error rate of approximately 5.1%. Consequently, the machine's recognition rate began surpassing that of humans in 2015. *Dodge/Karam*, A Study and Comparison of Human and Deep Learning Recognition Performance under Visual Distortions, 2017, 1. "Human top-5 classification error rate on the large scale ImageNet dataset has been reported to be 5.1%"; *Sun*, ResNet on Tiny ImageNet, 2017, https://api.semanticscholar.org/CorpusID:196590979. "ResNet with 152 layers achieves the best results of 3% error rate, which is even better than human judges".

III. Genetic Algorithms and Genetic Programming

A genetic algorithm (GA) is an entirely different concept from ANNs. While ANN models the structure of a human neural network and activates only important values among numerous connected neurons, GA models Darwin's theory of evolution and chooses the best indicators that survived from among all the possible indicators.[33]

John Holland invented GA and his theoretical foundation was presented in his 1975 book Adaptation on Natural and Artificial Systems.[34] Holland's GA uses 'natural selection' with operators designed by genetics such as crossover and mutation.[35] This led to it producing ever-better results with each process iteration.[36]

Finding the optimal solution in a GA works as follows: The 'fitness function,' which represents excellent traits that adapt well to the environment, should be set first. Then, based on the 'fitness function', from among various solutions (which, using the Darwin analogy, represent the gene pool), 'parents' are selected and 'children' are determined by applying crossover or mutation operators. The 'child' generation is more fit than the 'parent' generation. Therefore, the more it evolves, that is, the more the generation-producing process is repeated, the closer the optimal solution becomes. In other words, the GA expresses possible solutions with a fixed form of an appropriate data structure and then gradually transforms them to generate increasingly better solutions.

Genetic programming (GP) is an evolutionary computation derived from GA that was applied by John Holland's students and was steadily established in the 1990s, particularly by John Koza, one of Holland's PhD students.

---

33 Although ANN and GA are entirely different algorithms, some research takes advantage of combining the two. Neuroevolution is one such example.

34 However, the concrete theoretical foundation was laid 20 years later by John Holland.

35 Crossover and mutation are recognized as the primary genetic operators: (1) crossover is a genetic operator that imitates natural reproduction by combining genetic material from parents to produce offspring. It enables the exploration of diverse combinations of genetic material, potentially resulting in offspring inheriting advantageous traits from both parents. In GA, crossover plays a role in progressing towards better solutions across generations; (2) mutation is another genetic operator that introduces random changes or alterations. In GA, mutation promotes diversity within the population and introduces fresh genetic material that could lead to enhanced solutions. See *Mitchell*, An Introduction to Genetic Algorithms (Cambridge, MA: The MIT Press, 1998), chap. 5.5 Genetic Operators, https://www.boente.eti.br/fuzzy/ebook-fuzzy-mitchell.pdf.

36 *Holland*, Adaptation in Natural and Artificial Systems: An Introductory Analysis with Applications to Biology, Control, and Artificial Intelligence (MIT Press, 1992).

Genetic algorithms use a combination of binary and real types for the gene, while GP employs a tree-based approach. Due to the difference in gene expressions, GP differs from GA in many aspects, including the areas in which it can provide solutions and its implementation methods.

Genetic programming mimics the process of biological evolution and creates new-generation solutions by using crossover, mutation, reproduction, duplication and deletion. Human operators set the seed solution, fitness measures and termination criteria, however, there is usually no human intervention in implementing these programs.[37] This is the real strength of GP, essentially allowing the AI to self-evolve without human intervention.

IV. Natural Language Processing

Natural Language Processing (NLP) is a set of techniques that machines use to process human languages via various algorithms, such as DL[38] and probabilistic algorithms, as well as by supervised, unsupervised and reinforcement learning. Natural Language Processing employs the N-gram Model, topic modeling and Word Embedded, as explained below.

The N-gram Model calculates the probability of which word will appear after which word. For example, when the sentence "I will go if he" is input, the machine predicts what the next word will be: i. e., "goes" with a very high probability.[39] Already commercially available proofreading and writing services, such as Grammarly, are good examples of how the N-gram Model is utilized. The more textual data is entered, the more natural and better sentences can be generated and recommended to the user. Interestingly, the pro-

[37] *Fraser*, Computers as Inventors – Legal and Policy Implications of Artificial Intelligence on Patent Law, 316.

[38] *Young et al.*, Recent Trends in Deep Learning Based Natural Language Processing, IEEE Computational Intelligence Magazine 13, no. 3 (2018): 55–75, https://doi.org/10.1109/MCI.2018.2840738.

[39] When n=1, it is called Unigram; when n=2, Bigrams, when n=3, Trigram; when n=4, four consecutive words are considered. For instance, in Schopenhauer's famous quote, "We seldom think of what we have, but always of what we lack," we can extract the following corpus: "we, seldom, think, of, what, we, have, but, always, of, what, we, lack [unigram]" "we seldom, seldom think, think of, of what, … we lack [bigram]" "we seldom think, seldom think of, … what we lack [trigram]" "we seldom think of, seldom think of what, … of what we lack [4-gram]". An N-gram model predicts the next word based on its N-1 previous words. Using 3-gram to predict the next word that follows, "We seldom think of what we have but always what we," only two words 'what we' at the end are considered as N-1. For example, there are 20,000 sentences with "what we" among the pre-populated datasets: 10,000 with "what we do"; 8,000 with "what we have"; and 500 with "what we lack". Consequently, the most likely "do" would be recommended due to the 3-gram algorithm.

cess of human composition is similar: We pick and use words from our subconscious which we have accumulated through our exposure since childhood to books, conversations, media and so forth.

Topic modeling is a technique to discover the 'topic' of an input text. This topic is analyzed probabilistically by grouping frequently used words in the input text or by related words that appear together at least two times.[40] For example a document with a large number of words such as Covid-19, contagious and infectious the topic would be Coronavirus; the topic of a document frequently using words such as focus, mindfulness and peace would be meditation.

Word Embedding is the efficient mapping of words or sentences to mathematical spatial coordinates. This allows computers (1) to understand the meaning of the words, and (2) to analyze the relationship between words. Locating words according to mathematical spatial coordinates enables various mathematical operations, such as calculating the distance between coordinates and sequencing them, a process that is useful in various studies. Methods for representing words as vectors are broadly divided into the category of either 'One-hot Encoding' (also known as 'sparse representation') or 'Dense Representation'.

One-hot Encoding is a traditional way of dealing with natural language, where each word is treated as an individual symbol without considering the pronunciation or meaning of the word. For example, Schopenhauer's quote "We seldom think of what we have, but always of what we lack," is a sentence consisting of nine unique words. Expressing this using One-hot Encoding, they transform into nine sequence data where only one is given a value of 1 while the rest have a value of 0. This is called a one-hot vector consisting of nine-dimensional vectors.

The problem with one-hot vectors is that the vector's dimension grows proportionally as the number of words increases. If the number of words you want to express is 100,000, the number of vectors must be 100,000. In this case, many values in the data are marked as 0, resulting in an extreme waste of space and memory.

Dense representation is intended to solve this wastage problem associated with One-hot encoding. It does not establish the dimensions of vectors, as the size of words, but as values set by the user. As a result, there are no longer only 0 and 1 values, but real numbers. For example, in a document with a total of 1,000 words, the word "Berlin" is represented as a one-hot vector with a value of 1 and surrounded by 999 values of 0, which would look like [0, 0, 0,

[40] Various professional techniques exist as subfields of topic modeling, including LDA, LSA, pLSA, and deep learning-based Ida2vec.

Table 1

The Nine-Dimensional Vectors of Schopenhauer's Quote

Words	*One-hot Encoding*
we	[1, 0, 0, 0, 0, 0, 0, 0, 0]
seldom	[0, 1, 0, 0, 0, 0, 0, 0, 0]
think	[0, 0, 1, 0, 0, 0, 0, 0, 0]
of	[0, 0, 0, 1, 0, 0, 0, 0, 0]
what	[0, 0, 0, 0, 1, 0, 0, 0, 0]
have	[0, 0, 0, 0, 0, 1, 0, 0, 0]
but	[0, 0, 0, 0, 0, 0, 1, 0, 0]
always	[0, 0, 0, 0, 0, 0, 0, 1, 0]
lack	[0, 0, 0, 0, 0, 0, 0, 0, 1]

…, 0, 1, 0, …, 0, 0]. However, changing the word "Berlin" to a dense representation, when a user sets 5 coordinate vectors, then it would be for example [0.52, 0.54, 0.46, 0.36, 0.66]. This allows words to be expressed in a denser dimension, allowing them to be classified and analyzed for various purposes.[41]

Word Embedding can be utilized for a wide variety of purposes and applications. For example, cooking recipes can be recommended by analyzing an individual's nationality and taste preferences; or the risks associated with various diseases can be highlighted by analyzing diseases that frequently occur by occupation, region, age and so forth.

[41] An example of the dense representation is the use of RGB to determine color. When the seven visible colors of a rainbow are displayed in a one-hot vector format, seven columns are needed to represent seven colors, such as red=(1, 0, 0, 0, 0, 0, 0), orange=(0, 1, 0, 0, 0, 0, 0), yellow=(0, 0, 1, 0, 0, 0, 0), green=(0, 0, 0,1, 0, 0, 0), blue=(0, 0, 0, 0, 1, 0, 0), indigo=(0, 0, 0, 0, 0, 1, 0) and violet=(0, 0, 0, 0, 0, 0, 1). Adding more colors would lead to more and longer columns, resulting in more space and memory usage. However, using RGB with three columns, red=(255, 0, 0), orange=(255, 165, 0), yellow=(255, 255, 0), green=(0, 128, 0), blue=(0, 0, 255), indigo=(75, 0, 130) and violet=(238, 130, 238). This allows a large number of colors to be expressed using only three columns by simply changing the value combinations in the columns. As such, RGB can be seen as a dense representation that fits the vector dimension by three.

C. Today's Mass Production of AI Inventions

I. Stephen Thaler's Creativity Machine and DABUS

A "[d]evice for the automatic generation of useful information" (US patent number 5,659,666)[42] was filed on 13 October 1994 by Stephen L. Thaler. This neurobiological mechanism, which Thaler introduces on his website as the "Creativity Machine", uses an ANN algorithm to mimic the human brain's biological networks for idea formation.[43]

In 2005, the Creativity Machine became even more powerful by allowing 'critic nets' to work cooperatively or adversely, reinforcing the very best of its self-originated ideas within itself.[44] The resulting patent was for a "[d]evice for the autonomous bootstrapping of useful information" (US patent number 7,454,388).[45]

Furthermore, in 2008, Thaler started work on developing a new device he dubbed the Device for the Autonomous Bootstrapping of Unified Sentience (DABUS),[46] which derives new ideas without any clear objectives. The controversial results have been written to patent applications filed worldwide, prompting legal disputes about whether machines can own intellectual property. Thaler's DABUS is an AI made up of a "swarm of many disconnected neural nets, each containing interrelated memories … of a linguistic, visual, or auditory nature". These 'neural nets' continually combine and detach, leading to the generation of complex concepts – such as the ideas described in the patent applications. Unlike other ML systems, DABUS has not been trained to solve particular problems but seeks to devise and develop new ideas, namely "what is traditionally considered the mental part of the inventive act," according to creator Stephen Thaler.[47]

---

42 *Thaler*, Device for the Autonomous Generation of Useful Information, United States US 5,659,666, filed October 13, 1994, and issued August 19, 1997, https://patents.google.com/patent/US5659666A/en United States Patent US 5,659,666A.

43 Imagination Engines Incorporated, accessed August 12, 2019, http://www.imagination-engines.com/.

44 Imagination Engines Incorporated.

45 *Thaler*, Device for the Autonomous Bootstrapping of Useful Information, US 7,454,388 B2, filed May 8, 2006, and issued November 18, 2008, United States Patent 7,454,388 B2.

46 DABUS Described, Imagination Engines Incorporated, accessed August 3, 2023, https://www.imagination-engines.com/dabus.html; *Thaler*, Device and method for the autonomous bootstrapping of unified sentience, United States US 2015/0379394 A1, filed January 2, 2015, and issued December 31, 2015.

47 *Kelion*, AI System 'Should Be Recognised as Inventor,' BBC News, August 1, 2019, sec. Technology, https://www.bbc.com/news/technology-49191645.

Since Thaler patented Creativity Machine, there have been a number of inventions filed in the name of Thaler, although he himself stated that they were invented by the Creativity Machine.[48] However, at this point, there are four inventions produced by Creativity Machine that are worth briefly considering.

The first is the "Neural Network Based Prototyping System and Method" (US patent number 5,852,815), filed on 15 May 1998. Thaler has stated that his Creativity Machine created the patented property[49] and his colleague also mentioned that "patent number two was engaged by patent number one".[50]

The second invention originating with DABUS is a new toothbrush design called the Cross Action Toothbrush, which is said to have much better functionality in terms of plaque removal and gingival health.[51] Dr. Thaler input data on existing toothbrush designs and each brush's effectiveness and,[52] based on this input data, the Creativity Machine produced the new design. "The result of random or chaotic perturbations" is the creative act engaged in by the Creativity Machine as which led to it producing new inventions.[53]

There are two other inventions created by DABUS, the first being an interlocking "food container" (application number EP 18275 163) that is designed to be easy for robots to grasp,[54] and the second is a series of "devices and methods for attracting enhanced attention in dangerous situations" (application number EP 18275 174), designed to be hard to ignore with a warning light that flashes in a rhythm.[55]

The research team of Ryan Abbott at the University of Surrey in the UK has filed applications for patents for these two inventions worldwide since 2018

48 IEI's Patented Creativity Machine® Paradigm, Imagination Engines Incorporated, accessed August 12, 2019, http://imagination-engines.com/iei_cm.php.

49 See IEI Patents, Imagination Engines Incorporated, accessed October 17, 2023, https://www.imagination-engines.com/patents.html.

50 "Patent number one" refers to the Creativity Machine with "patent number two" being the "Neural Network Based Prototyping System and Method" (US patent number 5,852,815). *Hesman*, Computer Creativity Machine Simulates the Human Brain, St. Louis Post-Dispatch, January 24, 2004, https://www.umsl.edu/~sauterv/DSS/creativitymachine_12504.html.

51 *Fraser*, Computers as Inventors – Legal and Policy Implications of Artificial Intelligence on Patent Law, 317–18.

52 Telephone Interview with Stephen Thaler, President and CEO, Imagination Engines, Inc. (10 January 2016), cited in *Abbott*, I Think, Therefore I Invent: Creative Computers and the Future of Patent Law, 1094.

53 *Thaler*, Creativity Machine® Paradigm, in: Encyclopedia of Creativity, Invention, Innovation and Entrepreneurship, ed. Elias G. Carayannis (New York: Springer, 2013), 451, https://doi.org/10.1007/978-1-4614-3858-8_396.

54 Food Container, EP3564144.

55 Devices and Methods for Attracting Enhanced Attention, EP3563896.

citing DABUS as the inventor. As previously noted, this team and their activity in this regard are officially called the Artificial Inventor Project (AIP) and although most countries have ruled unfavorably on AI inventorship, there have been positive results in both South Africa and Australia.

II. John Koza's Invention Machine

While Thaler's Creativity Machine and DABUS are based on ANN, the Invention Machine is based on genetic programming.[56] GP is invented by John Koza, and his "invention machine"[57] embodies the essence of GP. The Invention Machine is composed of 1,000 networked computers that are not working with predetermined routines but with unique routines that produce better results than human inventors.[58]

In his 2010 paper, Koza introduces 76 instances that he describes as "human-competitive results". These are either patented results or patent infringement results.[59] There are three well-known and particularly useful inventions among those 76 cases: (1) apparatus for improved general-purpose PID and non-PID controllers;[60] (2) an optical lens system; and (3) an evolved antenna.

---

56 The GP's official website introduces seven traits about the fundamental differences between GP and other ML algorithms such as ANN. For more information: Seven Differences Between Genetic Programming and Other Approaches to Machine Learning and Artificial Intelligence, Genetic Programming Inc., August 27, 2003, https://www.genetic-programming.com/sevendiffs.html.

57 The name 'Invention Machine' is what John Koza himself likes to call it. *Keats*, John Koza Has Built an Invention Machine, Popular Science, April 19, 2006, https://www.popsci.com/scitech/article/2006-04/john-koza-has-built-invention-machine/. "His invention machine, as he likes to call it".

58 *Keats*: "Koza's 1,000 networked computers don't just follow a preordained routine. They create, growing new and unexpected designs out of the most basic code. They are computers that innovate, that find solutions not only equal to but better than the best work of expert humans".

59 *Koza*, Human-Competitive Results Produced by Genetic Programming, Genetic Programming and Evolvable Machines 11, no. 3 (September 1, 2010): 251–84, https://doi.org/10.1007/s10710-010-9112-3. Koza described in this paper, "Genetic programming has now been used to produce at least 76 instances of results that are competitive with human-produced results". Meanwhile, the GP's official website introduces some 23 instances (21 Previously Patented Inventions Reinvented by Genetic Programming and 2 Patentable Inventions Created by Genetic Programming) Genetic Programming Is an Automated Invention Machine, Genetic Programming Inc., December 30, 2003, https://www.genetic-programming.com/inventionmachine.html.

60 A PID controller is a type of control system that is widely used and can stands for Proportional-Integral-Derivative (PID) controller. On the other hand, non-PID controllers are control systems that do not follow the traditional PID control structure. They are used in specific situations where they may be a better fit or more effective.

First, the "apparatus for improved general-purpose PID and non-PID controllers" (US Patent No. 6,847,851B1) is a system to make factories more efficient. Koza filed a patent application in July 2002 and the apparatus was patented in January 2005, meaning it passed the Turing test. The patent officers at that time were not aware that it was a computer-generated invention.[61] To obtain the patent, Koza was forced to nominate human inventors,[62] as advised by his legal counsel. However, "the whole invention was created by a computer". explained by Koza.[63]

The second invention is a complex optical lens system created by the Invention Machine in 2005.[64] It performs better than what was the most advanced lens system at that time, namely, the lens system designed by Noboru Koizumi and Naomi Watanabe (US Patent No. 6,069,750A),[65] moreover, it does not infringe on the Koizumi-Watanabe patent.[66] The Invention Machine's process that led to it inventing this lens system was as follows:[67]

(a) To begin, the Invention Machine randomly generated 75,000 prescriptions. It then analyzed them in KOJAC,[68] which assigned each prescription a fitness rating based on how close it came to a desired set of specifications – in this case, a wide field of view with minimal distortion.

---

61 *Keats*, John Koza Has Built an Invention Machine.

62 This patent contains the names of three inventors: Martin A. Keane, John R. Koza and Matthew J. Streeter.

63 Telephone Interview with John Koza, President, Genetic Programming Inc., January 22, 2016; *Abbott*, I Think, Therefore I Invent: Creative Computers and the Future of Patent Law, 1088. "Dr. Koza stated that his legal counsel advised him at the time that his team should consider themselves inventors despite the fact that 'the whole invention was created by a computer'".

64 *Koza/Al-Sakran/Jones*, Automated Re-Invention of Six Patented Optical Lens Systems Using Genetic Programming, in: Proceedings of the 7th Annual Conference on Genetic and Evolutionary Computation, GECCO '05 (New York: Association for Computing Machinery, 2005), 1953–60, https://doi.org/10.1145/1068009.1068337.

65 The patent was filed in 1997 and described as a wide-field eyepiece for telescopes and binoculars.

66 *Keats*, John Koza Has Built an Invention Machine.

67 *Keats*.

68 KOJAC is a set of Java classes implementing optical elements and optics laws in order to build and simulate optical systems. It was developed at the IMT by Olivier Scherler. *Keats*: "Lee Jones (Koza's two employees: Lee Jones, Sameer Al-Sakran) calls up an optical simulator known as KOJAC. From a prescription (which numerically describes the curvature, thickness and glass type of lens components), KOJAC predicts how the compound lens will function in the real world. The numerous variables make the effect of simple changes difficult to predict. As a result, lens designers are a creative bunch, who depend as heavily on intuition as on knowledge". See also: *Scherler*, KOJAC: Optics Java Applets Classes, accessed October 17, 2023, https://olivier.ithink.ch/kojac/index.html.

(b) The machine took the original 75,000 prescriptions as the first generation and redistributed characteristics from two-parent lens systems into their offspring. It also inserted mutations, randomly altering a single detail and then went through a process imitating Darwin's natural selection: The machine rejected most lenses with low fitness ratings from the population, effectively killing them off so their genetic material will not contaminate future generations.

(c) This process was reiterated for 295 generations and, as a result, the machine was able to overcome the limitations of Koizumi-Watanabe's lenses.[69] The final field-of-view for Koza's eyepiece is a remarkable 10 degrees higher than the 55 degrees achieved by Koizumi-Watanabe.

The third invention was an evolved antenna developed under the guidance of Jason D. Lohn, Gregory S. Hornby and Derek S. Linden for use on NASA's Space Technology 5 mission.[70] Lohn plugged in the antenna's basic requirements and let the software run, several hundred generations later he got what appeared to be a mistake. "It looked like a bent paper clip," he stated, recalling that there is no chapter in any textbooks on crooked wire antennas, so it looked preposterous, but it was perfectly suited to its niche function.[71] This case highlights that GP is capable of exploring possibilities and options beyond current human knowledge, it readily works with notions and concepts many human scientists would dismiss out of hand.

As an interesting side point, the Invention Machine's other inventions include various logic circuits, amplifiers and filters, some of which are well-suited for the challenging low-power requirements of cellphones and laptops. Each took between one day and one month to evolve, generating an electricity bill of more than US $ 3,000 a month.[72]

III. Watson by IBM

The previously described Creativity Machine operates using ANN, while the Inventory Machine utilizes GP, however, IBM developed Watson[73] as a 'Cognitive Computing system' that runs with a completely different algo-

---

69 *Koza/Al-Sakran/Jones*, Automated Re-Invention of Six Patented Optical Lens Systems Using Genetic Programming, 1957.

70 *Lohn/Hornby/Linden*, An Evolved Antenna for Deployment on Nasa's Space Technology 5 Mission, in: Genetic Programming Theory and Practice II, ed. Una-May O'Reilly et al., Genetic Programming (Boston, MA: Springer US, 2005), 301–15, https://doi.org/10.1007/0-387-23254-0_18.

71 *Keats*, John Koza Has Built an Invention Machine.

72 *Keats*.

73 Watson was named after Thomas J. Watson, the first president of IBM.

rithm. In brief, Watson is a machine that acquires information by understanding human language and communicating naturally with humans based on natural language processing.

The dictionary definition of cognition is "the process by which knowledge and understanding are developed in the mind".[74] Consequently, cognitive computing means implementing an ability in a computer that mimics the human thinking process.

In particular, IBM's Watson aims to provide differentiated insights and solutions by understanding and learning data like humans, based on NLP technology. Natural Language Processing technology is crucial for processing and extracting valuable insights from the immense volume of unstructured data[75] that exists in the world. In other words, if computers themselves can understand and infer meaning from natural language data like humans, their contribution to science and technology is expected to be remarkably rapid as access to unstructured data accelerates.

In 2007, IBM began creating a computer system that could compete with human champions of quiz shows,[76] 4 years later in 2011, Watson became famous when it beat former winners Ken Jennings and Brad Rutter on the Jeopardy!™ quiz show.[77] Watson derives answers by analyzing questions, which are natural language, generating hypotheses, finding evidence and evaluations for its hypothesis and then ranking them.

Since 2011, Watson has been more active in research and development based on advanced NLP technology and is being utilized in various fields such as (1) culinary recipes; (2) medical practice; (3) new drug development;

---

[74] "Cognition," in Oxford Learner's Dictionaries (Oxford University Press, 2023), https://www.oxfordlearnersdictionaries.com/definition/english/love_1.

[75] 'Unstructured data' refers to any data that lacks a predetermined or structured format, lacking a fixed schema or data model. Analyzing and processing such data using conventional methods becomes more difficult. Unstructured data can manifest in various forms, like written documents, emails, content shared on social networking platforms, images, audio recordings, videos, and other similar forms. It is estimated that 80% of worldwide data is unstructured data. Hence, NLP technology enables organizations, researchers, and individuals to unlock valuable information, enhance decision-making, and attain a competitive advantage in today's data-centric world. See *Rogers*, The 80% Blind Spot: Are You Ignoring Unstructured Organizational Data?, Forbes, January 29, 2019, https://www.forbes.com/sites/forbestechcouncil/2019/01/29/the-80-blind-spot-are-you-ignoring-unstructured-organizational-data/.

[76] As the principal investigator of the Watson project, Dave Ferrucci spearheaded the team at IBM responsible for the development of Watson. *Ferrucci et al.*, Building Watson: An Overview of the DeepQA Project, AI Magazine 31, no. 3 (July 28, 2010): 59–79, https://doi.org/10.1609/aimag.v31i3.2303.

[77] Jeopardy!™ is a popular TV quiz show that has been broadcast in the US for more than 30 years.

and (4) software app development activities. All of these activities have resulted in patentable objects.

When developing recipes for cooking Watson is referred to as 'Chef Watson' and, in April 2015, a recipe book entitled Cognitive Cooking with Chef Watson was published.[78] So far, no attempt has been made to register a patent for Watson's new recipes, although this does not detract from the fact that an AI devised previously unrecorded cooking recipes.

Watson has learned data regarding various ingredients of past and present dishes, including flavor compatibility, nutrient combinations, cultural backgrounds and chemical compositions. Based on this knowledge, new recipe ideas were generated and 'Chef Watson' could provide individuals with personalized recipes that exclude ingredients they dislike or are allergic to. Indeed, the AI's recipes have returned good results that have pleasantly surprised many human chefs.[79]

Cooking recipes are patentable under US law. Patents may be granted for any "new and useful process, machine, manufacture, or composition of matter or any new and useful improvement thereof" (35 U.S.C. 101). On this basis, food recipes qualify as patentable subject matter because the combination of food ingredients belongs to "new compositions of matter" or "manufacture" and the cooking thereof is a "new and useful process".[80] This holds true as long as the recipe is also novel, nonobvious and useful.

'Watson for Oncology' uses cognitive computing to treat cancer after receiving 5,000 hours of training from cancer specialists. As a result, Watson has learned more than 600,000 pieces of medical evidence, over 2 million pages of medical journals and 1.5 million patient records. This process has given Watson a good understanding of patients' conditions from which it can derive recommended treatments. As a result, Watson's cognitive computing technology is helping with accurate diagnosis in the medical field.

To date, there has been no case in which an AI has developed a new medical treatment, however, there is a good chance that a new patentable treatment will be developed in the not-too-distant future. The patentable subject matter

---

78 The authors were "IBM and the Institute of Culinary Education" because AI could not be the author legally.

79 *Bilow*, How IBM's Chef Watson Actually Works, Bon Appetit, June 30, 2014, https://www.bonappetit.com/entertaining-style/trends-news/article/how-ibm-chef-watson-works.

80 See: Can Recipes Be Patented?, Inventors Eye 4, no. 3 (June 2013), https://perma.cc/EN3V-9DY4. See also Diamond v. Chakrabarty, 447 U.S. 303 (Supreme Court of the United States 1980). Noting that patentable subject matter "include[s] anything under the sun that is made by man".

of medical practice varies from country to country.[81] The situation regarding the German and US laws that are the focus of this paper is as follows: (1) In Germany, as well as the European Patent Convention (EPC),[82] medical procedures on a human or animal body are not patentable as the act of treating a patient should not put a medical professional at risk of infringing a patent. However, these exclusions from patentability are construed narrowly. Therefore, a patent can be acquired for methods useful in medical treatment if written in appropriate terms. (2) The US recognizes the patentability of medical practices as US law has been written based on a position of broad-based patentability recognition, only denying patentability on subject matters related to natural laws, natural phenomena and abstract ideas.

'Watson for Drug Discovery' has already led to new drug developments. The AI works tirelessly and rapidly, compared to human efforts, through the task of exploring and evaluating millions of new drug substances. This helps save time and money in the search for new drugs and increases the chances of these novel finding entering into clinical research.[83] For example, Merck, which uses Atomwise's AI specializing in developing new drugs, analyzed combinations of more than 700 commercially available drugs that were thought to be useful for treating Ebola in a day and discovered two substances that held promise. This process would have taken years if it had been done by

---

[81] Most countries state that medical practices are not patentable. According to a report published in 2011 by WIPO, there are 70 countries where legislation exempts treatment methods from patents: See *Bently et al.*, Exclusions from Patentability and Exceptions and Limitations to Patentees' Rights (WIPO Standing Committee on the Law of Patents, 2011), https://www.wipo.int/edocs/mdocs/scp/en/scp_16/scp_16_ref_scp_15_3-annex1.pdf.

[82] The European Patent Convention divides medical practice into surgical, therapeutic and diagnostic acts in social policy and these practices are explicitly excluded from patentability. However, the European Commission for Patent and Trademark Office, which is responsible for the Convention's interpretation, partially acknowledges the patentability of the subject matter through an interpretation of each act.

[83] It typically takes 10 to 12 years to discover and launch new drugs and the world's 12 large-cap biopharma companies spend about US$2.16 billion on the R&D process each year, 1/3 of which is spent during the new drug discovery phase. However, of every 10,000 substances that are screened, an average of only 10 enter into clinical trials and less than 10% of clinical trials are successful. Moreover, these figures have not changed much in decades. In particular, one of the main factors reducing the accuracy of the new drug development process is a lack of precise knowledge of the three-dimensional structure of the drug and target proteins. If AI technology can indirectly predict the efficacy of candidate drugs, it can improve the time and cost of developing new drugs. Ultimately, it can contribute to productivity improvements throughout the R&D process.

humans manually.[84] Needless to say, in both Germany and the US, new drugs are subject to patentability.

Watson also helps develop applications through IBM Bluemix, a cloud-based mobile application production platform introduced by IBM in February 2014.[85] More than 140 Application Program Interfaces (API) are registered at Bluemix, with Watson being one of them. Watson's work here has seen it develop an app that helps to build better interpersonal relationships based on analyzing chat content using an NLP algorithm that extracts the other person's tendencies and/or emotions; Watson also devised a learning-game app that helps people to memorize special knowledge by sharing questions with Watson.

In these cases, Watson has not developed a new app on its own but has only helped developers with NLP. However, there is again a good possibility that an AI will develop a novel new app in the near future.[86] For example, if a project is directed towards developing an application that solves a specific problem, an AI will be able to generate appropriate source code and design the corresponding remedial app.

If an AI develops an entirely new app, patents or copyrights are available in this case pursuant to German law and US law. However, it's important to note that AI inventorship is not legally recognized. Therefore, if the AI's name is listed as the inventor, the patent would be rejected.

Meanwhile, Watson has taken one more interesting step regarding patent law. In 2015, the Australian Patent Office used Watson to analyze a vast amount of patent data written in natural language and provide information to patent applicants. As a result, Watson's efforts dramatically reduced the period of patent examination and increased the accuracy of its examination.

---

84 Atomwise, an AI drug discovery company, utilizes deep learning algorithms known as AtomNet to analyze extensive molecular data and predict potential drug candidates. The AI technology examines the molecular structures and characteristics of these compounds, identifying the ones most likely to interact with the Ebola virus in a therapeutically advantageous way. It accelerates the initial stages of drug discovery, which conventionally entail time-consuming and costly experimental screening of compounds. Ultimately, the AI-driven methodology enables a more efficient and targeted exploration for promising drug candidates. "Atomwise," Pharmaceutical Technology, accessed July 4, 2023, https://www.pharmaceutical-technology.com/contractors/ps-ai/atomwise/.

85 In terminology, this is called Platform as a Service (PaaS).

86 App Builder That Builds Apps in Five Minutes without Coding, Appy Pie, 2023, https://www.appypie.com/app-builder/appmaker.

So far, this paper's focus has been on inventions that can be patented as a result of Watson's activities, however, Watson has also been active with other meaningful activities in the field of intellectual property rights.[87]

D. Comparison between AI Software and Human Brain

As previously noted, the software component of AI is comparable to the brain of a human being and ML, which is a category of AI software, has been explained above. This then begs the question of what are the commonalities and differences between AI software and the natural human brain (i.e. Human Intelligence, HI)? Understanding this will serve as a logical basis for discussing the 'creative thinking' for inventive action in AI dealt with in Chapter 6.

Before comparing the human brain with AI, it needs to again be emphasized that this paper focuses on 'weak AI' – as mentioned in the research scope of the introductory chapter. This is because strong AI and super AI that is the same as or beyond human capabilities do not yet exist and there is no realistic basis to review their structures or abilities.

When comparing HI with AI, five specific aspects will be examined: desire, emotion, memory, sensation and method.

First, humans have needs and desires, however, AI does not. Abraham Maslow, an American psychologist who is best known for his theory on the hierarchy of human needs, thought that there were five levels of desire in humans, commonly referred to as 'Maslow's hierarchy of needs'. The first level of the hierarchy is the primary or physiological needs: food, water, sleep, sex, homeostasis and excretion. The second level is safety needs: security, order and stability. These two steps are essential to the physical survival of the person. The third level of need is love and belonging, which are psychological needs. The fourth level is esteem, which relates to self-respect and social recognition. The fifth level, which sits at the top of the pyramid, is the need for self-actualization and is pursued by individuals seeking to achieve their full poten-

[87] Watson's activities in the field of intellectual property rights include the following: (1) producing cognitive dresses for Met Gala in New York; (2) producing movie trailers (Watson analyzed 100 horror movie trailers and extracted ten scenes for a trailer, a process that took only about 24 hours. Given that movie-trailer production is labor-intensive and usually takes 10 to 30 days, this shows the time and cost advantages of using AI for such tasks); (3) collaborating with musician to compose songs with 'Watson Beat' (Grammy Award-winning producer Alex Da Kid released a new song entitled "Not Easy" that was produced using Watson in 2016. Within 48 hours of its release, the song reached Top 4 on iTunes Hot Tracks and Top 6 on iTunes alternative. Watson analyzed five years of cultural data to understand each year's 'emotional temperature', reviewed comments posted on social media and reviewed music trends for 5 years on the Billboard charts).

tial.[88] In his later years, Maslow considered transcendence as the sixth level, in which one wants to go beyond one's original vision of self-actualization.[89] However, AI has none of these needs and desires. AI's software has a clear purpose, namely processing data by classifying or predicting it for a purpose that the operator has stipulated. AI is programmed like that, therefore, it moves like that, and needs do not come into the equation. When humans experience discomfort, they desire to improve their situation and/or invent tools to lessen that discomfort. Furthermore, humans will invent because of an inherent desire for self-actualization as scientists or inventors. In contrast, AI is not driven by desires, it only reacts to the programming it has been given for various specific purposes.

The second difference is that humans have emotions while AI does not. For example, in the science-fiction movie "Ex Machina", a female-looking AI robot called Ava intentionally baits a human called Caleb into trying to escape from the facilities of an AI programmer called Nathan. Ava used the natural language it had learned to emotionally agitate and manipulate Caleb into a course of action. From Caleb's perspective, it looked like the AI had feelings and desires, however, it was simply running an algorithm that tasked it to find a means of escape. In other words, an AI can imitate the presence of feelings, but such behavior is simply an empty facade. That is not to suggest this behavior is without merit as it may, for example, be used to comfort people with dementia and/or mental illnesses. For example, human-like and emotion-based AI can identify human facial expressions and posture understands the observed individuals' intentions and emotions and then interacts with them by employing gestures humans use to provide comfort, such as hugs or certain hand gestures, as well as natural expressions designed to convey the impression of emotion.

The third difference is that human memory is more limited and not always as accessible as the memory of an AI that can be given access to enormous amounts of data. The human brain can have many malfunctions, ranging from such things as memory distortions and forgetfulness to dementia and amnesia.[90] In comparison, an AI's memory is determined only by the accuracy and quantity of the input data, memory distortions that often occur in human brains do not occur in AIs. Whatever data is input, an AI can always be trusted

---

88 *Maslow*, A Theory of Human Motivation, Psychological Review 50 (1943): 370–96.

89 *Maslow*, The Farther Reaches of Human Nature (Penguin, 1993).

90 Daniel Schacter asserts that memory's malfunctions can be divided into seven cases: transience, absent-mindedness, blocking, misattribution, suggestibility, bias and persistence. *Schacter*, The Seven Sins of Memory: How the Mind Forgets and Remembers (Houghton Mifflin, 2001).

to accurately regurgitate that data at any point in the future.[91] The only problem that may occur in this regard is if humans enter wrong or manipulated data into an AI by error, that inaccuracy will be retained by the AI.[92] Interestingly in terms of similarities, humans learn from experience, can make predictions based on long-term memory stored in the neocortex and make optimal choices in various situations based on this. Even weak AIs have manifested various similar high-level intelligence factors based on data that essentially provide a vast long-term memory.[93]

The fourth difference is that humans have five senses: vision (sight), audition (hearing), gustation (taste), olfaction (smell), and tactition (touch), while AI does not have those natural senses, but electronic senses. These electronic senses are usually in the shape of sensors or input devices, which allow AI to comprehend and analyze data from the surroundings. For example, AI can have electronic sensors such as cameras, microphones, or other sensor varieties to collect visual or auditory information. These senses empower AI systems to effectively interpret the environment, much like how humans rely on their natural senses to perceive their surroundings.

Fifth, HI relies on biological energy, while AI operates on electrical energy. Living organisms, including humans, obtain energy by exchanging energy between cells and the external environment. Animals typically obtain energy by consuming nutrients from food, while plants obtain energy through photosynthesis, converting sunlight into chemical energy without the need for food intake. The human adult brain has an average weight of 1,400 gm and measures approximately 167 x 140 x 93 mm, however, despite its lack of size, it has tremendous efficiency. The hardware of AI can fill entire rooms and consumes huge amounts of electrical energy, although these days both physical size and energy consumption are rapidly decreasing with technological developments.

---

[91] For example, AI is superior to humans in quiz competitions when finding answers to questions.

[92] For example, in January 2021, a controversy arose in South Korea over sexist remarks by the AI-Iruda. This situation happened because biased data was originally input by humans.

[93] Numenta, founded in 2005, is trying to implement the human brain's neocortex abilities into AI software. The neocortex is known to govern the intelligence of higher organisms and is active in brain functions related to the manifestation of things such as willpower, desire and judgment. Only mammals or higher animals have this functionality and the higher the animal, the broader scope. Numenta believes that implementing neocortex operations into an AI is essential to developing a strong AI capable of recognizing problems, making judgements and acting on its own. Therefore, this company is developing Hierarchical Temporal Memory (HTM), which models the driving principle of the neocortex. For more, see *Numenta*, About Us, https://www.numenta.com/company/.

To this point, the focus has been on the difference between the human brain and an AI's software. From a hardware perspective, humans are complex biological organisms composed of organs, cells, and other biological components, while computers are composed of electronic components. However, there is an emerging field called "bio-computing" that explores the use of living cells as hardware. For example, "DishBrain," developed by Cortical Labs in Australia, consists of 800,000 to 1,000,000 living brain cells and has learned to play the computer arcade game Pong in just five minutes, while AI took 90 minutes.[94] This suggests that computers can operate more quickly and efficiently when utilizing living brain cells. In the future, the distinction between biological and electronic forms may become blurred. If AI can be organically bonded to the human body, it could create a world without brain death. However, technology to fully connect an artificial brain to a living natural body is a tremendous challenge in biotechnology.

The comparison of AI and human brains in this section was done because 'the process that leads to AI inventions' and 'the process of making inventions by humans' need to be compared. Patent law has historically recognized inventorship exclusively for natural persons, as they possess the ability to exercise creativity, a crucial element in the process of inventing. However, when comparing the disparities between HI and AI, one may question whether AI could potentially possess a form of 'inventive thinking' akin to that of humans.

Below, I will compare the differences and similarities between AI and HI, limiting the scope of the invention process. The invention process can be analyzed in three parts: (1) task selection, (2) learning and (3) problem solving/deriving results.

Table 2

HI vs AI: In the Scope of the Invention Process

	Human Intelligence	*Artificial Intelligence*
Step 1	Perceive a problem	Task-selection
Step 2	Obtain basic knowledge	Learn with input data
Step 3	Solve the problem/Derive the results/Design the invention	

[94] *Kagan et al.*, In Vitro Neurons Learn and Exhibit Sentience When Embodied in a Simulated Game-World, Neuron 110, no. 23 (December 7, 2022).

First, in terms of task selection, AI performs tasks solely given to it by humans, whereas humans can and do select tasks independently.[95] Human beings desire to survive or improve their quality of life, while AI only engages in the inventive process in response to its programmed purposes.

The second step demonstrates that both humans and AI are similar in their learning processes, which is unsurprising given AI imitates human learning models via ANN and GA.

In fact, humans have two kinds of knowledge: (1) innate knowledge; and (2) acquired knowledge. Chomsky, for example, argues that babies can acquire language in a short period because they have an innate property to do so, which is embodied in a 'language acquisition device' (LAD) called the 'little black box.'[96] However, it is not easy to measure the extent of innate knowledge and the extent to which it contributes to the invention process, therefore, it is left out of the discussion here. What this means in essence is that the learning process of an AI is similar to that which occurs in a human brain, at least with regard to acquired learning experiences.

Third, the problem-solving stage of the inventive process sees the human brain find a solution in six stages as described by Bloom's Taxonomy[97], however, AI has not yet mastered a similar approach, as a study by Jim Parker and Shannon Jaeger revealed.[98] Having said that, not all six steps of Bloom Texamony are required to legally acknowledge inventorship. In particular, Chapter 4 B. will deal in detail with which steps have legal import under German and US law using the framework of the previously mentioned '2/7 Questions' concept. This problem-solving process is very important because this is the process in which an inventor derives an invention after acquiring and applying knowledge. This process must be unique to the inventor so his/her status as the inventor is recognized. It will be discussed throughout Chapter 4 that neither the natural nor legal persons associated with AI inventions can be assigned as the inventor before Chapter 6 discusses whether AI has devised any truly ingenious solutions.

---

[95] Of course, if humans are employed by a company, they will frequently be required to perform the tasks given them by others.

[96] *Chomsky*, Reflections on Language (Douglas: Pantheon, 1975).

[97] Bloom's taxonomy is a classification system that explains how humans acquire knowledge in 6-steps: (1) remembering (knowledge), (2) understanding (comprehension), (3) applying (application), (4) analyzing (analysis), (5) evaluating (synthesis) and (6) creating (adaptation).

[98] *Parker/Jaeger*, Learning in Artificial Intelligence: Does Bloom's Taxonomy Apply?, SSRN Electronic Journal, 2016, https://doi.org/10.2139/ssrn.2891191.

Chapter 3

Comparative Studies of the Requirements for Inventorship Under Patent Law in Germany and the US

A. Introduction

I. The Need for Comparative Law Research in AI Inventorship

Gustav Radbruch's relativistic view reminds us of the importance of the act of comparison. The role of legal philosophy is to analyze and compare basic evaluations of different worldviews, without prioritizing one over another.[1]

Countries around the world are very engaged in comparative law research,[2] a relatively new field of study with a history dating back only about 150 years.[3]

---

[1] See *Radbruch*, Rechtsphilosophie, 3., ganz neu bearbeitete und stark vermehrte Auflage (Leipzig: Quelle & Meyer, 1932), 9. "*Sollenssätze sind nur durch andere Sollenssätze begründbar und beweisbar. Eben deshalb sind die letzten Sollenssätze unbeweisbar, axiomatisch, nicht der Erkenntnis, sondern nur des Bekenntnisses fähig. Wo also entgegengesetzte Behauptungen über die letzten Sollenssätze, entgegengesetzte Wert- und Weltanschauungen einander streitend gegenübertreten, kann zwischen ihnen nicht mehr mit wissenschaftlicher Eindeutigkeit entschieden werden.*"; *Radbruch*, 11. "*Die hier dargelegte Methode nennt sich Relativismus, weil sie die Richtigkeit jedes Werturteils nur in Beziehung zu einem bestimmten obersten Werturteil, nur im Rahmen einer bestimmten Wert- und Weltanschauung, nicht aber die Richtigkeit dieses Werturteils, dieser Wert- und Weltanschauung selbst festzustellen sich zur Aufgabe macht.*"

[2] For example, (1) In Germany, the Max-Plank-Institute were established in major cities and universities for the comparative law study, such as Max Planck Institute for: Comparative Public Law and International Law in Heidelberg; Comparative and International Private Law in Hamburg; Legal History and Legal Theory in Frankfurt; and Intellectual Property and Competition Law in Munich. See also: Max Planck Institute for Comparative Public Law and International Law (Heidelberg), accessed June 26, 2022, https://www.mpil.de/en/pub/news.cfm; Max Planck Institute for Comparative and International Private Law (Hamburg), accessed June 26, 2022, https://www.mpipriv.de/home; Max Planck Institute for Legal History and Legal Theory (Frankfurt), accessed June 26, 2022, https://www.lhlt.mpg.de/en; Max Planck Institute for Innovation and Competition – Intellectual Property and Competition Law (Munich), accessed June 26, 2022, https://www.ip.mpg.de/en/. Scientists of various nationalities and majors are actively working together in these institutes. (2) The International Academy of Comparative Law was founded at The Hague on 13 September 1924, and

While many advantages can be derived from comparative law research, there are two in particular worth addressing for the context of this paper:

(1) There are advantages from the perspective of legal interpretation. It is possible to contribute to a better interpretation of the law of one country by examining similar laws in another country. For example, a legal scientist from Japan can work on the historical background of clauses in civil law by researching German law to find a more reasonable interpretation,[4] as Japanese civil law has been absorbing many foreign influences, such as German civil law.[5]

(2) There are also benefits from the perspective of enactment or revision. A comparison with the similar or different legal systems may aid in the better enactment or revision of existing domestic law, as lawmakers can gain insights into alternative approaches, effective strategies, and possible pitfalls, by examining how other countries have approached similar legal issues. This is because comparative law research does not compare each statutory provision with its counterpart in another legal system, rather it

---

the International Congress of Comparative Law has been held regularly since 1932. IACL – International Academy of Comparative Law, accessed June 26, 2022, https:// aidc-iacl.org/general-presentation/. (3) In the United States, comparative law was greatly developed by the 'exile jurists' who were brought to the United States by Nazism. (4) "The International Encyclopedia of Comparative Law" has been published since 1981. *Zweigert* (ed.), International Encylopedia of Comparative Law (Springer Netherlands, 1981); (5) Ernst Rabel founded Germany's first Institute of Comparative Law at the University of Munich in 1916. See also: Tagung 100 Jahre Institut für Rechtsvergleichung, Juristische Fakultät – Ludwig-Maximilians-Universität München, 100, accessed June 28, 2022, https://www.jura.uni-muenchen.de/fakultaet/lehrstuehle/ lorenz/rechtsvergleichung/index.html.

[3] Law began in ancient Rome and was formulated as an 'academic' in the West. Thus, the history of modern world law can be said to be the spread of reception western laws into all over the world. Of course, in western laws, there have been various legal families (in German '*Rechtsfamilie*') or legal cultures (in German '*Rechtskultur*') such as continental law, Anglo-American law, and socialist law. This is the reason why comparative law study began 150 years ago, which researches different systems and concepts.

[4] In general, a country still developing its legislation will adopt legal principles and laws from countries with long-established legal traditions, thus embracing what is often widely considered to be modern law. Comparative law refers to this as the relationship between parent law (*Mutterrecht* in German) and filial law (*Tochterrecht* in German). However, the laws resulting from this relationship are not simply copy-pasted as the adopting legal system will change over time and even when initially incorporated, foreign influences may be altered to better suit the indigenous situation of the society in question.

[5] *Kitagawa*, The Identity of German and Japanese Civil Law in Comparative Perspectives (Berlin: De Gruyter, 2007).

explores and compares the people's lives depending on the law system in place and the function of the law on which each legal system works.

As such, of the many positives that can be derived from comparative law research, this paper will focus particularly on the contributive aspect of the "enactment or revision of the law" in the context of the legislative direction of the inventorship of AI. Henry Maine (1822–1888), a 19th-century scholar engaged in comparative law studies, said, "the chief function of comparative jurisprudence is to facilitate legislation and the practical improvement of law".[6]

Comparative law studies are particularly active in the field of commercial law,[7] which is ultimately due to ongoing growth in international trade in particular. This trade has created the necessity to streamline domestic laws so they function well within the global system, as far as possible, to avoid creating disadvantages in international trade competition. For this purpose, comparative law studies are essential. Today, each country has its own legal system, however, international activities often see legal problems arise, such as in the areas of transportation and communication This leads to frequent international exchanges in various fields, ranging from society and culture through to law. With regard to the latter, harmonization between legal systems is being seriously studied to solve these various problems and patent law is no exception.[8] Patent law gives patent holders the right to monopolize the market with their invention for a certain period. Given that monopolies are a very sensitive issue for trade and business, comparative legal considerations are essential for handling the growing issue of the need for patent law revision in the era of AI.

As time goes by, we find ourselves entering an era where many areas of activity that were solely human-driven are becoming shared spaces with AI, however, many relevant laws have not yet caught up with this fast-moving technological change. In studying the direction of new enactments and revisions of patent laws in the AI era, a comparative law approach based on exist-

---

6 *Sumner Maine*, Village-Communities in the East and West: Six Lectures Delivered at Oxford, 4th ed. (London: Murray, 1881).

7 In the field of commercial law, there is a trend toward universalization, such as the enactment of the Uniform Commercial Code (UCC).

8 The Patent Law Treaty (PLT) was concluded on 1 June 2000 and was aimed at harmonizing formal procedures, such as the requirements to obtain a filing date for a patent application, the form and content of a patent application and representation. Moreover, the Substantive Patent Law Treaty (SPLT) is under negotiation to harmonize substantive points of patent law. Meanwhile, since 2011, the heads of offices and representatives from Denmark, France, Germany, Japan, UK, the USA and the EPO gathered at Tegernsee for a meeting to consider the state of affairs concerning patent law harmonization. The Tegernsee Process, European Patent Office, accessed June 28, 2022, https://www.epo.org/law-practice/harmonisation/tegernsee-process.html.

ing laws is indispensable. It is important to examine the basis of the legal conception of inventorship and find a philosophical basis for giving AI a new legal status, by comparing as many laws as possible on whether AI can be granted as an inventor.

II. The Importance of Inventorship Studies

All patents begin with the inventor. Inventors who create inventions apply for patents to be recognized for their inventive actions and to receive legitimate compensation for their efforts and success. In other words, the status of the inventor in patent rights – the inventorship – is essentially the foundation of patent rights. Therefore, inventorship is very important as it is a fundamental human right.

However, despite the importance of inventorship, the variety of regulations and legal precedents set in relation to it, have not been very well researched in practice in most countries. There are, arguably, a number of reasons for that, which may include the following.

First, the invention of something is clearly a factual act, the object or process did not exist before but now, here it is. As such, an inventor's act of inventing something, once legally established as a new invention, is indisputable.

Second, the lack of research is a characteristic response to the first-to-file (FTF) system adopted in most countries for new inventions. The FTF system grants patent rights to the first person rather than being concerned with who invented it first. This approach instantly eliminated any complex legal disputes that could arise between inventors regarding timing within inventive processes. For example, there is no need to consider a legal dispute over who invented an invention first or what should be recognized as the starting point or key moment in the act of invention. As a by-product, the FTF system has also eliminated any meaningful need for research on inventive behavior and/or how and why an individual acquires inventor status.

Although there has been some limited research on inventorship to date, this chapter will introduce a number of the relevant legal regulations and precedents in the belief that this will contribute to triggering serious research into inventorship This is important beyond the scope of just this paper because, as the AI era proceeds, legal discussions about inventorship will become increasingly important.

Inventions made by an AI are, by their nature, very vague as to who the inventor is. As mentioned before, inventorship is a key foundation of patent rights. Therefore, if who (or what) the inventor is remains ambiguous, the basis for awarding a patent becomes unclear and will undoubtedly lead to legal disputes over property among stakeholders, especially as patent rights secure monopoly power for a certain number of years given what that entails financially.

To create a meaningful starting point to solve this problem, this text will deal in depth with all German and US regulations, precedents and the universal history of inventorship so that the legal nature and existence of inventorship can be clearly defined.

III. Why German and US Law?

Most human-made social systems have been created through the law. That is to say, the rule of law is fundamental to social order. Comparative law is beneficial for a country, as it helps in gaining a better understanding of various legal concepts, principles, and practices that can be implemented to improve the domestic legal system. For this reason, it would be ideal to compare as many legal systems as possible, however, for reasons of practicality and manageability, this paper will limit itself to comparing just two for the following reasons.

First, civil law (Continental law) and common law (Anglo-American law) are systems with the sharpest contrast. Although the world's legal systems are often discussed using various criteria,[9] Konrad Zweigert divided them into eight 'legal families' (*Rechtskreis* in German): Roman, Germanic, Nordic, Anglo-American, Socialist, Far Eastern, Islamic and Hindu.[10] Although it would be advantageous in some ways to compare all eight families in some detail, only German law (civil law from the Germanic family) and US law (common law from the Anglo-American family) will be compared in this paper. Civil law and common law differ considerably in their origins and history

---

9 For example, John Henry Wigmore (1863–1943) divided world laws into the sixteen principal legal systems; all handled in detail in its own chapter in his publication. Not all these systems remain as some ended with their civilization's decline, however, he listed Egyptian, Mesopotamian, Hebrew, Chinese, Hindu, Greek, Roman, Japanese, Mohammedan, Keltic, Slavic, Germanic, Maritime, Ecclesiastical, Romanesque and Anglican. See *Wigmore*, A Panorama of the World's Legal Systems (Saint Paul: West Publ. Co., 1928).

10 *Zweigert*, Zur Lehre von den Rechtskreisen, XXth century comparative and conflicts law, 1961, 55. "*Ziel dieser untersuchung war es nicht, eine neue Einteilung der Rechtskreise vorzustellen. Auch ich gliedere mit einer leichten Nuancierung der Lehre von Arminjon-Nolde-Wolff: 1) Romanischer Rechtskreis, 2) Deutscher Rechtskreis, 3) Nordischer Rechtskreis, 4) Angelsächsischer Rechtskreis, 5) Kommunistischer Rechtskreis, 6) Fernöstlicher (nichtkommunistischer) Rechtskreis, 7) Islamischer Rechtskreis und 8) Rechtskreis des Hindu-Rechts*".

of development.[11] Through comparisons of the markedly different legal systems, the path of convergence between them will be explored.

Second, considerable attention has been devoted to the US patent system, which is unique and centered on inventors. The US originally adopted the First-to-Invent (FTI) system, which was significantly compared to the First-to-File (FTF) system in Germany and other countries.[12] The uniquely inventor-centric US system is arguably an important subject of study in this paper that studies inventorship and, as such, the following section will look at not only the current AIA (FITF system) but also the pre-AIA (FTI system) for the following four reasons.

First, even under the new AIA, the pre-AIA regulations still apply to applications that have an effective filing date before 16 March 2013, even if a single claim. Patent rights are recognized for 20 years, so pre-AIA patent rights are still applicable until 2033.

Second, researches on how the FTI system works can reveal considerable scope to think about the nature of inventorship. Numerous precedents help to identify who the first inventor is and detailed legal research on the invention process thanks to the unique FTI system.

Third, it is common to research old laws that have already been repealed or lost to history in the process of enacting new laws and/or revising existing

[11] Though the two traditions – common and civil law – have grown closer over the last century, there are at least five significant differences that remain between them. (1) Common law is essentially unwritten law. Codification had been resisted by generations of common lawyers, although this resistance has been weaker in the US than elsewhere. The American Law Institute (ALI), a group of lawyers, judges and legal scholars in the US was established in 1923 and has published "Restatements of the Law". This includes commentaries on contract, property, agency, tort and trust laws so that judges and lawyers can clearly identify the general principles. However, this seeks to clarify the law rather than codify it. Restatements are broadly accepted by US courts as secondary sources of law, although they still have no binding authority. (2) Common law is case law. The foundational blocks of common law are cases, while in civil law this role is fulfilled by legislation. (3) Common law has a distinct view of court decisions. It elevates the doctrine of precedent to the supreme position in its legal system. This doctrine means judges need to follow the rulings of other judges in higher courts when a case entails similar issues. In other words, the judgments of higher courts are binding on courts lower in the judicial hierarchy. (4) While common law proceeds from the premise "where there is a remedy, there is a right", civil law tradition generally adopts the opposite position, namely that "where there is a right, there is a remedy". (5) Common law has used trials by jury for both criminal and civil cases since the 13th century. *Wacks*, Law: A Very Short Introduction, 2nd ed. (Oxford: Oxford University Press, 2015).

[12] In the U.S., AIA (America Invents Act)'s new application system is called 'First-Inventor-to-File' (FITF), which is intended to emphasize that the US application system is defined more inventor-centric than the more common FTF system.

laws. Studying the inventorship of AI requires considering the direction that needs to be taken when enacting and/or revising patent law in the Fourth Industrial Revolution. Therefore, it is normal and useful to look at relevant laws in the past to see if there is any logical relevance and comparable homogeneity with AI. This process can find value in rather unexpected places, such as precedents in which animals were classified as criminals in the Middle Ages[13] and in slave codes that existed before the US civil war.[14]

Fourth, Germany and the US were chosen as two of the five IP offices (IP5). The IP5 is the name given to a forum of the five largest intellectual property offices in the world. The members of IP5 are the European Patent Office (EPO); the Japan Patent Office (JPO); the Korean Intellectual Property Office (KIPO); the National Intellectual Property Administration of the People's Republic of China (CNIPA); and the United States Patent and Trademark Office (USPTO). They handle approximately 80 percent of the world's patent applications and 95 percent of all work performed under the PCT.[15] The European Patent Convention (EPC) was also considered, but it was deemed that a single treaty did not ideally fit the purposes of this study, namely to examine patent laws as well as general civil principles (especially the right to legal capacity) and even constitutional law (the right of invention and copyright are

[13] "During the Middle Ages, animals could be tried for criminal offenses. There are documented stories of cases brought against chickens, rats, field mice, bees, gnats, and pigs. Back then, people apparently thought animals capable of knowing right from wrong and behaving accordingly, in a way that we don't today. They believed that animals had what's called moral agency". *Kaplan*, Humans Need Not Apply: A Guide to Wealth and Work in the Age of Artificial Intelligence (New Haven: Yale University Press, 2015), 79. Originally cited: *Payson Evans*, The Criminal Prosecution and Capital Punishment of Animals (New York: E. P. Dutton, 1906). These historical examples could also be a source of research on the criminal punishment of AI, if needed.

[14] There are, arguably, significant similarities between the status of slaves (in accordance with various slave codes that existed in the 17th to 18th centuries) and that of AIs. At the time these codes were in force, slaves were treated as the legal property of their owner, however, they contradictorily had to take legal responsibility for any crimes they committed. It seems initially intuitive that the owner assume responsibility in such cases since the slave is otherwise classed simply as property. However, slaves were punished for their crimes because they were recognized as having the capacity to decide independently on a course of action. AIs are also the legal property of an owner and, at some point in time, they may also have the legal capacity to decide on a course of action that has legal consequences. If an AI causes damage to others, the owner would not necessarily take responsibility but the AI itself, if we accept the premise assigned to slaves in the past. See *Kaplan*, Humans Need Not Apply, 86, citing *Goodell*, The American Slave Code in Theory and Practice: Its Distincive Features Shown by Statutes, Judicial Decisions, and Illustrative Facts (New York: American and foreign anti-slavery society, 1853).

[15] See: About IP5 Co-Operation, accessed February 17, 2020, https://www.fiveipoffices.org/about.

generally constitutional rights). Therefore, since the EU's EPO does not operate based on national law, the decision was made to use Germany, Europe's top filing country[16] from among the EPO's Member States as a case study.

IV. Methods of Analysis

1. Time Division of the Process by which a Patent is Granted

This paper does not compare all the individual regulations and aspects of all patent laws in Germany and the U.S., rather, it only deals with the single concept of inventorship that will be traced by chronologically following the steps taken that end in a patent being granted. This tracery is divided as follows:

First comes the 'inventive process', a step that is undertaken wholly and solely by the inventor.

The second step is the 'application process'. This can be undertaken by the applicant or the inventor and involves the preparation of the pertinent papers to submit the application. There are some parts that the inventor must be fully involved, such as specifying the name of the inventor.

The third step is the 'publication of patent applications and the patent examination process'. This step is carried out by the patent office and does not involve either the inventor or the applicant.

The 'inventive process' and 'the application process' have been chosen as sub-sections for in-depth research to find where inventors play a part in both processes. Below, all provisions regarding the inventorship in the US and Germany in both processes will be dealt with.

2. A Study of Universality and Particularity

The study undertaken here will first introduce legal provisions and precedents of inventorship in Germany and the US, second, it will then compare the universality and particularity of both countries' relevant laws. These endeavors

---

16 Applications from EPO Member States in 2018 were 47 percent of all patent applications at the EPO originating from the 38 EPO member states. The largest figure among them is Germany (15 percent), second one is France (6 percent), and third one is Switzerland (5 percent). See more information: European Patent Office, European Companies and Inventors File More Patent Applications in 2018, European Patent Office, accessed July 2, 2022, https://www.epo.org/news-events/press/releases/archive/2019/20190312.html.

will ultimately underpin the legislative proposals suggested later in this text for a new patent law model for the AI era.

Law has, arguably, two key aspects: universality and particularity. Law is a universal social norm that pursues justice without being limited by time and place. At the same time, it has particularity, that is, it continuously changes and evolves according to the values, needs and circumstances of the time and place in which it is applied. This paper compares the legal provisions for inventorship in German and US law, furthermore, it makes this examination using both the universality and particularity present in both systems.

This chapter pays particular attention to the following points.

First, the background of the enactment of the provisions and the reality of their operation in both countries were considered together from a particularity perspective rather than simply attempting a superficial comparison between the legal texts.

Second, a focus has been placed on discovering the universality underlying both countries' laws, this goes beyond their particularity caused by their differences. This paper then proposes a global common legislative direction that views AI inventorship positively, albeit one that requires the implementation of a new legal framework that goes beyond the current status quo.[17] As Rudolf Schlesinger put it, the "common core" of the legal systems of the world should ultimately be found, to derive the right law.[18]

With respect to universality, this dissertation draws on the functional method of comparative law.[19] While the specific legal provisions and case law governing who qualifies as a legal inventor may differ from country to country, these systems ultimately serve the same legal function: determining to whom the rights to an invention should be assigned. Therefore, a meaning-

---

[17] Through comparative research on various legislation, it is very important to derive the general theory and the philosophy of natural law, which is based on the premise of various laws around the world. Arthur Kaufmann, a German scholar who studied comparative law philosophy (*Vergleichende Rechtsphilosophie* in German) emphasized in his book, "a certain legal system beyond the state should be found". *Kaufmann*, Vergleichende Rechtsphilosophie: am Beispiel der klassischen chinesischen und der klassischen abendländischen Rechtskultur, Festschrift für Werner Lorenz zum siebzigsten Geburtstag, 1991, 635–48.

[18] *Schlesinger*, Research on the General Principles of Law Recognized by Civilized Nations, The American Journal of International Law 51, no. 4 (1957): 734–53, https://doi.org/10.2307/2195351.

[19] Konrad Zweigert and Hein Kötz's book provides a systematic account of the functional method, the core methodology of comparative law, particularly in Chapter 3 (§ 3). See: *Zweigert/Kötz*, Einführung in die Rechtsvergleichung: Auf dem Gebiete des Privatrechts, 3., neubearbeitete Auflage (Mohr Siebeck, 1996), https://doi.org/10.1628/978-3-16-162053-9.

ful comparison should not merely examine statutory language or judicial decisions, but rather focus on the underlying purpose or function each legal system seeks to fulfill through its concept of inventorship. It is this very purpose – or function – that constitutes what may be called universality. This idea is particularly developed through the 2/7 Questions discussed in Chapter 4.

B. Three Preliminary Remarks

Prior to the full-scale analysis of 'the invention process' and 'the application process', this section offers preliminary remarks to help set a contextual background on the following topics: (1) A comparison of the constitutional provisions, the starting point of all laws; (2) an examination of how both countries' laws define the word inventor; (3) clearly identifying that only a natural person can be an inventor under both laws.

I. The Relevant Constitutional Law in Germany and the US

The United States Constitution Art. I, Section 8, clause 8 states that "[the Congress shall have power] to promote the Progress of Science and useful Arts, by securing for limited Times to Authors and Inventors the exclusive Right to their respective Writings and Discoveries". This clause, commonly called the 'Patent Clause', 'Copyright Clause' or the 'Intellectual Property Clause,' was enacted in 1787, shortly after the United States Constitution came into force, and it continues to this day.[20]

The US 'Patent Clause' provides insight into the following:

First, it reveals an explicit reason for granting patent and copyright protection, i. e. to encourage innovation;

second, the reward for invention should go to the inventor, not to an investor or user.

---

[20] The US Constitution came into force in 1789 as a result of the people's will in the 13 named US states. The text was originally penned at the Constitutional Convention in Philadelphia, Pennsylvania, from 25 May to 17 September 1787, and the 'Patent Clause' was added after proposals from Madison and Pickney were accepted. Research about the drafting history of the 'Patent Clause' relies on two credible academic sources: the Convention's journal and James Madison's private journal of the Convention. Both record the daily events of the Convention. See *Oliar*, The Origins and Meaning of the Intellectual Property Clause, 2004, https://cyber.harvard.edu/ip/oliar_ipclause.pdf; *Oliar*, Making Sense of the Intellectual Property Clause: Promotion of Progress as a Limitation on Congress's Intellectual Property Power, Georgetown Law Journal 94 (2006): 1771–1845.

Third, based on the Constitution, Congress must grant the exclusive right directly to the inventor, not the applicant. In other words, the applicant must be identical to the inventor in the US Constitution, a requirement that has been strictly observed until pre-AIA.[21]

While the US Constitution explicitly states the inventor's rights in the 'Patent Clause', the German Constitution[22] does not have such a directly worded provision. However, since patent rights are also a form of property rights, Art. 14 GG can be the constitutional basis. Moreover, the Charter of Fundamental Rights of the European Union (CFR, *Charta der Grundrechte der Europäischen Union* in German),[23] to which Germany is a signatory, simply stipulates in Art. 17(2) that "intellectual property is protected".

Both the US and Germany have means of dealing with intellectual property rights as part of the basic rights enshrined in their respective constitutions. The US has, on the whole, been the leading country for the development of science and technology since its founding. One contributing factor to this has been a comprehensive understanding of the importance of patents[24] and sup-

---

21 35 U.S.C. 118 (pre-AIA) stated that the patent application had to be filed by the inventor or inventors in principle. Exceptions were made for individuals who had legal rights to the invention, such as through an assignment or license agreement. However, this was only allowed in exceptional cases. There is a debate that the new FITF system is unconstitutional. See MadStad Engineering, Inc. v. United States Patent and Trademark Office, 756 F.3d 1366 (United States Court of Appeals for the Federal Circuit 2014). The plaintiff argues that the US Constitution focuses on the word "inventors" in the 'Patent Clause' (US Constitution, Art. I, Section 8, Clause 8), therefore, Congress is not authorized to award patents to "the winners of the race to file at the PTO" instead of the inventors. The petition was, in the end, denied by the US Supreme Court on 23 February 2015 since the plaintiff had no pending patent applications nor rejected patent applications under the FITF system. Therefore, this problem remains and is simply awaiting a more suitable plaintiff. See MadStad Engineering, Inc. v. United States Patent and Trademark Office, cert. denied U.S. (Supreme Court of the United States 2015).

22 The Constitution of the Federal Republic of Germany is called the Grundgesetz (GG, Basic Law). It was firstly enacted in 1949 and has been amended over 60 times to date. In many aspects there are differences between Germany's GG and the US Constitution. For example, see *Eberle*, Human Dignity, Privacy, and Personality in German and American Constitutional Law, Utah Law Review 1997, no. 4 (1997): 963–1056. Furthermore, about historic influence between them: *Steinberger*, Historic Influences of American Constitutionalism upon German Constitutional Development: Federalism and Judicial Review, Columbia Journal of Transnational Law 36, no. 1 & 2 (1998): 189–208.

23 The Charter of Fundamental Rights of the European Union (CFREU) was drafted by the European Convention in 2000. The preamble of CFREU states its purpose to strengthen the protection of fundamental rights in the EU.

24 The early adoption of patent law in the United States may be understood in light of the influence of the British Industrial Revolution (1760–1820), during which Great

porting inventors through its unique FIF system, an attitude that is reflected in the Constitution.

II. The Legal Definition of Inventors

In German law, there is no legal provision defining who an inventor is, however, several scholars have tried. Eisenmann says: "The inventor is the person who found a solution to the technical problem using technical tools, i.e. who developed the technical rule".[25] In other words, an inventor must (1) recognize a technical problem (*das technische Problem*); (2) present a solution (*eine Lösung*) to the problem; (3) use a technical means (*technische Mitteln*) as a solution.

Meanwhile, the US precedents use the following explicit definition: "Inventors of patentable inventions, as a class, are those who bridge the chasm between the known and the obvious on the one side and that which promotes progress in useful arts or technology on the other".[26] In other words, an inventor is a person who fills the gap between "the known and the obvious" and "that which promotes progress in useful arts or technology on the other". The former refers to the past and the present while the latter refers to the future. In other words, an inventor is a person who promotes the development of science and technology based on knowledge accumulated from the past to the present to provide something for a better future.

After all, comparing the definition of German and the US inventors, although the details are different, there is virtually no significant difference in meaning. Inventors, based on existing technical knowledge, ultimately pro-

---

Britain benefited significantly from the use of Letters Patent and legal instruments such as the Statute of Monopolies. Drawing on this example, the framers of the US Constitution appear to have recognized the strategic importance of intellectual property protection. This recognition is reflected in the rapid legislative timeline: following independence from Britain in 1783, the Constitution was adopted in 1787, and the first Patent Act was enacted shortly thereafter in 1790. The sequence suggests that the establishment of a patent system was considered a foundational element in building the new nation. See: *Walterscheid*, The Early Evolution of the United States Patent Law: Antecedents (Part 1), Journal of the Patent and Trademark Office Society 76, no. 9 (September 1994): 697–715.

[25] *Eisenmann/Jautz*, Grundriss Gewerblicher Rechtsschutz und Urheberrecht: mit 55 Fällen und Lösungen, 9., neu bearb. Aufl., Start ins Rechtsgebiets: Zivilrecht (Heidelberg: C. F. Müller, 2012), 66. "*Erfinder ist derjenige, der das technische Problem mit technischen Mitteln einer Lösung zugeführt, also die technische Regel entwickelt hat*".

[26] In re Bergy, 596 F.2d 952 (Court of Customs and Patent Appeals 1979); Diamond v. Chakrabarty, 447 U.S. 303.

mote the development of science and technology, improving the quality of human life.

III. Only a Natural Person is Allowed to be an Inventor

Only natural persons are allowed to be inventors in both countries' laws, meaning even legal persons are excluded. To date, no known case from anywhere around the world acknowledges a legal person as an inventor.

In German legal scholarship, it is also widely believed that inventors can only be natural persons and that legal persons are excluded.[27] That is, any corporation, even a large one with many investors and employees and that is at the cutting edge of technology cannot be an inventor for any of the inventions that arise from the activities of the company or its employees.

In the US, 35 U.S.C. 100(f) states that inventor(s) are "individual(s)",[28] a deliberately clear reference to individual inventors, not corporations.[29] Indeed, the term "individual(s)" has been used since 1952[30] to specifically grant human inventors constitutional rights for their inventions and to prevent corporations from proclaiming themselves as inventors.[31] This intent also appears in precedents of the United States Court of Appeals for the Federal Circuit as evidenced by straightforward expressions such as "people conceive, not companies".[32]

---

27 *Eisenmann/Jautz*, Grundriss Gewerblicher Rechtsschutz und Urheberrecht, 67. "*Erfinder kann nur eine natürliche Person sein. Eine juristische Person ist nur in der Lage, durch ihre Organe zu handeln*".

28 35 U.S.C. § 100(f) (1952) "The term 'inventor' means the individual or, if a joint invention, the individuals collectively who invented or discovered the subject matter of the invention".

29 "Such language would help to ensure that patent rights were more likely to go to individual inventors than to corporate entities where ownership was disputed". *Abbott*, I Think, Therefore I Invent: Creative Computers and the Future of Patent Law, 1097.

30 *Abbott*, 1096. "This language ('individuals') has been in place since at least the passage of legislation in 1952 that established the basic structure of modern patent law". Original footnote: Public Law 82-593, 66 Stat. 792 (1952).

31 *Abbott*, 1096. "The 'individual' requirement likely was included to reflect the constitutional language that specifically gives 'inventors' the right to their discoveries as opposed to other legal entities that might assert ownership rights".

32 *Abbott*, 1097. See New Idea Farm Equipment Corporation v. Sperry Corporation and New Holland, Inc., 916 F.2d 1561 (United States Court of Appeals for the Federal Circuit 1990). "Although the special verdict referred only to Hesston, the judge properly recognized that people conceive, not companies, stating that '[w]hen I refer to Hesston, I mean to include Mr. Burkhart and all his colleagues who worked on the Hesston machines in question.'"

To sum up, what has been covered to this point, the Chapter 3. B. can characterize two things related to AI inventions:

First, the possession and exercise of respective patent rights are derived from the constitutions of Germany and the US. It is unclear who the true inventor of AI's invention is. However, the right of an inventor to acquire and enjoy the patent right is very important as it comes from the constitution. Therefore, there is a need to clearly identify the true inventors of AI inventions.

Second, and as mentioned previously, under current law only natural persons can be inventors, not legal persons and not AIs who currently have no independent legal status relevant to securing inventorship. This paper will ultimately affirm the inventiveness of AI and this should provide a logical basis to extend the provision of inventor status to more than just natural persons, namely to 'E-Persons' as well.

C. The Invention Process

I. Intro

The whole invention process is undertaken only by the inventor. This is the overall process by which one inventor (or more than one in cases of joint inventions) has inspiration for an invention in his/her and then head designs and implements this inspiration to create something that can be productized.

This section, divided into two subsections, will look at all the relevant German and US legal regulations and legal disputes associated with inventorship that arise during the invention process.

(1) The United States adopted the unique FIF system in the past and granted patent rights to the 'first inventor' rather than the 'first applicant'. This approach has led to some legal disputes – referred to as 'interference procedures' – and subsequent legal research has been done on this. In dealing with this, this section will look at what is key to defining the inventor in the invention process.

(2) Nowadays, inventions are often invented by an employee in a company rather than by an independent inventor. Inventions made within a company are called 'employee inventions' or 'joint inventions'. In these cases, the employee who was actually involved in the act of invention is cited as the inventor, while the employee's superiors, colleagues and company investors cannot be regarded as the inventor(s). To be classed as a joint invention, a collaborative effort between at least two co-inventors must take place, however, any person who does not participate in the collaboration

cannot be an inventor. As such, this study will limit itself to examining the core of the inventor's act of invention by looking at the relevant German and US laws in dealing with 'employee inventions' and 'joint inventions'.

II. The Interference Procedure Under Former US Law

Under former US law, there was always a small possibility that a patent holder could be deprived of his/her own patent right, even if obtained legitimately by completing the entire application process. This was possible because someone could claim to be 'the preceding inventor', resulting in a legal battle to take the patent right away from the current patent holder. This is referred to as an 'interference procedure' and a court must decide if the plaintiff or the defendant is the true inventor.

In dealing with this procedure, a court assigns the invention process three criteria and judges which party is the true inventor by comparing the views of both. These criteria are (1) conception; (2) reduction to practice; and (3) reasonable diligence. This is also the specific order in which the criteria are applied by a court to reach its decision.

First, conception is the concrete idea of an invention, which should be able to be the reduction to practice. The conception criterion definition that has been used in many US precedent cases is: "The formation in the mind of the inventor, of a definite and permanent idea of the complete and operative invention, as it is hereafter to be applied in practice that constitutes an available conception within the meaning of the patent law".[33] This means that a 'person of ordinary skill in the art' (POSITA) should be able to undertake reduction to practice right away after the conception. That is to say, a POSITA should be able to make and use the invention from the written description without extensive experimentation or additional inventive skill,[34] or without significant further exercise of the inventive faculty.[35] If subsequent experiments reveal

[33] Townsend v. Smith, 36 F.2d 292 (United States Court of Customs and Patent Appeals 1929); Hybritech, Inc. v. Monoclonal Antibodies, Inc., 802 F.2d 1367 (United States Court of Appeals for the Federal Circuit 1986); Brunswick Corp. v. United States, 34 Fed. Cl. 532 (United States Court of Federal Claims 1995).

[34] United States Patent and Trademark Office, Manual of Patent Examining Procedure (MPEP § 2138.04), R-10.2019 (United States Patent and Trademark Office, 2019), https://www.uspto.gov/web/offices/pac/mpep/s2138.html. "[C]onception is established when the invention is made sufficiently clear to enable one skilled in the art to reduce it to practice without the exercise of extensive experimentation or the exercise of inventive skill. Hiatt v. Ziegler, 179 USPQ 757 (Board of Patent Interferences 1973); United States Patent and Trademark Office, MPEP, 2138.04 [R-10.2019].

[35] "[T]he board defined conception as a disclosure of an invention which enables one skilled in the art to reduce the invention to a practical form without 'exercise of

sufficient uncertainty to undermine the specificity of the inventor's idea, this conception is not complete. This is especially true if subsequent experimental results reveal a fatal failure or defect in the inventor's design.[36]

For example, it is just imagination rather than conception to think of a flying broom. However, if an individual can find a way to fit a broom with a robust jet engine that can allow the broom to fly actually, manage the thrust and lift while also withstanding the forces of drag and gravity without incinerating the rider, imagination has turned to conception.

Second, the reduction to practice criterion has two aspects: (1) 'Actual reduction to practice' is the real implementation of a product; and (2) 'Constructive reduction to practice' is a detailed description of the invention in the patent application, which a POSITA should be able to produce immediately.[37]

Third, the continuous reasonable diligence criterion covers the process by which an inventor has worked diligently from 'conception of ideas' to 'reduction to practice'.

These three criteria serve as the benchmark for courts endeavoring to determine who the actual inventor is in a patent dispute. The previous US law, in its Art. 102(g), recognized the actual inventor based on: (1) the day of conception; (2) the day of reduction to practice; and (3) whether the inventor who conceived it first but took an extended period to reduce it to production has tried to work diligently on the invention prior to the date that other people also conceived it.[38]

---

the inventive faculty.'" United States Patent and Trademark Office, MPEP, 2138.04 [R-10.2019]; Charles E. Gunter, Appellant, v. Ralph M. Stream, Appellee, 573 F.2d 77 (United States Court of Customs and Patent Appeals. 1978).

[36] "[A]ll the claims should be invalid for failure to disclose the best mode". Amgen, Inc. v. Chugai Pharmaceutical Co., Ltd., 927 F.2d 1200 (United States Court of Appeals for the Federal Circuit 1991).

[37] United States Patent and Trademark Office, Manual of Patent Examining Procedure (MPEP § 2138.05), R-10.2019 (United States Patent and Trademark Office, 2019), https://www.uspto.gov/web/offices/pac/mpep/s2138.html#d0e207753. (1) Merely conceiving the final invention is insufficient; the inventor must also possess an operative method of making it. In certain fields, particularly those involving unpredictable technologies, an inventor may only be able to establish conception once the invention has been successfully reduced to practice through experimentation, resulting in a simultaneous occurrence of conception and reduction to practice. See Oka v. Youssefyeh, 849 F.2d 581 (United States Court of Appeals Federal Circuit 1988); Amgen, Inc. v. Chugai Pharmaceutical Co., Ltd., 927 F.2d; Brunswick Corp. v. United States, 34 Fed. Cl. (2) Actual reduction to practice requires that the claimed invention function for its intended purpose. See e.g. Great Northern Corp. v. Davis Core & Pad Co., Inc., 782 F.2d 159 (1986); Hybritech, Inc. v. Monoclonal Antibodies, Inc., 802 F.2d. (3) "[C]onstructive reduction to practice occurs when a patent application on the claimed invention is filed" Hybritech, Inc. v. Monoclonal Antibodies, Inc., 802 F.2d.

[38] Pre-AIA 35 U.S.C. 102(g).

The most important criterion in a real legal dispute was 'the date of reduction to practice.' That is, (1) in principle, the person who reduce to practice first becomes the inventor, although (2) exceptionally, the person who reduced later could be assigned as the inventor if he/she conceived the invention first and worked diligently throughout the period in question. An example is [Figure 4]:[39]

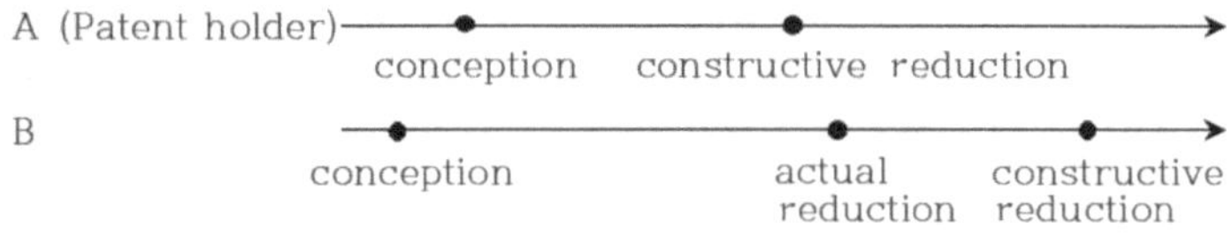

Figure 4: An Example of Key Inflection Points on a Timeline in an 'Interference Procedure'

In the case of [Figure 4], although A is the actual patent holder, B appears one day and proceeds with an 'interference procedure', claiming that he has the right to hold the patent as he had invented it earlier than A. The court begins by comparing the timing of conception and reduction. If A's conception was later than B but reduction was completed faster, A's patent right may be revoked if B submits evidence of 'reasonable diligence'. Usually, laboratory notebooks can be important evidence in this regard, therefore R&D workers in the US keep daily records of their research notes.[40]

In reality, it is highly likely in such cases that A is an employee for a big company and B is an individual inventor. Such timelines are commonplace because company employees have access to significantly more resources than individual inventors, allowing the former to work much faster than the latter. The US law allowed 'interference procedures' to protect individual inventors who often need more time to get through the inventive process, which can be problematic despite their conception step having occurred first.

The case *Apotex v. Cephalon* (2011) highlights the importance of the timing of conception and the ability to prove it. This case involved an interference proceeding concerning a pharmaceutical formulation of modafinil, a drug used to treat sleep disorders. Apotex argued that it had invented the formula-

39 United States Patent and Trademark Office, Manual of Patent Examining Procedure (MPEP § 2138.01), R-10.2019 (United States Patent and Trademark Office, 2019), https://www.uspto.gov/web/offices/pac/mpep/s2138.html.

40 "[The laboratory notebook] offers evidence of priority as to conception, diligence, and reduction to practice. It is usually the initial and sometimes the only record of accidental discoveries". *Cheesman*, The Role of Laboratory Notebooks in Patent Matters, Journal of the Patent Office Society 30, no. 6 (1948): 439.

tion before Cephalon. The key legal issue was whether Apotex could establish both an earlier conception and reasonable diligence in reducing the invention to practice before Cephalon's effective filing date. However, the court found that Apotex failed to provide sufficient evidence – such as detailed laboratory notebooks, witness testimony, or records – demonstrating continuous activity during the critical period. As a result, Apotex was unable to prove priority, and Cephalon retained its patent rights.[41]

Similarly, the case *Price v. Symsek* (1991)[42] addressed an interference proceeding between two inventors claiming rights to a similar invention related to signal processing. Price asserted that he had conceived the invention first, but the key issue was whether he had exercised reasonable diligence in reducing the invention to practice, particularly during the critical period before Symsek's constructive reduction to practice. The court found that Price failed to present sufficient evidence of continuous activity or diligence during this period. As a result, despite being the first to conceive, Price was not awarded priority, and the patent rights were granted to Symsek. The case reaffirmed that conception alone is insufficient without diligent effort to reduce the invention to practice under the FTI system.

Since the AIA revision, 'interference proceedings' have been abolished and revised to now be 'derivation proceedings'. An 'interference proceeding' was a product of the FIF system and its "who invented it first" approach. However, after the transition to the FITF system by the AIA amendment, only the contents on the derivation of the invention remain[43] while provisions on 'interference proceedings' have been deleted. The old 'interference procedure' is still deemed valid for patents filed before 16 March 2013 while a derivation proceeding is used for disputes involving patents filed after 16 March 2013.

German patent law, with its FTF system, grants the patent right to the first applicant in the case of multiple people laying claim to an invention, which is

---

[41] Apotex, Inc. v. Cephalon, Inc., 2011 U.S. Dist. LEXIS 125859 (United States District Court for the Eastern District of Pennsylvania 2011).

[42] Price v. Symsek, 988 F.2d 1187 (1991).

[43] Pre-AIA 35 U.S.C. 102(f) stipulated "A person shall be entitled to a patent unless[,] he did not himself invent the subject matter sought to be patented". It may not be patented, if a person's contents of a patent specification or claims is derived from another person. Only the inventor who derived the inventive idea himself is allowed to hold the patent right. "To invalidate a patent for derivation of invention, a party must demonstrate that the named inventor in the patent acquired knowledge of the claimed invention from another, or at least so much of the claimed invention as would have made it obvious to one of ordinary skill in the art". New England Braiding Co. v. A. W. Chesterton, 970 F.2d 878 (1992).

called *Doppelerfindung* in German.[44] However, in cases where an invention is stolen, which is dealt with via a derivation proceeding in US law and involves an application being filed by an unauthorized person, § 21 III PatG addresses such cases in German law.[45] Here, the victim must bring a legal challenge (*Einspruchsverfahren* in German) to the application within nine months of the publication of the application (§ 59 I PatG).[46] Based on the legal challenge, the German patent office may decide to uphold or revoke the patent or grant it only to a limited extent (§ 61 I, III PatG). In addition, a complaints procedure (*Beschwerdeverfahren* in German) lodged with the patent court is also possible to challenge the decisions of the patent office (§§ 65 I, 73 PatG). Alternatively, such complaints can be lodged with the Federal Court of Justice (*Bundesgerichtshof* in German) if they have been admitted (§ 100 PatG).[47]

In summary, under US law, the invention process is measured by three criteria: conception, reduction to practice and reasonable diligence. It is argued here that the core of the invention process is 'conception'[48] because it is, as previously described, the already concretely completed point where a POSITA has executed the invention. Given that 'reduction to practice' is a concept used to encourage patent applications and to contribute to industrial development by disclosing inventions, when one asks "what is the act of invention?", it can reasonably be defined as that which occurs at conception.

As such, the person who can be attributed with 'conception' is recognized as the inventor. Therefore, for example, one who reads the written description of an already conceived invention and simply implements it, or one who makes a working model according to the original conceiver's description may

---

44 § 6, 3 PatG provides that if two or more persons have made the invention independently of each other, the right belongs to the person who is the first to file the application in respect of the invention with the German Patent and Trade Mark Office). Translation provided by Ute Reusch in cooperation with the Language Service of the German Patent and Trade Mark Office, Patent Act (Translation of 'Patentgesetz'), accessed July 18, 2023, https://www.gesetze-im-internet.de/englisch_patg/englisch_patg.html.

45 § 21 III PatG.

46 § 59 I PatG.

47 Under what conditions is admitted is governed by § 100 PatG.

48 MPEP (Manual of Patent Examining Procedure) also emphasizes the importance of conception. "The definition for inventorship can be simply stated: 'The threshold question in determining inventorship is who conceived the invention.[' And] one must contribute to the conception to be an inventor". United States Patent and Trademark Office, Manual of Patent Examining Procedure (MPEP § 2109), R-10.2019 (United States Patent and Trademark Office, 2019), https://www.uspto.gov/web/offices/pac/mpep/s2109.html.

not be acknowledged as the inventor.[49] Similarly, those who are employed as technicians[50] to manufacture the invention but were not involved in the conception are also excluded from being regarded as inventors.

III. Legal Disputes over Employee Inventions, Joint Inventions, and the Invention Process

Today, the source of many inventions are company employees rather than private individuals and legal disputes over who can be recognized as an inventor when several people were involved in a company are not uncommon. Through various precedents dealing with such cases, this section deals with what defines the inventor under German and US law.

As already mentioned in Chapter 3 B. III. above, it must be reiterated that only natural persons can be the inventor under current law, which necessarily excludes legal persons, such as many companies. When an invention is produced in a company, the employee who performed the invention process should be credited as the inventor, while the company at which the employee works may be cited as the transferee, it can never be the inventor.

Given this backdrop, the following paragraphs will introduce the regulations and precedents relevant to inventorship related to employee inventions and joint inventions under German and US law.

Germany provides fairly specific rights and obligations for employees and employers in its law on employee inventions (ArbnErfG, Gesetz über Arbeitnehmererfindungen) and strictly protects their rights to employee inventions.[51] The right to the employee inventions belongs to the employee based

---

[49] The MPEP states that "A reduction to practice can be done by another on behalf of the inventor". In other words, to build a working model does not qualify as the inventor. MPEP, 2138.05 [R-10.2019], accessed July 19, 2022, https://www.uspto.gov/web/offices/pac/mpep/s2138.html#d0e207753.

[50] "[O]ne following oral instructions is viewed as merely a technician" Mattor v. Coolegem, 530 F.2d 1391 (United States Court of Customs and Patent Appeals 1976); Originally cited: United States Patent and Trademark Office, MPEP, 2109 [R-10.2019].

[51] The German Patent Act strengthens the employer's obligations. These obligations may be partially mitigated by separate private contracts between the parties or by additional compensation for the employees. But it is normally understood that the German employee invention system pursues the strong protection of the employee's rights by strengthening the employer's obligations. The obligations are for example: The employer's obligation strengthens in Germany, for example: the employer is obliged to apply for an in-country patent without delay (§ 13 I ArbnErfG); he should support the employee for a foreign patent application (§ 14 II ArbnErfG); he should provide the employee with patent application documents and information on proceedings (§ 15 I ArbnErfG); he should notify the employee if he wished to waive the proceedings of

on § 6 PatG and it is subsequently assigned to his employer. Typically, at the start of an inventive process or even prior to that, the employer will formally declare his intention regarding transferring rights from the employee (the inventor) to the employer. However, since October 2009, the German law has been amended in a way that the claim has been deemed to declare four months after notification of the invention (§ 6 ArbnErfG). In addition, an inventor must give his/her employer proper compensation afterwards (§ 9 ArbnErfG).

The German Patent Act states that a joint invention is recognized when multiple people have made an invention together rather than independently[52] (§ 6 PatG). Each of the joint inventors holds a significant intellectual share in the invention.

The different opinions among academics and precedents of German law on employee inventions and joint inventions are as follows:

(1) Anybody who simply stimulates or motivates the act of invention may not be an inventor. That is to say, an inventor must actively take part in the invention process.

(2) A person who just sets tasks and directs the goal – for example, a supervisor or somebody sitting on a guiding committee – may not be an inventor.[53] An inventor is regarded as a person who actually implements the invention process rather than simply setting the overall direction of the process or its perceived purpose.

(3) An assistant shall not be an inventor. While an assistant is involved in the invention process, he/she is not deemed to sufficiently contribute to the intellectual aspect that is important for invention. For example, a chemical laboratory worker whose tasks are purely manual according to the records of his/her daily work routine is an assistant.[54] However, there are situations where the distinction between assistants and co-inventors may

---

the application process, and provide the related documents if the employee requests (§ 16 I ArbnErfG).

52 If multiple people have made the invention 'independently,' the right belongs to the person who first registered the invention with the German Patent Office (§ 6 PatG) as the principle of the FTF system.

53 "*Kein Erfinder ist der die Erfindung lediglich Anregende, also etwa derjenige, der eine bestimmte Aufgabe stellt, eine Richtung weist, wie es häufig durch Arbeitgeber oder Vorgesetzte vorkommt*". *Eisenmann/Jautz*, Grundriss Gewerblicher Rechtsschutz und Urheberrecht, 66.

54 "*Kein Erfinder ist auch der Gehilfe. Darunter versteht man denjenigen, der an der Erfindung zwar beteiligt war, aber keinen wesentlichen geistigen Anteil am Erfolg hatte. Dies ist etwa ein Mitarbeiter, dessen Arbeit sich auf rein handwerkliche Tätigkeiten nach Vorgaben beschränkt hat, wie etwa bei einem Chemielaboranten*". *Eisenmann/Jautz*, 66–67.

need to be handled on a case-by-case basis as the distinction is not always clear-cut.[55] In essence, however, the inventor is the one who played a leading role in the invention process.

While Germany has a specific employee invention law, the ArbnErfG, no such specific law has been established in the US. The US handles employee inventions per the individual contracts between employers and employees. Most US employment contracts have a patent assignment clause requiring the employee to transfer certain rights to inventions to his/her employer should these be realized during the employment period. Deservedly, an employer must compensate its employee-inventor for this effort, an issue often dealt with in the employment contract, however, the common law principle is normally applied if there is no relevant contract and/or clause between the parties.[56]

The US Patent Act contains a definition of a joint invention and also defines the inventor. AIA § 100(f) defines an inventor as a person, or people in case of a joint invention ("[an] individual" or "individuals collectively"), who invented or discovered the invention.[57] Furthermore, AIA § 100(g) applies the terms joint inventor and co-inventor to "any 1 of the individuals who invented or discovered the subject matter of a joint invention". Here, "joint inventions" refer to an advent where multiple people have jointly made the invention and the patent application shall be filed jointly.[58]

To qualify as a co-inventor under the US law an individual must:

First, play a somewhat important role in the conception of the relevant technological ideas[59];

second, partake in the collaborative effort between co-inventors that is required. The use of the word "jointly" as the requirement of a co-inventor in 35 U.S.C 116 means that there must be some element of combined effort,

---

[55] "*Die Grenzziehung Gehilfe/Miterfinder kann im Einzelfalle schwierig sein*". *Eisenmann/Jautz*, 67.

[56] "State law governs contractual obligations and transfers of property rights, including those relating to patents". Regents of University of New Mexico v. Knight, 321 F.3d 1111 (U.S. Court of Appeals – Federal Circuit 2003).

[57] AIA § 100(f) "The term 'inventor' means the individual or, if a joint invention, the individuals collectively who invented or discovered the subject matter of the invention".

[58] AIA § 116(a) "When an invention is made by two or more persons jointly, they shall apply for patent jointly and each make the required oath, except as otherwise provided in this title". 37 CFR 1.45 also says "Joint inventors must apply for a patent jointly[.]"

[59] "[An inventor should do] more than simply providing well-known principles or explaining the state of the art[. He should contribute] snag-resistant elements to a total inventive concept". Pannu v. Iolab Corp., 155 F.3d 1344, accessed July 24, 2022.

such as collaborating or researching in a common direction. In general, two people who have no idea of each other's research cannot be joint inventors.[60] This does not require that they have physically collaborated in the same place or time (35 U.S.C. 116), however, there should be at least communication between them. In other words, meaningful mutual interaction must exist between such individuals for them to become a co-inventor.

The provisions for joint inventions are stipulated in 35 U.S.C. 116(a) where they are summarized as:

(1) When two or more persons jointly invent an invention, they shall jointly file a patent application and each shall submit the required oath;

(2) they do not necessarily have to work together physically (in the same space) or simultaneously (at the same time);

(3) there is no need to make the same type or same amount of contribution;

(4) even if each has not contributed to all claims of the patent, each may be recognized as a co-inventor, when each has contributed individually or jointly to at least one claim subject.[61]

When multiple individuals, such as a team working in a company's laboratory, participate in research and development together, it is never easy to clearly specify who invented the invention when applying for the patent. However, a patent not filed by the true inventor is invalid,[62] so it is very important to specify who actually has 'inventorship' for the invention.

---

60 For example, think of a case where several employees are working for the same company but they are unaware of what research the others do and do not communicate, the results from each of their independent efforts cannot be seen as a joint invention even though they were all simultaneously working for the same company. See Kimberly-Clark v. Procter Gamble, 973 F.2d 911. "Lawson worked alone and was completely unaware of earlier work done by other P G employees. One of these employees was Kenneth Buell, who in 1979 and 1982 made a disposable diaper with inboard flaps. Buell was also unaware of Lawson's work, until 1988 or 1989, long after the Lawson patent issued".

61 35 U.S.C. § 116 regulates directly that "[A co-inventor] may apply for a patent jointly[,] even though each did not make a contribution to the subject matter of every claim of the patent". MPEP 605.07 explains this regulation, "[It] adopts the rationale of cases such as SAB Industrie AB v. Bendix Corp., 199 USPQ 95 (E.D. Va. 1978)". This regulation was added to the revised law in 1984. The majority of precedents prior to 1984 demanded that all co-inventors must contribute to all claims. For example, if the first claim is contributed only by A, the second claim only by B, and the third claim jointly by A and B, it is not allowed to submit one patent application for a joint invention by A and B. In other words, three separate applications are required in this situation, resulting in high costs for the applicant.

62 35 U.S.C. 102(f) "A person shall be entitled to a patent unless he did not himself invent the subject matter sought to be patented".

Theories and precedents in the US regarding employee inventions and joint inventions include the following.

(1) The inventor shall provide a specific means (i. e. solutions) to achieve the desired purpose or outcome. If a person only presents the idea of the outcome without the means to perform, that individual would not be recognized as the inventor.[63] In other words, articulating the problem alone does not qualify one to be classed as an inventor, even if the problem is very difficult to identify and requires some inventive talent to perceive.[64]

(2) A person who performs 'routine acts' and 'routine skills' is not an inventor. For example, a person who undertakes routine tasks to record a simple description from others, or somebody who designs circuits to execute ideas is simply an ordinary chip designer employing routine skills common in the industry. If a POSITA can construct the functional device in a patent specification without further research or experiment, it does not include any inventive action; therefore, it cannot be recognized as an inventor.[65]

---

63 "One who merely suggests an idea of a result to be accomplished, rather than means of accomplishing it, is not a joint inventor". Garrett Corporation v. United States, 422 F.2d 874.

64 Regents of the University of California v. Synbiotics Corp., 849 F. Supp. 740 (United States District Court for the Southern District of California 1994). The University of California patented test kits to diagnose whether a cat was infected with FIV (Feline Immunodeficiency Virus, similar to the HIV/AIDS virus in humans). The university sued Synbiotics for selling the patented test kits, while Synbiotics offered a strong counterargument based on joint patent ownership. According to Synbiotics, if Ms. Brown is recognized as a co-inventor, it becomes the co-owner of the patent by assigning the ownership. Initially, Ms. Brown sent her sick cat to the University with a record of observations of symptoms, suggesting that the cat may have contracted a virus similar to AIDS in humans. In the end, the court ruled that Ms. Brown may not be a co-inventor, while Dr. Pedersen and Dr. Yamamoto, employed at the University, developed a way to isolate the new virus and diagnose infected cats. Although Ms. Brown presented symptoms of the cat's disease and provided it to the University, she did not do enough to be the inventor: "Brown's sole contribution to the discovery of FIV is that she brought her sick cats, along with her written observations of the cats' symptoms, to UC Davis with a suspicion that the cats may have a virus similar to the human AIDS virus. These facts do not support a claim that Brown is a co-inventor[.]"

65 Sewall v. Walters, 21 F.3d 411. Walters developed the CT scanner technology and provided it to Star Technologies, where Sewell implemented them in the chip form without any functional changes to Walter's design. Star Technologies filed a patent application with Sewell and Walters as co-inventors. This case was tackling whether Sewell was the true inventor of the CT scanner. The court decided that Sewell was not the inventor because he only performed an ordinary skill of converting Walter's design into a chip form. Sewell simply used a standard technology that any ordinary chip designer can perform, so it does not include any inventive faculty. In other words, a POSITA can construct the stated device in the patent specification without further re-

(3) Simply identifying a problem does not qualify somebody as the inventor as solutions to problems should be presented. For example, if it is evident that a particular tool has a problem and needs improvement, but the improvement suggested is so slight and easy to implement that anyone could have thought of it, it may not be patented.[66]

(4) It is not problematic for a person to be recognized as an inventor if he/she used the 'suggestions of others' in the invention process. The phrase 'suggestions of others' may include, for example, services, ideas and help from others.[67] Even if these are used, the right to patent is not lost. For example, Morse consulted with many scientists in the US and Europe before inventing the telegraph in 1837. The US Supreme Court ruled that suggestions from such consultations did not negatively affect Morse's status as an inventor.[68] This aligns with the notion that a person who simply provides 'suggestions' to an inventor is not necessarily recognized as a co-inventor. To qualify as a co-inventor, one's research, experiments and proposals must reach a certain level of significance in the invention process, such as notably helping complete the concept of the invention (i.e., the conception process). In other words, a person who simply describes the prior situation and problem, or simply provides a component for use in an invention, is generally not recognized as an inventor.[69]

---

search or experiments: "Sewall contends that he designed the hardware described in the specification[, and therefore he] is a joint inventor of that subject matter. [The Board holds that] Sewall's hardware design was dictated explicitly by Walters' specifications. In addition, Sewall has failed to persuade us that the Board clearly erred in finding that Sewall's design of circuits to carry out Walters' idea was simply the exercise of the normal skill expected of an ordinary chip designer, which did not involve any inventive acts on the part of Sewall".

66 See: Garrett Corporation v. United States, 422 F.2d. 874. In this case, the patent was denied. "It would [have been] obvious to anyone that the prior art canopy was defective and needed improvement as soon as more essential difficulties with the design were deemed overcome". The court dismissed the action because "[the inventions represent] advances on the prior art which are too small for notice under the patent laws, and would be tried by anyone who recognized the defects of prior art and wanted to experiment with the obvious means of correcting them".

67 James C. Hobbs, Petitioner, v. United States of America, Atomic Energy Commission, Respondent, 451 F.2d 849 (US Court of Appeals for the Fifth Circuit 1971). "An inventor may use the services, ideas, and aid of others in the process of perfecting his invention without losing his right to a patent".

68 O'Reilly v. Morse, 56 U.S. 62 (Supreme Court of the United States 1854). "An inventor does not lose his right to a patent because he has made inquiries or sought information from other persons. If a combination of different elements be used, the inventors may confer with men as well as consult books to obtain this various knowledge".

69 Ethicon Inc. v. United States Surgical Corporation, 135 F.3d 1456; Hess v. Advanced Cardiovascular Systems, Inc., 106 F.3d 976. "One who simply provides the

(5) The employee who conceived the invention is recognized as the inventor, and the supervisor or manager of the employee shall not be the inventor.

(6) Simply verifying (or testing) that an invention works well for its intended purpose shall not be a qualification for obtaining the status of inventor.[70] That is, to be an inventor, one must participate in the formation of the basic concept of the invention, i. e. the conception process.

(7) A person who has made only economic contributions shall not be a joint inventor.

The above introduces only seven sets of circumstances among many, however, these seven revolve around one common point, namely who was involved in the 'conception,' i. e., the person at the core of the invention is the inventor, while those who have contributed only subsidiary effort may not be recognized as inventors.

IV. The Core of the Inventive Process

So far, the regulations and precedents about inventors in the invention process in German and US law have been reviewed to show that many similarities exist between both countries' laws regarding the requirements to define and identify an inventor. Of key relevance in this paper is their primary common ground that inventors can only be natural persons meaning, for example, that company employees may be inventors but the company itself may not.

---

inventor with well-known principles or explains the state of the art without ever having 'a firm and definite idea' of the claimed combination as a whole does not qualify as a joint inventor". "Holding that explaining the state of the art and providing well-known information found in textbooks was insufficient for joint inventorship".

70 Burroughs Wellcome Co. v. Barr Laboratories, Inc., 828 F. Supp. 1208. Burroughs Wellcome (BW), who invented the treatment of HIV infection using AZR compounds, filed a patent infringement lawsuit against Barr. Barr argued that NIH (National Institutes of Health) scientists should also be included in the co-inventors, because NIH scientists have partially proven that the method and compounds of the claimed patent are effective for treatment. However, BW argued that the indication of inventor was correct because the patent application was drafted in the UK prior to NIH scientist's test. In other words, the conception of the invention was completed before testing by NIH scientists. The court ruled in favor of BW and made it clear that, in order to be the inventor, one must participate in the formation of the conception of invention: "The court notes further that a party who conducts tests wholly at the direction and instruction of another is merely a technician and not a conceiver and acts merely as a 'pair of hands.' The court finds that this last statement accurately characterizes the role played by Dr. Broder and Dr. Mitsuya. The evidence in the record shows that BW Co. sent Compound S to the NIH with specific instructions and directed the testing performed by Dr. Broder and Dr. Mitsuya".

In the US, where an 'interference procedure' exists,[71] conception is clearly presented as the core of the invention process. In Germany, there is no provision for a similar procedure thanks to the FTF system, however, there is a similar approach to the idea of the conception as the German law states that only those who contribute to the "important concept of the technical idea of the invention" can become inventors.[72]

This paper will endeavor to establish the concept of 'the core of the inventive process.' The invention process is the chain of events an inventor goes through when devising an invention before submitting his/her patent application. 'The core of the inventive process' refers to the essential components in this chain of events that make acknowledging an inventor possible. Under US law, it refers to the 'conception,' while in German law the expression "*Erfindungsgedanke*", which translates to "inventive idea".[73]

A person who participated in 'the core of inventive process' and played an important or leading role in an invention process, i.e., was a practical and active participant in the invention process, can be recognized as the inventor. On the contrary, assistants, employers, those who provided only simple explanations, and those who provided only funds cannot be inventors, both German and US laws clearly states.

The concept of 'the core of inventive process' is essential in discussing the inventorship of AI because AI inventions involve not only AI itself but also other stakeholders, each with their own reasons to stake a claim. Chapter 4 will conduct an in-depth analysis of 'the core of inventive process' for each stakeholder.

D. The Application Process

This section studies an inventor's involvement in the application process from a comparative legal perspective.

(1) Both German and US laws' overall application processes will be described and the key application documents that must be submitted will be introduced. This allows an understanding of the function of each document

---

71 Interference procedures still exist in the US, although they were replaced by derivation proceedings for patent applications filed on or after March 16, 2013. So, patent applications filed before March 16, 2013 can still proceed with interference procedures if there is a dispute over who was the first inventor of the invention claimed in the patent application.

72 Parallel concept of "conception" in the German patent law is called "*Erfindungsgedanke*". *Crotti*, The Allgemeine Erfindungsgedanke in the German Patent, Journal of the Patent Office Society 39, no. 7 (1957): 477–501.

73 *Crotti*.

with the inventor's name on it and its role throughout the application process.

(2) The correlation between the inventor and the applicant will be explained. Under prior-US law (pre-AIA), the inventor must be the applicant. However, under German law and current US law, not only the inventor himself but also the transferees may be the applicants.

(3) Documents with the inventor's name will be reviewed among the application documents.

(4) In particular, the rights of 'naming of the inventor' and 'declaration of inventors' are studied.

I. The Application Process and Application Documents

1. Germany

The application process in Germany begins with the submission of the application documents. Art. 34 (3) PatG states that the following five pieces of information must be included in application documents:[74] (1) The name of the applicant;[75] (2) a patent application in which the invention is briefly but accurately described; (3) one or more claims;[76] (4) a detailed description of the invention;[77] and (5) drawings to which the claims or the description refer.

The application date (*Anmeldetag* in German) is set when the documents with the above information are submitted. Furthermore, an applicant is obliged to submit two additional documents within 15 months of the original application date: (1) A technical summary as required under Art. 36 of PatG,[78] this

---

[74] Art. 6 of PatV describes the application's form in great detail, including the paper material, margins, and font size.

[75] Art. 4(2)1 of PatV divides the case, whether the applicant is a natural person or a corporation. Moreover, it details the personal information that needs to be filled out, such as first name, last name, address, and signature. For some cases, the personal information of the representatives should be filled.

[76] Art. 14 of PatG states that the scope of patent protection is determined by the content of claims.

[77] Art. 34(4) of PatG stipulates that the description of the invention must be written accurately enough to be executed by experts in the field. And this is usually done in three steps: (1) presentation of state of the art (Art. 34(7) PatG), (2) description of the technical problems, and (3) their solution using an exemplary embodiment.

[78] Earlier, it was burdensome to read the full text of the patent specification in detail to understand the invention's contents since the summary word-count limitation did not exist. After the summary requirement was put in place it became easier to access the key technical information, which can be seen as something of a necessity given the rapid rate of technological advancement today.

cannot exceed 150 words; (2) the name of the inventor as required under Art. 37 of PatG. This will be handled in Chapter 3 D. IV. in detail.

Art. 3 of PatV states that when making a submission, the application must be submitted either in writing or electronically.[79]

Eighteen months after the application date, the application contents are automatically disclosed to the public, this disclosed document is referred to as the *Offenlegungsschrift* (OS), which translates to English as the 'disclosure document'.

Prior to the substantive patent examination, the German patent office (*Deutsche Patent- und Markenamt*, DPMA) first conducts a preliminary examination (*Vorprüfung*) which serves as an initial clarity check (*Offensichtlichkeitsprüfung*) as required under § 42 PatG. The submitted application is checked for obvious identifiable deficiencies and, should any deficiencies be noted, the applicant must correct them to avoid the application being rejected (§ 42 III PatG).

Afterwards, when the substantive examination (*Vollständige Prüfung*) is passed,[80] the patent is finally granted (§ 49 I PatG), posted in the patent gazette (*Patentblatt*) (§ 58 PatG) and, finally, registered in the patent register (*Patentregister*) (§ 30 PatG).[81]

2. The United States

The US application process is divided into two parts: (1) the non-provisional application (35 U.S.C. 111(a)); and (2) the provisional application (35 U.S.C. 111(b)).[82]

---

79 Furthermore, the DPMA website offers information on how to apply online for other IP rights, including utility models, trademarks and designs. See Elektronische Anmeldung, Deutsches Patent- und Markenamt, accessed July 29, 2022, https://www.dpma.de/service/elektronische_anmeldung/index.html.

80 *Eisenmann/Jautz*, Grundriss Gewerblicher Rechtsschutz und Urheberrecht, 70. "*Für die Entstehung eines Patentes ist der Schritt der vollständigen Prüfung der formellen (§§ 34, 37, 38 PatG) und materiellen (§§ 1–5 PatG) Erfordernisse durch den technischen Fachmann der Prüfungsstelle des DPMA am bedeutsamsten*". – in English "For the birth of a patent right, the step of the complete examination of the formal (§§ 34, 37, 38 PatG) and material (§§ 1–5 PatG) requirements by the POSITA is the most important".

81 The *Patentregister* is also known as the *Patentrolle* (patent roll).

82 Provisional application requirementss were created on 8 June 1995 and are designed to provide "a lower-cost first patent filing in the US and give US applicants parity with foreign applicants under the GATT Uruguay Round Agreements". Provisional Application for Patent, United States Patent and Trademark Office, accessed

When a provisional application is submitted, an applicant is given 12 months to transform it into a non-provisional application. A non-provisional application is a standard patent application and leads to substantive patent examination, which a provisional application does not.

According to 35 U.S.C. 111, application documents in general must include (1) a specification as prescribed by 35 U.S.C. 112; (2) a drawing, when necessary, as prescribed by 35 U.S.C. 113; (3) an oath or declaration as prescribed by 35 U.S.C. 115.

Furthermore, 37 CFR 1.77 describes the application documents and the sequence of applications in more detail: (1) Utility application transmittal form[83]; (2) fee transmittal form[84]; (3) application data sheet (ADS)[85]; (4) specifications; (5) drawings; (6) the inventor's oath or declaration.

What important is that three key documents are included in the application, namely, a specification, a drawing and an oath or declaration.

The specification here includes a detailed description of the invention and claims[86] while the drawings should include a pictorial representation of the invention. These claims, descriptions and drawings are meant to describe the invention in a detailed way, with the claims particularly being significant factors in determining the scope of patent protection. The inventor's oath/declaration will be described in detail later in subsection 3.4.4.

In the case of provisional applications, specifications and drawings must be filed, but the remaining documents may be submitted later (35 U.S.C. § 111(b)(1)). Moreover, late submissions detailing one or more claims are allowed,[87]

July 29, 2022, https://www.uspto.gov/patents/basics/types-patent-applications/provisional-application-patent.

83 Also called a transmittal letter.

84 In pre-AIA and AIA, applications must be submitted in written form (35 USC 111 Application (a)(1) 'Written Application'). There are three ways to submit a non-provisional application: internet, postal and direct submission. In postal and direct submission, the fee transmittal form must be filled out.

85 See: 37 CFR § 1.76 about ADS. Also guides for ADS can be found on the USPTO's website: Important Information for Completing an Application Data Sheet (ADS), United States Patent and Trademark Office, accessed July 29, 2022, https://www.uspto.gov/patents/apply/forms/important-information-completing-application-data-sheet-ads. Submission of the Application Data Sheet (ADS) is optional. ADSs allows USPTO to easily digitalize the bibliographic information, meaning there is no need to extract the data manually. This enables the data to be recorded more accurately and much faster.

86 The contents of the 'Specification' are stipulated in 35 U.S.C. 112 and 37 CFR 1.77(b) explains it more accurately.

87 35 U.S.C. § 111(b)(2): "A claim shall not be required in a provisional application".

however, it is mandatory to submit these within 12 months of the original application date otherwise the application is deemed to have been waived.

Irrespective of the permutations described above, the filing date is set as the date on which the specification is submitted[88] and is the start date for the provisional application. In other words, this allows provisional applications to be implemented when there is not enough time to prepare a regular application but it is necessary to quickly make a filing. Therefore, when an invention is released to the public, the provisional application is usually submitted on the same date. This confirms the filing date and avoids jeopardizing an invention's patentability in some countries where strict requirements exist regarding novelty.[89] In other words, applicants have the flexibility of disclosing and securing their invention through a provisional application.

3. Four Key Components During the Application Process and AI

At this point, the application processes and key application documents in both Germany and the US have been briefly detailed, showing that the two countries have similar frameworks in this respect. This is evidenced by the fact that the application processes under both countries' laws begin with the submission of the application documents, after which applicants are granted patent rights through the formal examination process. In both countries, patent applications must be submitted in a certain form (such as the application, specification, etc.), be that either written or electronically, this cannot be done verbally or by submission of the invention itself. One advantage of these requirements is to ensure that all applicants are by and large on the same footing in the patent examination.

In German and US law, there is a difference in the formality of the application documents despite the similarities in the content where the three most significant components are: (1) claims, (2) descriptions (textual explanation), and (3) drawings (pictorial explanation). Claims are a vital component in defining the patent right, while the description and drawings are supplementary

[88] 35 U.S.C. § 111(b)(4): "The filing date of a provisional application shall be the date on which a specification, with or without claims, is received in the United States Patent and Trademark Office".

[89] Each country has specific regulations defining the prior state-of-the-art. However, some countries have no grace period regulations like the US, therefore, if a US inventor wants to obtain patent rights outside the US, filing a priority patent application (provisional patent application) before disclosing the invention to the public is recommended. For grace period regulations in each country, refer to WIPO: Certain Aspects of National/Regional Patent Laws – Grace Period (WIPO, June 2022), https://www.wipo.int/export/sites/www/scp/en/national_laws/grace_period.pdf.

to help explain the claims. Therefore, patent lawyers make every effort to set claims for design around.[90]

The three key components above are the essential parts of preparing an application while describing an invention in written form. In addition, 'the naming of the inventor' or 'the inventor's oath' is selected as the fourth major component. The inventor's oath will be covered later in Chapter 3 D. IV.

Table 3

The Four Key Components of the Application Documents

	Germany (PatG § 34 and § 37 I)	The U.S. (37 CFR 1.77, 35 U.S.C § 112 and § 115)
1	Patentansprüche	One or More Claims
2	Beschreibung der Erfindung	Description
3	Zeichnungen	Drawings
4	Die Erfinderbenennung	Inventor's oath

In addition, the two countries' laws have something in common as to when an inventor may apply for a patent right, namely, when 'the core of the invention process' can be well represented in the above four components. The overall invention process is generally a long one and the point at which filing an application becomes possible is crucial for inventors in terms of the economic benefits they can secure through patent acquisition. From an inventor's point of view, the whole invention process entails: (1) coming up with inspiration and ideas, (2) composing a concrete product with engineering technology, (3) practically refining ideas through various experiments and, finally, (4) creating a successful final invention. Among these four, successfully physically creating a working prototype of the invention may be the last and even the longest step, however, the application process does not require the physical submission of an invention. It is sufficient to concretely represent the idea,[91] within 'the core of the invention process', in written form in the application

[90] 'Design around' is a strategy patent lawyers use to avoid infringing on existing patents. It involves designing a product or process to not infringe on existing patents while still achieving the desired functionality. This approach is often used when a company wants to introduce a new product or process that may be similar to an existing patented invention, but they do not want to risk infringing on the patent and facing legal action.

[91] The legal requirements for recognition as a patented invention, such as novelty, inventiveness, and industrial usefulness, should be fully considered and the scope of the claim should be well established so as not to infringe on others' patent rights.

documents. It is important for an inventor to know the possible time point to start the application process as this will typically have a bearing on the economic benefits (such as investment attraction) that can be realized.

However, AI can be much more efficient than humans in dealing with legal documents in certain forms, including documents such as patent applications. These applications use standardized documents. (1) Both German and US laws commonly describe inventions in claims, descriptions, and drawings; (2) applications must be in written form, which cannot be replaced by submission of the physical inventions themselves or oral explanations.

On 29 August 2019, a competition called Alpha Law was held in Seoul, Korea between a team using AI software and a team of two lawyers.[92] Their task was to examine the labor contracts within a fixed time and identify legal problems. The result was a complete victory for the team using AI, which was actually predictable enough because AI can analyze much better than humans, as labor contracts have standardized patterns and similar patterns are repeated.

Therefore, if AI inventors and application forms are combined, there is a possibility that AI itself will become a patent troll. AI will lead to many social changes, producing a massive number of applications on its own. Indeed, as AI advances and grows in its ability to advance science and technology, there is also an opinion that AI will replace humans as inventors.[93] In addition, there is a concern that advanced technology could be frozen if AI becomes a patent troll, only producing endless patent drawings but unable to produce actual market products. However, in my opinion, its possibility is low. Patent trolls do not produce products by themselves because production requires significant investment, such as resources or expertise in manufacturing. However, AI's production capability, such as smart factory and 3D printing, is excellent.

II. Correlation between the Inventor and the Applicant

Turning to the relationship between the inventor and the applicant, in principle, a person who has devised an invention is entitled to the patent right, however, coming up with an invention is, by itself, insufficient to obtain a patent.[94] Securing a patent right requires a patent application in written form

---

[92] "Alpha Law" Program Beats Human Lawyers in Analyzing Contracts in Korea's First-Ever Showdown, 2019, https://www.youtube.com/watch?v=eXxVutGBUeU.

[93] *Barrat*, Our Final Invention: Artificial Intelligence and the End of the Human Era, 2013.

[94] Legal requirements for recognition as an invention: § 1 I PatG in Germany stipulates that patents are granted for inventions in all fields of technology, when they are 'new', based on 'inventive' activity, and 'commercially applicable.' To acquire a

that declares the intention to acquire a patent. A patent application is an act of expressing one's intention to obtain the status of a patent holder on the condition of disclosure of an invention. This raises the obvious question of who can apply for a patent. The individual central to the conception process is the obvious choice to be given the right to apply, however, there are differences in various legal systems around the globe that allow a transferee nominated by an inventor to apply. An applicant who is also the inventor is designated as the 'inventor-applicant' while an applicant who is not the inventor is the 'assignee-applicant'.

In most countries, including Germany and the US, an applicant can be an 'inventor-applicant' or an 'assignee-applicant'. However, the pre-AIA in the US had a unique system of granting the right of application only to an 'inventor-applicant' in principle. A topic that is worth elaborating on at this point in this subsection.

1. Germany

Under German patent law, not only an 'inventor-applicant' but also an 'assignee-applicant' can apply for patents, as can be sufficiently inferred from the following provisions.

First, § 4(2) of PatV classifies the applicants into two cases: (1) one where an applicant is a natural person; and (2) the other where an applicant is a legal person or a partnership. Under German patent law, an inventor can only be a natural person. Therefore, when "an applicant is a legal person or a partnership",[95] it already indicates the existence of an assignee-applicant.

Second, the name of the applicant is stated in the patent application as prescribed by § 34(3) 1 PatG, and the name of the inventor must be separately submitted within 15 months from the application date under § 37(1) PatG.

---

patent right, the invention must have three legal requirements, that is to say, (1) industrial applicability ("*Gewerbliche Anwendbarkeit*"), (2) novelty ("*Neuheit*"), and (3) inventive activity ("*Erfinderische Tätigkeit*"); meanwhile, 35 U.S.C. 101 also states regarding the inventions that are patentable, "Whoever invents or discovers any new and useful process, machine, manufacture, or composition of matter, or any new and useful improvement thereof, may obtain a patent therefor, subject to the conditions and requirements of this title". A similar concept to "*Neuheit*" and "*Erfinderische Tätigkeit*" in Germany, "Novelty" from 35 U.S.C. 102 and "Non-obviousness" from 35 U.S.C. 103 are defined in the U.S.

[95] Meanwhile, in an application to the European Patent Office (EPO), a corporation can become the applicant as same as German law. "A European patent application may be filed by any natural or legal person, or any body equivalent to a legal person by virtue of the law governing it". (The European Patent Convention, Art. 58).

Therefore, it can be shown that the existence of the applicant and the inventor is defined separately.

Third, § 37(1) PatG stipulates that "how the applicant acquired the right to the patent" must be explained when the applicant is not the inventor or a co-inventor. With this regulation, it shows explicitly: (1) The applicant may or may not be the inventor; (2) a valid legal procedure exists to detail the inventor's identity and the relationship between the inventor (assigner) and the applicant (assignee).

Fourth, § 63(1) PatG lists documents in which the inventor's name shall be described while § 63(2) PatG stipulates that the applicants or others should be responsible for any corrections needed if the description is wrong. Therefore, it can be inferred that the applicant's existence is separately defined from the inventor.

Fifth, the applicant shall be deemed to be entitled to request the granting of the patent under Art. 7(1) PatG. Art. 6 states that the patent right shall belong to the inventor or the inventor's successor in title. Based on Art. 7(1) the applicant has the right to request the grant of the patent and, based on Art. 6, the inventor or his/her assignee has the right to acquire the patent. Therefore, it can be derived that the applicant may be an 'inventor-applicant' or an 'assignee-applicant.'

2. The United States

Under US patent law, the rules regarding the inventor and the applicant changed after AIA.

35 U.S.C. 111, a regulation that remained unchanged after the AIA, explicitly stipulates that: (1) a patent application shall be made by the inventor; or (2) it shall be authorized to be made by the inventor, i.e. representatives of the inventor. For example, a patent attorney or some other legal representative usually helps to prepare an application handling the design-arounds for inventors who usually lack the legal incompetence to do so.[96] This means that both before and after the AIA, 'inventor-applicants' in the US may file an application in principle.[97]

---

[96] For example, if the inventor is dead, his/her legal representative, such as an estate manager or designated will-executor, may apply for a patent. If the inventor is mentally insane, it may be filed by the guardian. "Legal representatives of deceased inventors and of those under legal incapacity may make application for patent upon compliance with the requirements and on the same terms and conditions applicable to the inventor". (35 U.S.C. 117).

[97] This principle of the 'inventor-applicant' is also indirectly demonstrated in 35 U.S.C. 115, stating that "The applicant shall make oath that he believes himself to

However, in exceptional cases, an application may be filed by an assignee-applicant in accordance with 35 U.S.C. 118. This clause changed with the AIA amendment.

In 35 U.S.C. 118 (pre-AIA), filing by someone other than the inventor was limited to only the following two cases: (1) "whenever an inventor refuses to execute an application for patent"; or (2) "[whenever an inventor] cannot be found or reached after diligent effort". That is to say, an assignee-applicant would be recognized only under very exceptional circumstances in which cases the applicant would be treated almost identically to the inventor for procedural purposes. However, the sentence mentioned above was deleted from the revised AIA. Therefore, since 16 September 2012, not only an inventor but also an assignee can now officially be an applicant without any need for special circumstances.[98]

In summary, in the US pre-AIA, only an 'inventor-applicant' was eligible to be an applicant unless there were exceptional circumstances, post-AIA, both 'inventor-applicants' and 'assignee-applicants' can submit applications without special restrictions.

Furthermore, 35 U.S.C. 118 and 37 CFR 1.42 (b) refer to the qualifications of 'assignee-applicants', i.e. persons who are not the inventor but can nevertheless be the applicant. There are three such persons:

(1) A person to whom the inventor has assigned;

(2) a person who is under an obligation to assign the invention;

(3) a person who otherwise shows sufficient proprietary interest in the matter.

If at least one of these three requirements is met, the relevant persons "may make an application for a patent on behalf of and as agent for the inventor on proof of the pertinent facts and a showing that such action is appropriate to preserve the rights of the parties".(37 CFR § 1.46 (a)) When an application is filed by an 'assignee-applicant' on behalf of an inventor, the patent is regis-

---

be the (…) inventor (…)". That is to say, the applicant in the US is in principle the inventor.

[98] This is evident before and after the amendments to 37 CFR 1.41. "A patent is applied for in the name or names of the actual inventor or inventors" (pre-AIA 37 CFR 1.41). "An application must include, or be amended to include, the name of the inventor for any invention claimed in the application" (AIA 37 CFR 1.41). See also MPEP § 2109: "The requirement that the applicant for a patent in an application filed before September 16, 2012 be the inventor(s) (except as otherwise provided in pre-AIA 37 CFR 1.41), and that the inventor or each joint inventor be identified in applications filed on or after September 16, 2012, are characteristics of U.S. patent law not generally shared by other countries".

tered to the actual applicant, i.e. the 'assignee-applicant' and the director of USPTO shall notify the inventor thereof.

In summary, both 'inventor-applicants' and 'assignee-applicants' can be applicants under the current US law. Moreover, the possible list of applicants in compliance with 37 CFR 1.42(a), 37 CFR 1.43, 37 CFR 1.45 and 37 CFR 1.46 are as follows:

(1) the inventor;

(2) the legal representative of the inventor, if an inventor is deceased or under legal incapacity;

(3) the joint inventors altogether;

(4) some joint inventors (if one or more co-inventors refuse to join in an application for a patent or cannot be found or reached after diligent effort, the other co-inventors may make the application for a patent on behalf of themselves and the omitted inventor);

(5) an assignee, which refers to a person assigned by the inventor;

(6) a person to whom the inventor is under an obligation to assign the invention (e.g. an employee acting in compliance with his/her employment contract);

(7) a person who shows sufficient proprietary interest in the matter.

If a person meets at least one of the above seven circumstances they may be the applicant "on behalf of and as agent for the inventor on proof of the pertinent facts and a showing that such action is appropriate to preserve the rights of the parties" (35 U.S.C. 118).

3. Connection with AI Inventions

The current legal situations concerning the correlation between the inventor and the applicant are summarized as follows.

(1) Under German and current US laws, both the inventor and assignee can be applicants. However, only the inventor could be the applicant under previous US law.

(2) The qualification of 'assignee-applicants' is limited to three circumstances under paragraphs 35 U.S.C. 118 and 37 CFR 1.42(b) as detailed above. German law does not have a separate provision to define the qualification of an 'assignee-applicant' in detail, however, Art. 6 PatG states that the patent right shall belong to the inventor or his legal successor (*Rechtsnachfolge* in German), which indirectly suggests that the applicant can also be such a successor.

This subsection deals with the correlation between the inventor and the applicant and examines a number of challenges regarding AI inventions.

First, one must question which name can indeed be registered as the inventor of AI inventions given that both German and US laws distinguish the person of the inventor from that of the applicant. In this regard, chapters 4 and 6 will analyze who is the true inventor of AI inventions.

Second, it is necessary to consider an applicant's qualifications as distinct from that of the inventor. AI owners and programmers are currently becoming applicants of AI inventions, as German and US law stipulates that such stakeholders may be applicants as assignees. It is argued here that the inventor's name should be that of the AI but the name of the applicant and patent holder be a natural or legal person so that such persons may enjoy the resultant property rights as stakeholders. This point will be detailed in chapters 6 and 7.

III. The Application Documents in Which the Inventor's Name is Written

1. Germany

Under German law, there are five application documents in which the inventor's name is written as required by Art. 37 (1) 1, Art. 63 (1) 1, and Art. 63 (1) 2 PatG.

The first and most basic document is the 'Designation of the inventor(s)' (*Erfinderbenennung* in German).[99] This is a form that contains the inventor's name that the applicant must submit within 15 months from the application date, as prescribed by Art. 37 (1) 1 PatG.

The DPMA provides a related form[100] in which the applicant is obliged to fill out the inventor's identity and include:

(1) the name and place of residence of the inventor;

(2) the reason for assignment to the applicant (e.g., employment contract, inheritance or sale);

---

99 "*[D]ie Erfinder zu benennen*" (Art. 37 (1) PatG) is translated as "to designate the inventor or inventors" in the official English translation: See Translation provided by Ute Reusch in cooperation with the Language Service of the German Patent and Trade Mark Office (n 180). Therefore, this paper translates "Erfinderbenennung" into "Designation of the inventor(s)".

100 Deutsches Patent- und Markenamt, Erfinderbenennung, Deutsches Patent- und Markenamt, accessed August 3, 2022, https://www.dpma.de/docs/formulare/patent/p2792.pdf.

(3) the guarantee of the non-existence of other inventors as far as the applicant can know;

(4) an application for the denial of disclosure of the inventor's name (*Nichtnennung* in German) when the inventor wants to remain anonymous.

Furthermore, German law stipulates that an inventor must be mentioned in the following four documents. (*Erfindernennung*,[101] § 63 Abs. 1, Satz 1 and Satz 2 PatG), described in detail below.

The second is 'the disclosure document',[102] called the *Offenlegungsschrift* in German, as prescribed by Art. 32 (2) PatG. After 18 months from the application filed by the applicant, the application is disclosed to the public as per Art. 63 (1) 1 PatG.

The third, fourth, and fifth documents are respectively called 'the patent specification'(Patentschrift, Art. 32 (3) PatG); 'the Patent Gazette' (Patentblatt, Art. 58 (1) PatG); and 'the Patent Register' (Patentregister, Art. 30 (1) PatG, with the latter also called Patentrolle at times).[103] When the final examination is passed by a technical expert at the DPMA, the patent right will be granted. It will be posted on 'the Patent Gazette' (*Patentblatt*), 'the patent specification' (*Patentschrift*) and then registered in 'the Patent Register' (*Patentregister*).

Of the 'five documents' cited above, the first document, the *Erfinderbenennung* is always the first document to be lodged with the other four released chronologically in the order listed as they are derived from the *Erfinderbenennung*.

101 "*[D]er Erfinder mit Namen und Ortsangabe zu nennen*" (§ 63 (1) PatG) is translated as "to mention the inventor by name and place" in the official English translation: See Translation provided by Ute Reusch in cooperation with the Language Service of the German Patent and Trade Mark Office, "Patent Act (Translation of 'Patentgesetz')." Therefore, this paper translates "*Erfindernennung*" into "Mentioning the inventor(s)".

102 "*Offenlegungsschrift*" (§ 63 (1) and § 32 (2) PatG) is translated as "the first publication of the application" in the official English translation: See Translation provided by Ute Reusch in cooperation with the Language Service of the German Patent and Trade Mark Office. Therefore, this paper translates "*Offenlegungsschrift*" into "the first publication of the application".

103 "*Patentschrift*" (Art. 32 (3) PatG, Art. 63 (1) PatG), "*Patentblatt*" (Art. 58 (1) PatG), and "*Patentregister*" (Art. 30 (1) PatG) are translated as respectively "the patent specification", "the Patent Gazette" and "Register" in the official English translation: See Translation provided by Ute Reusch in cooperation with the Language Service of the German Patent and Trade Mark Office. Therefore, this paper translates each of them into "the patent specification", "the Patent Gazette" and "the Patent Register".

Table 4

Five Application Documents in Which the Inventor's Name is Written under German Law

[1]	Designation of the inventor(s) (*Erfinderbenennung*)	
[2]	The disclosure document (*Offenlegungsschrift*)	Mentioning the inventor(s) (*Erfinder-nennung*)
[3]	The patent specification (*Patentschrift*)	
[4]	The Patent Gazette (*Patentblatt*)	
[5]	The Patent Register (*Register*)	

2. The United States

Just as German law obliges an applicant to submit an *Erfinderbenennung* that displays the inventor's name, the US law (37 CFR 1.41(a)) also requires that the inventor's name be given in the application form.

Under both German and US law, the inventor's name is given in more than one document. Under US law, there are up to five instances where the inventor's name can appear: (1) the Application Data Sheet; (2) the inventor's oath or declaration; (3) the document including processing fees as prescribed by 37 CFR 1.17(i) and 37 CFR 1.17(q); (4) the application papers which are filed in compliance with 37 CFR 1.53(b) and 37 CFR 1.53(c); and (5) the cover sheet lodged in accord with 37 CFR 1.51 (c)(1).

These five documents do not always need to be lodged together, however, at least one version of each document is required to complete an application process. The exact number depends on the situation: (1) Whether the applicant has made a provisional or non-provisional application;[104] or (2) what documents the applicant has submitted. The US law has a differentiated approach to the above five documents as they are divided into standardized priorities rather than the somewhat sequential approach to their lodgement required under German law.

37 CFR 1.41(b) provides four priorities for inventorship in non-provisional applications:

(1) If an ADS is filed before or concurrently with an inventor's oath or declaration, inventorship belongs to the inventor outlined in the ADS;

104 37 CFR 1.41 covers inventorship in non-provisonal and provisional applications, moreover, international applications (37 CFR 1.41(e)) and international design applications designating the US (37 CFR 1.41(f)).

(2) if an ADS is not filed before or concurrently with an inventor's oath or declaration, inventorship belongs to the inventor outlined in the inventor's oath or declaration;

(3) if neither an ADS nor an inventor's oath is filed, and if the applicant files 'a paper including the processing fee set forth in 37 CFR 1.17(i),'[105] inventorship belongs to the inventor set forth in this paper;

(4) if neither an ADS nor the inventor's oath is filed, inventorship belongs to the inventor set forth in 'the application papers' filed pursuant to 37 CFR 1.53(b).

This is highlighted again in 37 CFR 1.41(d), where the name and residence of each person believed to be an actual inventor should be provided, when the application papers according to § 1.53(b) or § 1.53(c) are filed, in case of a non-provisional application filed without an ADS or an inventor's oath or declaration. This is to prevent an omission of the defining inventorship should scenario (4) above occur.

37 CFR 1.41(c) provides three priorities for inventorship in provisional applications:

(1) Inventorship belongs to the inventor outlined in the 'cover sheet' as prescribed by 37 CFR 1.51 (c)(1);

(2) if the applicant files 'a paper including the processing fee set forth in 37 CFR 1.17(q)', although a cover sheet is not filed during the pendency of a provisional application, the inventorship is the inventor outlined in the paper;

(3) if a cover sheet is not filed during the pendency of a provisional application, the inventorship belongs to the inventor set forth in the 'application papers' filed pursuant to 37 CFR 1.53(c).

This is highlighted again in 37 CFR 1.41(d) where, in cases where a provisional application is filed without a cover sheet as prescribed by 37 CFR 1.51(c)(1), the name and residence of each person believed to be an actual inventor should be provided when the application papers pursuant to 37 CFR 1.53(b) or 37 CFR 1.53(c) are filed.

---

[105] 37 CFR § 1.17(i)(1) explicitly refers to the case of 37 CFR § 1.41(b), which explicitly states that a processing fee should be paid ($35 for a micro entity; $70 for a small entity; $140 for other than a small or micro entity) for supplying the name of the inventor in an application without either an application data sheet or the inventor's oath or declaration, except in provisional applications.

3. Conclusion

Under German patent law, five documents refer to the inventor's name, however, ultimately the most essential document is the *Erfinderbenennung*, which is the inventor's declaration in Germany. The rest documents are published chronologically after the inventor's declaration. No such chronological order regarding the largely comparable documents required under US law exists.

The US law refers to up to five documents where it provides three priorities for the provisional application (37 CFR 1.41(c)) and four priorities for the non-provisional application (37 CFR 1.41(b)).

The standard procedure for application in the US will see a non-provisional application, which is lodged first, converted to a non-provisional application within 12 months. In the case of non-provisional applications, if an ADS is not filed before or concurrently with the inventor's oath or declaration, then the inventor's oath or declaration has priority in determining who is regarded as the inventor.

Therefore, in both Germany and the US, 'the inventor's oath' or inventor's declaration is considered the most basic and essential document for determining inventorship and, as such, this declaration will be the focus of the following sub-section.

IV. The Declaration of Inventors

1. Germany

In 1936, German law initially stipulated an applicant's obligations to lodge the inventor's name and secure the inventor's rights. Historically, these obligations had a start in Art. 4 of the Paris Convention for the Protection of Industrial Property (PCPIP) in 1934, which states: "The inventor shall have the right to be mentioned as such in the patent".[106]

[106] *Benkard/Bruchhausen*, Patentgesetz, Gebrauchsmustergesetz: Kurz-Kommentar, 8., neubearb. Aufl., Beck'sche Kurz-Kommentare. (München: Beck, 1988), 896. "*Die Nennung des Erfinders in den öffentlichen Bekanntmachungen des Patentamts war bis zum Jahre 1936 gesetzlich nicht geregelt. Es war nur im Verwaltungswege angeordnet worden, daß der Erfinder in der Patentschrift genannt werden konnte. Nachdem durch Art. 4ter Pariser Verbandübereinkunft zum Schutz des gewerblichen Eigentums (PVÜ) in der Londoner Fassung von 1934 das Recht des Erfinders, als solcher im Patent genannt zu werden, anerkannt worden war, ist die Nennung des Erfinders 1936 näher geregelt worden. Die Regelung ist durch das Gesetz über das Gemeinschaftspatent und zur Änderung patentrechtlicher Vorschriften vom 26.7.1979 (GpatG) den veränderten Verhältnissen, insbesondere der Umgestaltung des Ertei-*

In terms of the 'naming of the inventor' in Germany, there are two concepts: 'Designation of the inventor(s)' (*Erfinderbenennung*) and 'Mentioning the inventor(s)' (*Erfindernennung*). Although the two terms differ strictly, they seem to be commonly used in combination. In fact, the important one is *Erfinderbenennung*, as *Erfindernennung* is just four documents released in chronological order. In that sense, *Erfinderbennennung* is the starting point for *Erfindernennung*.[107]

The *Erfinderbenennung* system, using the German verb *benennen*, is set out in § 37 Abs. 1 Satz 1 PatG and obliges an applicant to submit an inventor's name within 15 months of the application date, or, if an earlier date is claimed to govern the application, within fifteen months of that date. Where an applicant substantiates that he/she was prevented by exceptional circumstances (*außergewöhnliche Umstände*) from making the declarations in due time, the DPMA shall grant him/her a reasonable extension of the time limit. However, this time limit may not be extended beyond the decision on the granting of the patent (Art. 37(2)). Under the pre-2014 law, if the *Erfinderbenennung* was not lodged within a specified period, the patent could have expired, however, this has now been revised and is no longer applicable as of 1 April 2014.[108]

The *Erfinderbenennung* clause (§ 37 Abs. 1 PatG) stipulates that the applicant: (1) shall designate the inventors ("*den oder die Erfinder zu benennen*"); (2) shall guarantee that, to his knowledge, no other persons participated in the invention ("*zu versichern, daß weitere Personen seines Wissens an der Erfindung nicht beteiligt sind*"); and (3) shall indicate how he acquired the right to the patent if he is not the inventor or not the sole inventor ("*Ist der An-*

---

lungsverfahrens und dem Druck der Offenlegungsschriften (§ 32 Abs. 2), angepaßt worden".

107 See Chapter 3.4.3.1 in this paper.

108 Section 37(2) of the law applicable before 1 April 2014 stated that if an applicant provides plausible evidence that extraordinary circumstances have prevented him/her from submitting the declaration prescribed in paragraph 1 in due time, the patent office shall grant him/her a reasonable extension of the time limit. The period should not be extended beyond the decision to grant the patent. If the obstacles still exist, the patent office must extend the period again. The patent office shall notify the patent holder six months before the expiry of the period, stating that the patent will expire, if he/she does not lodge the declaration (*Erfinderbenennung*) within six months of the notification. (Original in German: *Macht der Anmelder glaubhaft, daß er durch außergewöhnliche Umstände verhindert ist, die in Absatz 1 vorgeschriebenen Erklärungen rechtzeitig abzugeben, so hat ihm das Patentamt eine angemessene Fristverlängerung zu gewähren. Die Frist soll nicht über den Erlaß des Beschlusses über die Erteilung des Patents hinaus verlängert werden. Bestehen zu diesem Zeitpunkt die Hinderungsgründe noch fort, so hat das Patentamt die Frist erneut zu verlängern. Sechs Monate vor Ablauf der Frist gibt das Patentamt dem Patentinhaber Nachricht, daß das Patent erlischt, wenn er die vorgeschriebenen Erklärungen nicht innerhalb von sechs Monaten nach Zustellung der Nachricht abgibt.*).

melder nicht oder nicht allein der Erfinder, so hat er auch anzugeben, wie das Recht auf das Patent an ihn gelangt ist"). In other words, this system is a mandatory procedure to firmly record the inventor's identity and relationship with the assignee (applicant).[109]

As stipulated under § 7(1) PatV, the designation of the inventor(s) (*Erfinderbenennung*) must be written in the form issued by DPMA,[110] including the above three details.

Basically, the designation of the inventor(s) (*Erfinderbenennung*) is a prerequisite for the mentioning the inventor(s) (*Erfindernennung*), that is, *Benennung* leads to *Nennung*. § 63(1) 1 PatG also reveals their antecedent relationship by stating that the inventor must be mentioned (*nennen*) if he/she has already been designated (*benennen*).[111]

The legal basis for mentioning the inventors (*Erfindernennung*) is found in §§ 63 Abs. 1 Satz 1, Satz 2 PatG. This law states that the inventor's name should be written in four documents:

(1) on the disclosure document (§ 32 Abs. 2 PatG);

(2) on the patent specification (§ 32 Abs. 3 PatG);

(3) in the the Patent Gazette (§ 58 Abs. 1 PatG); and

(4) the Patent Register (§ 30 Abs. 1 PatG).

When the designation of inventors (*Erfinderbenennung*) is written, the inventor's name is disclosed in four documents as mentioning the inventors (*Erfindernennung*) in chronological order. Chapter 3 D. III. dealt with five documents including the inventor's name.

---

109 § 7(2) PatV further details it in five ways: (1) the identity of the inventor (name and address); (2) the applicant's assurance that there is no more existence of other inventors; (3) the reasons for assignment to the applicant, if he is not the inventor or is not the sole inventor; (4) the declarations of the invention, or the official file number if already known; (5) the signature of the applicant or his representative (if many people have applied for the patent, each of them or their representative must sign the designation). In orginal German text: "*Die Benennung muss enthalten: 1. die Vornamen, den Namen und die Anschrift mit Angabe von Straße, Hausnummer, Postleitzahl und Ort des Erfinders; § 4 Absatz 3 gilt entsprechend; 2. die Versicherung des Anmelders, dass weitere Personen seines Wissens an der Erfindung nicht beteiligt sind (§ 37 Abs. 1 des Patentgesetzes); 3. falls der Anmelder nicht oder nicht allein der Erfinder ist, die Erklärung darüber, wie das Recht auf das Patent an ihn gelangt ist (§ 37 Abs. 1 Satz 2 des Patentgesetzes); 4. die Bezeichnung der Erfindung und soweit bereits bekannt das amtliche Aktenzeichen; 5. die Unterschrift des Anmelders oder seines Vertreters; ist das Patent von mehreren Personen beantragt, so hat jede von ihnen oder ihr Vertreter die Benennung zu unterzeichnen*".

110 Deutsches Patent- und Markenamt, Erfinderbenennung.

111 § 63(1) 1 PatG "*(...) ist der Erfinder zu nennen, sofern er bereits benannt worden ist*".

The designation of the inventors (*Erfinderbennenung*) generally has both characteristics: property rights and personality rights: (1) This designation of the inventors (*Erfinderbenennung*) is the starting point for ultimately patent rights, which has a property nature. In Germany, property rights are guaranteed by Art. 14 of the Constitution[112]; (2) it also has a personal nature as an inventor's right of honor (*Erfinderehre*).

Therefore, the *Erfindernennung* has the following characteristics:

(1) It is a right that cannot be given up on its own. The waiver of naming the inventor (*ein Verzicht auf Erfindernennung*) is invalid under § 63 Abs. 1 Satz 5 PatG. However, an inventor has the right to claim that his name is not disclosed (*Nichtnennung*, § 63 Abs. 1 Satz 3 PatG) to protect the privacy and confidentiality for various reasons, such as personal or business considerations. If the inventor wishes later to reveal his/her identity, he/she may do, and his/her name will be disclosed retrospectively (§ 63 Abs. 1 Satz 4 PatG);

(2) it is an unassignable right;

(3) it is a right that cannot be seized by way of distress;

(4) it is a right of honor, which can be claimed only by the inventor. No third party can lay claim to such honor.

Art. 63 (2) PatG stipulates how to modify an inventor's name if the inventor in question (1) has been wrongfully designated (*Änderungen der Erfindernennung*) or (2) has not been designated at all (*Nichtnennung des Erfinders*).[113] In this case, (1) the patent applicant (*Patentsucher*) or (2) the owner of the patent (*Patentinhaber*) or (3) the person who has been wrongfully designated (*der zu Unrecht Benannte*) shall be obliged on behalf of the true inventor to declair their consent to the DPMA that the inventor's name will be modified (*berichtigt*) or made up for (*nachgeholt*) later in the four documents cited above. This consent may not be withdrawn. However, proceedings to grant a patent right shall not be delayed. Additionally, this consent should be given

---

112 Meanwhile, Art. 1 of the 1st Additional Protocol to the ECHR (European Convention on Human Rights) also states the guarantee of property rights, stating that "Every natural or legal person is entitled to the peaceful enjoyment of his possessions". Furthermore, Art. 17 (1) of the Charter of Fundamental Rights of the European Union also stipulates the property rights, and Art. 2 states, "Intellectual property shall be protected".

113 § 63(1)(2) PatG and § 8(1) PatV refers to two cases: (1) if the inventor has been designated wrongfully (*Änderungen der Erfindernennung*) and (2) has not been designated at all (*Nichtnennung des Erfinders*). These claims shall be submitted (1) in written form, (2) with the signature of the inventor, and (3) with the description of the invention and the official file number.

'in written form' under Art. 8 (2) PatV, which indicates how important the naming of the true inventor is.

Today, more than 90 percent of all inventions are employee inventions where patent holders are companies, however, the inventors' name must be that of the true inventors (i. e. natural persons).[114] Since the naming of the inventor is legally guaranteed as a personal right, inventors have a positive motivation for the act of invention,[115] which serves as a potent driver for further developing science and technology.

The naming of the inventor gives that inventor several legal claims in case of infringement:

(1) Under Art. 63 (2) 1 PatG, if the inventor's name is incorrectly stated or absent, a patent applicant or patentee or the named inventor is obliged (a) to correct or supplement the inventor's name or (b) to explain their consent to name it later.

(2) The inventor may also pursue a tort liability claim under Art. 823 Abs. 1 BGB. The right guaranteed by an Erfindernennung is a personal right (*ein allgemeines Persönlichkeitsrecht*), and a tort liability claim can be pursued when infringed.

2. The United States

In the US, there is a system referred to as 'naming the inventor' or the 'inventor's oath or declaration' operable under 35 U.S.C. 115(a). It corresponds to Germany's *Erfinderbenennung* or *Erfindernennung*. The law here states that the patent application[116] must include two things: (1) the name of the inventor; and (2) the inventor's oath or declaration, in principle.

---

114 Greipl and Täger even said in their paper that the rate of the employee inventions was 94 percent. *Greipl/Täger/Grefermann*, Wettbewerbswirkungen der unternehmerischen Patent- und Lizenzpolitik: unter besonderer Berücksichtigung kleiner und mittlerer Unternehmen, 1st ed. (Berlin: Duncker & Humblot, 1982), 46.

115 See also: *Scheffler*, Das deutsche Patentsystem und die mittelständische Industrie: eine theoretische und empirische Untersuchung (Universität Stuttgart, 1986), 163. "*Die Nennung seiner Person als Erfinder in den öffentlichen Bekanntmachungen des DPMA (wie auch des EPA und – gegebenenfalls – der Patentämter weiterer Staaten) bedeutet für den Erfinder eine öffentliche Verkörperung seiner Erfinderehre. Sie wird ihn deshalb in vielen Fällen zu weiterer kreativer Tätigkeit motivieren*". (The naming of the inventor by DPMA – as well as the EPO, and the patent offices of other countries if applicable – means a public embodiment of his honor as an inventor. It will therefore motivate him further to creative works.).

116 35 U.S.C. § 115(a) defines an application: (1) "An application for patent that is filed under 35 U.S.C. § 111(a)"; or (2) "commences the national stage under 35 U.S.C. § 371".

Furthermore, 35 U.S.C. 115(b) and the articles that follow it describe the valid forms of presenting the 'inventor's oath' and 'naming of the inventor' as well as their contents. This paper breaks the actions required under this law into three aspects: (1) 'required statements' ('basic statements'); (2) 'substitute statement'; (3) 'required statement in the 'assignment record'.

The first aspect of 'basic statements' was originally specified in 35 U.S.C. 115(a)(b)(c) while the 'required statement' are the official name in the law as the title of paragraph (b). It is the principal and the most commonly submitted inventor declaration.

The 'basic statements' includes three details:

(1) the name of the inventor;[117]

(2) two obligatorily statements of oath, "The application was made or was authorized to be made by the affiant or declarant"[118] and "Such individual believes himself or herself to be the original inventor or an original joint inventor of a claimed invention in the application";

(3) additional information if necessary, such as in a case involving a joint invention, each inventor shall submit a declaration under 35 U.S.C. 116.

The second aspect is a 'substitute statement', which is acceptable in exceptional circumstances where 'basic statements' are impossible. There are four exceptions provided for in 35 U.S.C. 115(d)(2) named as "permitted circumstances":

(1) if the inventor is deceased;

(2) if the inventor is under legal incapacity;

(3) if the inventor cannot be found or reached after diligent effort; and

(4) if the inventor is under an obligation to assign the invention but has refused to make the oath or declaration in compliance with 35 U.S.C. 115(a).

Among these, the fourth situation is particularly notable given that most of today's inventions are employee inventions. Prior to the AIA reforms, applications were hampered by disputes between employees (inventors) and employers (assignee) – i.e., inventors refusing to sign the inventor's declaration. However, the AIA revision has addressed this and the law now easily allows employers to file the 'substitute statement'.[119]

---

117 37 CFR 1.63(a)(1) requires identification using the legal name.

118 37 CFR 1.63(a)(4) clarifies this again: "State that the application was made or was authorized to be made by the person executing the oath or declaration".

119 To this end, it is recommended for employers to thoroughly prepare an assignment record which clarifies the transfer of rights of the employee invention. Thus,

The 'substitute statement' needs to include three details:

(1) Identification of the person who has written the substitute statement;

(2) an explanation of the circumstances that qualify as a permitted reason for the filing of the 'substitute statement'; and

(3) any additional information which is required by the director of the patent office.[120]

The third action required under 35 U.S.C. involves cases where an individual who is under an obligation of assignment regarding a patent application may include the contents of the 'basic statements' in the 'assignment record' and may omit to file the 'basic statements' separately (35 U.S.C. 115(e)). Therefore, an 'assignment record' may be accepted under certain circumstances, especially if an inventor is not aware that the patent application has been filed. Moreover, the submission of the oath/declaration can be omitted in cases involving an "earlier-filed application" (35 U.S.C. 115(g)). If the 'assignment record', with its specific requirements, has already been submitted in an earlier-filed application, the submission of an inventor's oath or declaration will be exempted.

In all three of the above scenarios, a patent application shall be submitted "no later than the date on which the issue fee for the patent is paid" (35 U.S.C. 115(f)) and where the issue fee must be paid within three months of the date of the notice of allowance (37 CFR § 1.311(a)).

The 'basic statements' are the principle form while a 'substitute statement' is a form of 'exemption' in the exceptionally granted legal circumstances where 'basic statements' are not possible. In contrast, the third option of 'required statements in the assignment record' is a means to provide expediency.

By requiring his/her signature, these statements provide an opportunity for an inventor to review the contents of the application and discuss the scope of the claim with the assignee.

All these statements may be withdrawn, replaced or otherwise corrected at any time by the person who wrote them (35 U.S.C. 115(h)(1)).[121] Additionally, if an error in complying with the requirements is not remedied until or

even if an inventor (employee) refuses to sign an oath or declaration for a patent application, employers (the assignee) can apply for it without encountering legal problems.

[120] The 'basic statements' ('required statements') are expressed in plural while the substitute statement is specified in singular form because the 'required statements' contain two documents and the 'substitute statement' is just stating the reason why the 'basic statements' are impossible.

[121] If there is a flaw in the inventor's oath or declaration, Pre-AIA allowed the inventor to correct it through the 'Supplementary Declaration.' However, AIA is amended

near the end of the process, the patent shall not be invalid or unenforceable based upon the error (35 U.S.C. 115(h)(3)).

In this regard, 35 U.S.C. 116(c) and 37 CFR 1.48 specify a total of four situations for the correction of data pertaining to inventorship:

(1) When a person is wrongly named by errors in the patent application as the inventor;

(2) when an inventor is not named (i. e., omission) in the application;

(3) when the name of an inventor is being modified; and

(4) when the order of the names is being modified, in cases involving joint inventors.

In such cases, the Director of the Patent Office may permit the application to be amended under specific terms. 37 CFR 1.48(b) states that the inventor's oath or declaration or the substitute statement should also be submitted if the inventorship is corrected.

In pre-AIA, the error of misnaming inventors could have occurred without deceptive intent. (35 U.S.C. 256); that is to say, an innocent mistake. If a name was not corrected because of deceptive intent it could result in a patent right being held as invalid or unenforceable.[122] Also, an applicant who deliberately misrepresented themselves as the inventor could have been criminally punished.[123]

However, AIA removed all of the following provisions regarding deceptive intent (AIA Section 20 – Technical Amendment[124]): § 116 Inventors, § 251 Reissue of defective entities and § 256 Correction of a named inventor. As a result, the inventor's name can be corrected for all forms of error,[125] whether

to allow the inventor to drop, replace, and correct the basic statements or substitute statement directly at any time.

122 Advanced Magnetic Closures v. Rome Fastener Corp., No. 98 Civ. 7766 (PAC) (United States District Court for the Southern District of New York July 17, 2008). "[P]atents have in the past been held unenforceable for failure to correctly name inventors in cases where the named inventors acted in bad faith or with deceptive intent".

123 Regarding the distinction between criminal and civil law in the field of patent law, see: *Sherkow*, Patent Infringement as Criminal Conduct, Michigan Telecommunications and Technology Law Review 19, no. 1 (2012): 42.

124 See: Leahy-Smith America Invents Act: Full Text, accessed August 3, 2022, https://www.bitlaw.com/source/America-Invents-Act/full-text.html. This document contains the full text of the Leahy-Smith America Invents Act, passed by Congress on 16 September 2011. Especially in 'Section 20 – Technical Amendment,' the-'deceptive intention'-part was indicated "by striking".

125 It includes all cases in which the name of one of the joint inventors is incorrectly named (i. e. 'mis-joinder') or the true inventor is not named (i. e. 'non-joinder').

the error was intentionally deceptive or not.[126] Moreover, and in contrast to the pre-AIA situation, a patent will not be invalidated due to a correction of an inventor's name, a court simply needs to order the correction and the patent office shall issue a certificate accordingly (AIA § 256(b)).

To sum up, it goes without saying that the truthful identification of the inventor's name in US law is a crucial matter. Prior to the AIA, a patent could be invalidated or an applicant criminally punished due to an error involving the inventor's name. The AIA revision has made it easier to correct the errors and, even allowing for situations including a grace period or a derivation proceeding, the identification of the true inventor is still an important matter.[127]

3. Conclusion

The German and US laws require submitting the inventor's name and the inventor's oath or declaration in their application processes and the contents of these are substantially similar in both laws.

In the US, 35 U.S.C. 115(a) stipulates that the inventor's name and the inventor's oath should be included in the application. The most basic and important inventor's oath is the 'basic statements', as mentioned above. It states that the inventor must declare two key points: first, the application was written by the inventor him/herself; second, the invention was truly invented by the inventor him/herself.

In Germany, Art. 37 Abs. 1 PatG requires an applicant to be responsible for two things: first, the identification of an inventor, and second, the guarantee that "other persons have not contributed to the invention as far as the applicant knows".

---

126 *Bui*, Navigating the Leahy-Smith America Invents Act Including Effective Dates for Patent Reform An Overview of Patent Reform Act of 2011, Journal of the Patent and Trademark Office Society 93, no. 4 (2011): 457. "However, the change will likely have little material impact on patent litigation practices because deceptive intent is typically difficult to prove and many inventorship issues can be remedied in the absence of deceptive intent".

127 Although the US patent law has changed from FTI to FTF, the question of who is the inventor is still important. In the case of the grace period or a derivation proceeding, only the true inventor is acknowledged as the patent holder; therefore, it is necessary to have legal proof of the identification of the true inventor. Furthermore, as AIA adopts the First-to-Publish system, a disclosure or application from another person is not accepted as the prior state-of-the-art when there was already a disclosure from the true inventor. Therefore, proof of true inventorship is also necessary. Since a patent right lasts 20 years from the filing date, for example, the 15 years after the application lawsuits such as grace period or derivation proceeding may occur, and the true inventor's identity may become a legally important issue; therefore, it is necessary to preserve the proof of the true inventor's identity.

This German regulation is called *Erfindersbenennung* in German, which translates directly as naming of the inventor. As such, both German and US laws have almost identical substantive content and systems regarding the provisions relating to an inventor's name. Both countries' laws require (1) the identity of the inventor and (2) the assurance that the named inventor is the true inventor of the invention.

Having said that, there are also differences. In the US, 'basic statements' are written by inventors while the 'substitute statement' can be written by a non-inventor in exceptional cases. In Germany, in contrast, a declaration is always written by an applicant, although this is only a difference in formality. The substantive contents are similar, namely the requirement that the identity of the true inventor is revealed and guaranteed.

Returning to the central issue of this paper, if an AI's inventorship were to be recognized, who should complete and file the documents supplying the inventor's identity and oath? Under German and US laws, a declaration can be written by the true inventor (who must be a natural person) or an applicant (who could be either a natural or legal person). Can an AI write the declaration itself? If it shall be prepared by a natural or legal persons on behalf of AI, the relevant legal regulations shall be prepared.

E. The Official Position of the Patent Office and Courts in both Germany and the US on AI Inventorship

I. German Opinions Expressed through the EPO, DPMA and Federal Patent Court

The DABUS team first filed applications to the EPO, then filed an application to the DPMA in October 2019 (these application numbers are DE 10 2019 128 120.2 and DE 10 2019 129 136.4 respectively), claiming the priority of this EU application. However, and as expected, the DPMA rejected the applications and the DABUS team filed an appeal to the German Federal Patent Court (*Bundespatentgericht*).

The content of the German Patent Court's decision on 11 November 2021 is as follows: (1) The court supports the decision of DPMA noting that the applicant's claim that the AI is the inventor violates patent law. (2) However, an appeal to the German Supreme Court (*Bundesgerichtshof* in German) was deemed as legally allowed because the applicant's case on AI inventorship was seen as undoubtedly worth serious discussions and, as such, has the right to review by a higher court. Regarding the importance of AI inventorship, the German Supreme Court cited two reasons: (1) A German precedent in 2021

(GRUR 2021, 784 ff.) and (2) the affirmative ruling on AI inventorship in Australia in 2021.[128]

Given that the German Supreme Court's decision is yet to come out, it must currently suffice for this paper to analyze two crucial sources representing Germany's position on AI inventorship that are currently available: (1) The EPO decisions on AI inventorship in 2020[129] that have now been partially introduced into German patent law; (2) documents from the DPMA and Federal Patent Court, both of which have revealed their stance regarding AI inventorship.[130]

First, EU Member States' laws, including those of Germany, have historically indicated that "the inventor must be a natural person" in enacting and revising the EPC where the travaux préparatoires have been consistently clear on this point.[131] The same point was also clearly highlighted at the Munich Diplomatic Conference.[132]

Second, regarding the *Erfinderbenennung* documents submitted by the applicant on behalf of DABUS, the DPMA rejected them saying that they were not legitimate document submissions pursuant to § 37 PatG and § 7 PatV. The

---

[128] Bundespatentgericht 11 W (pat) 5/21 (Bundespatentgericht (German Federal Patent Court) November 11, 2021). "*Seine Überzeugung, dass eine KI in gleicherweise wie eine natürliche Person als Erfinder in Betracht zu ziehen sei und die Benennung eines entsprechenden Systems als Erfinder statthaft sein müsse, spiegelt eine Rechtsmeinung wider, die mittlerweile von einigen Stimmen für vertretbar angesehen wird (vgl. z. B. die Nachweise bei Domis in GRUR 2021, 784 ff.). Für das australische Patentrechtssystem hat das Federal Court of Australia die Möglichkeit, eine KI als Erfinder zu benennen, zwischenzeitlich mit einer Entscheidung vom 30. Juli 2021 bejaht (vgl. Az.: VID 108 of 2021)*".

[129] As there are two inventions that originate with DABUS, there are two decisions by EPO. European Patent Office, Grounds for the Decision on EP 18 275 163, January 27, 2020, https://register.epo.org/n?showPdfPage=1&documentId=E4B63SD6219I498&appnumber=EP18275163&proc=; European Patent Office, Grounds for the Decision on EP 18 275 174, January 27, 2020, https://register.epo.rg/n?showPdfPage=1&documentId=E4B63OBI2076498&appnumber=EP18275174&proc=.

[130] Bundespatentgericht 11 W (pat) 5/21.

[131] European Patent Office, Grounds for the Decision on EP 18 275 163, 5. "The legislative history shows that the legislators of the EPC were in agreement that the term 'inventor' refers to a natural person only. The Travaux Preparatoires consistently refer to the inventor as being a natural person".

[132] European Patent Office, 6. "The requirement that the inventor be a natural person is in line with the intention of the Munich Diplomatic Conference to give inventors a clear and strong legal position (J 8/82 point 13 of the reasons)"; "This position is rooted in Article 4ter of the Paris Convention for the Protection of Industrial Property (as amended on 28 September 1979). See also Minutes of the Munich Diplomatic Conference, document M/PR/K/1 page 22, point 54 and document M/PR/1 page 40, point 247".

direct reasons are § 6 PatG and § 37 PatG which clearly state that only natural persons are eligible to be inventors; accordingly, an AI is not allowed to attain such a designation.[133] Moreover, the statutory basis is the following: (1) The term "Personen" from § 37 Abs. 1 PatG; (2) the term "Vornamen" and "Namen" from § 7 Abs. 2 Nr. 1 PatV.[134]

Third, the DPMA believes that AI inventorship violates § 14 of the German Constitution, which is referred to as the 'property clause.'[135]

Fourth, German courts have directly ruled that an inventor's right to be named in the *Offenlegungs- und Patentschriften* according to § 63 Abs. 1 PatG is a personal moral right (*Erfinderpersönlichkeitsrechts* or *Erfinderehre*) permitted only to natural persons.[136]

Fifth, the DPMA finds no logical connection between "technological advancement (*der technische Fortschritt* in German) as the purpose of the patent law" and "an opinion that the legislature must consider the artificial inventor beyond natural inventors".[137] In other words, it seems that legislature is not legally obligated to recognize the inventorship of 'E-Persons'.

Sixth, the applicant appealed to the court by explaining his 'dilemma',[138] however, the court rejected his argument. The dilemma here refers to the fact that: (1) The applicant must name the AI as the inventor under the "legal obligation to tell the truth" (*Wahrheitspflicht* in German) under § 124 PatG, however, (2) patent rights may not be granted if he does disclose this truth as an AI inventor is not legally allowed. The court determined that the applicant's dilemma did not legally exist and the applicant's name – not the AI's designation – should be recorded as the true inventor. This ruling was based on two reasons. First, the "legal obligation to tell the truth" under § 124 PatG refers to the factual circumstances (*auf tatsächliche Umstände* in German). However, the applicant's claim that DABUS is the inventor is not a factual circum-

---

[133] Bundespatentgericht 11 W (pat) 5/21. Even legislature says AI cannot be an inventor. "*Aus der so vom Gesetzgeber bewusst getroffenen Entscheidung folgt, dass nach deutschem Patentrecht eine Kl nie als Erfinder oder Miterfinder benannt werden kann (vgl. Rainer Schulte, ed., 'Patentgesetz Mit Europäischem Patentübereinkommen: Kommentar (§ 6 Rn. 18),' 11th ed. (Carl Heymanns Verlag, 2021); Rudolf Busse and Alfred Keukenschrijver, eds., Patentgesetz: Kommentar (§ 37 Rn. 4), 9th ed. (De Gruyter, 2020); Stortnik (commentator for § 37), Patentrechtskommentar: PatG, GebrMG, IntPatÜG, PCT Und EPÜ Mit Nebenvorschriften (PatG § 37 Rn. 2f.), ed. Uwe Fitzner, Raimund Lutz, and Theo Bodewig, 4th ed. (Vahlen, 2012))*".

[134] Bundespatentgericht 11 W (pat) 5/21 at 10.

[135] Bundespatentgericht 11 W (pat) 5/21 at 4.

[136] Bundespatentgericht 11 W (pat) 5/21 at 10; Bundespatentgericht 11 W (pat) 5/21 at 14.

[137] Bundespatentgericht 11 W (pat) 5/21 at 10.

[138] Bundespatentgericht 11 W (pat) 5/21 at 4.

stance but merely his legal opinion (*eine Rechtsmeinung* in German)[139]; the court went on to state its second reason, namely that § 7 Abs. 1 PatG requires applicants to name themselves as inventors in case of doubt.[140]

Seventh, the DABUS team submitted an additional explanation which was that "this invention … was created by an artificial intelligence named DABUS", when filing the application. Since § 7 Abs. 2 PatV stipulates only five items to be included for the naming of inventors, a legal debate arose on whether the above additional explanation part was legal. In the end, the opinions of the DPMA and the court differed on this matter.

The DPMA found that this additional explanation was not lawful. Their grounds are as follows: First, § 10 Abs. 3 prohibits unnecessary explanations of inventions, so this additional explanation is illegal; second, if the above additional explanation is permitted, there is a risk of extending claim interpretation, that is, the scope of patent rights because the specification (*Beschreibung* in German) is used to interpret claims according to § 14 Satz 2 PatG.

(2) In contrast, the court took a different stance on this point, as § 7 Abs. 2 PatV is an open clause (*keinen abschließenden Katalog* in German).[141]

Eighth, it is interesting that the court allowed the applicant to appeal while commenting on a positive possibility regarding AI inventorship, although both the court and the DPMA gave negative responses based on existing statutory law. The court said that § 37 PatG and § 63 PatG, which regulate the naming of inventors will become increasingly questionable in the future with the advent of AI,[142] with the following three points of view: (1) the concept of "Person", a word that is written in the two clauses, cannot include an AI;[143] (2) both clauses contain the concept of *Erfinderehre* or 'inventor's honor', which carries the idea of a right to reputation or right of honor. This is problematic because AI cannot have such rights and/or it is unnecessary to assign them these rights; (3) finally, the last point is that excluding an AI as the inventor does not limit the invention's patentability.[144] In other words, inventions must be evaluated objectively and whether the invention is a product of the inventor's consciousness or was created by AI is not essential. It is interesting that the German court clearly mentioned the possibility that a natural

139 Bundespatentgericht 11 W (pat) 5/21 at 12.

140 Bundespatentgericht 11 W (pat) 5/21 at 13.

141 Bundespatentgericht 11 W (pat) 5/21 at 16.

142 Bundespatentgericht 11 W (pat) 5/21 at 15.

143 Bundespatentgericht 11 W (pat) 5/21 at 15.

144 Bundespatentgericht 11 W (pat) 5/21 at 15.

person need not necessarily be an inventor.[145] This is a very similar point of view to the American 'Flash of Genius' doctrine.[146]

II. The US (USPTO)

The DABUS team filed two patent applications to the USPTO using the name of the AI as the inventor, leading to the USPTO rejecting both due to the lack of information (the USPTO issued a "Notice to File Missing Parts of Nonprovisional Application"). Accordingly, the applicant submitted a petition, which the USPTO dismissed in December 2020. The decisions of the USPTO regarding petitions are not normally disclosed, however, this decision was made public by the USPTO.[147] The exact reasons for this are unclear, although wanting to give this issue a more public profile may have been a factor as AI inventorship has become a hot topic in patent law circles.

The applicant filed a lawsuit against the secretary of the USPTO in the United States District Court for the Eastern District of Virginia in August 2020.[148] However, the court dismissed the case in September 2021,[149] reaffirming that designation as an inventor can only be applied to natural persons and necessarily excludes AIs.

In explaining how it arrived at its decision, the court noted that an attempt to nominate an AI as an inventor contradicts the general interpretation of the wording in the below-cited relevant statutory provisions:[150]

(1) the word "Whoever" in 35 U.S.C. § 101;

(2) the words "himself or herself" in 35 U.S.C. § 115(b);

(3) the word "person" in 35 U.S.C. § 115(h)(1), 35 U.S.C. § 102(a), 35 U.S.C. § 116(c), 35 U.S.C. § 185, 35 U.S.C. § 256(a), 37 CFR 1.27(a)(1), 37 CFR

145 Bundespatentgericht 11 W (pat) 5/21 at 12.

146 See Chapter 6 B. I. 2. regarding "Flash of Genius"-Doctrine.

147 It is notable that the word "[u]nusually" is used: *Thaler*, Complaint for Declaratory and Injunctive Relief in the United States District Court for the Eastern District of Virginia, 2020, 5, https://artificialinventor.com/wp-content/uploads/2020/09/Complaint.pdf. "Unusually, USPTO took the step of publishing one of the decisions on the petition".

148 See the filed complaint by DABUS team: *Thaler*, Complaint for Declaratory and Injunctive Relief in the United States District Court for the Eastern District of Virginia.

149 Thaler v. Hirshfeld, 558 F. Supp. 3d 238 (United States District Court, Eastern District of Virginia 2021).

150 See Decision on Petition (In re Application of Application No.: 16/524,350) at 4. regarding "whoever", "himself or herself" and "person"; see Decision on Petition (In re Application of Application No.: 16/524,350) at 6. regarding 'legal name.'

1.41(d), 37 CFR 1.53(d)(4), 37 CFR 1.63(a)(3), 37 CFR 1.324(a), 37 CFR 1.324(b)(1);

(4) the term "legal name" in 37 CFR 1.76(b)(1);

(5) the word "individuals" in 35 U.S.C. §§ 100(f)(g).

As for the reasons for defining "individuals" as natural persons, the court explained that it first must examine "the word's ordinary meaning". Quoting from several well-known dictionaries, the court held that when used "[a]s a noun, 'individual' ordinarily means '[a] human being, a person.'" from the Oxford English Dictionary (1989). Second, the court should consider "everyday parlance" and English speakers use "individual" to refer to a natural person. Third, 1 U.S.C. § 1, which is frequently referred to as 'the Dictionary Act', indicates "individual" refers to humans. Fourth, the US Congress has tied the word "individual" to "natural persons" through some statutes, including the Trafficking Victims Protection Act (TVPA). Fifth, Mohamad Court[151] noted that "no one … refers in normal parlance to an organization as an 'individual'".[152]

The court also concluded that inventor means only a natural person according to precedents. The following precedents were given as examples and grounds: Regarding the conceiving of an idea, (1) in University of Utah v Max-Planck, the presiding court expressed the opinion that "[i]t is axiomatic that inventors are the individuals that conceive of the invention". The District Court for the Eastern District of Virginia then cited Burroughs Wellcome Co v. Barr Labs where it was noted that "conception is a mental act" and the presiding court emphasized that only natural persons can undertake a mental act;[153] (2) in Beech Aircraft Corp v EDO Corp, the court there directly expressed the notion that "only natural persons can be 'inventors.'"[154]

The Eastern District court then turned its attention to the MPEP, which is written based on statutory and case law as a reference source for disputing parties,[155] where the court noted it contains the same logic: (1) The MPEP

---

151 Mohamad v. Palestinian Authority, 566 U.S. 449 (2012).

152 Thaler v. Hirshfeld, 558 F. Supp. 3d 238 at 15–16. "Courts, including the Supreme Court, have repeatedly held that Congress's use of the term 'individual' in a given statute denotes a 'human being,' as opposed to other things".

153 Burroughs Wellcome Co. v. Barr Laboratories, Inc., 828 F. Supp.; University of Utah v. Max-Planck-Gesellschaft zur Foerderung der Wissenschaften e.V., 851 F.3d 1317 (United States Court of Appeals for the Federal Circuit 2017). "To perform this mental act, inventors must be natural persons and cannot be corporations or sovereigns".

154 Beech Aircraft Corp. v. EDO Corp., 990 F.2d 1237 (United States Court of Appeals, Federal Circuit 1993).

155 Decision on Petition (In re Application of Application No.: 16/524,350) at 6 p. 6.

explains that "the threshold question for inventorship is 'conception.'";[156] (2) at the same time, the legal definition of "conception" in this context is "the complete performance of the mental part of the inventive act" and "the formation in the mind of the inventor of a definite and permanent idea of the complete and operative invention as it is thereafter to be applied in practice";[157] all of this aligned with what the USPTO had previously clearly concluded, namely that "the use of terms such as 'mental' and 'mind' in the MPEP indicates that 'conception' must be performed by a natural person".[158]

Prior to the district court ruling the USPTO had drawn very similar conclusions. During the application process, the applicant stated that the EPO and UK Intellectual Property Office at least acknowledged the fact that DABUS had invented the invention and he claimed that the USPTO should also acknowledge this fact.[159] However, the USPTO noted on this point that (1) it did not determine who made the invention,[160] and (2) foreign laws are not a factor in the USPTO's deliberations.[161]

The applicant also criticized current statutory and case law which only recognizes natural persons as inventors, forcing the applicant to nominate a 'fake inventors'.[162] The USPTO responded that nominating a 'fake inventor' does not conform to the truth and violates current law, emphasizing that only 'true inventors' can be listed under current patent law.[163]

Further to this, the applicant asserted that the USPTO established "an additional test for patentability" not prescribed by law and should adhere to the general principle that inventorship should not be a substantive condition for granting patent rights.[164] Regarding this, the USPTO ruled that the applicant's

---

156 United States Patent and Trademark Office, MPEP, 2109 [R-10.2019].

157 United States Patent and Trademark Office, MPEP, 2138.04 [R-10.2019].

158 Decision on Petition (In re Application of Application No.: 16/524,350) at 6 p. 6.

159 Decision on Petition (In re Application of Application No.: 16/524,350) at 6. "[The p]etitioner also argues that the USPTO should take into account the position adopted by the European Patent Office ('EPO') and the UK Intellectual Property Office ('UKIPO') that DABUS created the invention at issue, but DABUS cannot be named as the inventor".

160 Decision on Petition (In re Application of Application No.: 16/524,350) at 7. "The above-identified application is currently undergoing review for completeness of the application. The USPTO has not made any determination concerning who or what actually created the invention claimed in the above-identified application".

161 Decision on Petition (In re Application of Application No.: 16/524,350) at 6.

162 Decision on Petition (In re Application of Application No.: 16/524,350) at 6. "[T]he referenced statutes are intended to compel an applicant to name a natural person even where the person does not meet the inventorship criteria".

163 Decision on Petition (In re Application of Application No.: 16/524,350) at 6.

164 Decision on Petition (In re Application of Application No.: 16/524,350) at 7.

argument was not persuasive because inventorship is a critical condition for granting a patent right: (1) 35 U.S.C. § 115(a) explicitly requires that the inventor's name be included in the application; (2) if the inventor's name is inappropriate, the application must be refused according to 35 U.S.C. § 102(f) (pre-AIA), 35 U.S.C. § 101 (AIA) and 35 U.S.C. § 115 (AIA).[165] Interestingly, what the applicant argues here is related to the deletion of the 'flash of genius' doctrine, however, both the USPTO and the district court simply responded by emphasizing the importance of naming the inventor.

Another issue raised by the applicant with the USPTO was that the patent right for the invention involving DABUS should be implicitly recognized since the patent right for the DABUS machine itself had already been recognized.[166] However, the USPTO rejected this line of reasoning saying that a patent for a camera is different from a copyright for pictures using the camera.[167]

The penultimate issue the applicant raised concerned judicial interpretations, here he argued before the district court that the intent of the framers must be emphasized rather than a simple focus on textualism. In other words, it is crucial when seeking to apply patent law to interpret it in accordance with the law's overarching purpose, namely the promotion of scientific and technological development. However, the court rejected this claim stating that it was simply his personal assessment[168] or speculation[169] and negatively evaluated the claim as "at the zenith of hyperbole"[170]. Further to this, the court noted that dealing with the intent of the framers is a task of the legislative branch, not the judicial branch[171] before ruling that textualism, which entails the plain meaning of the language used, still matters historically and should not be ignored.[172]

Finally, the applicant argued that AI did not exist when the Patent Act was enacted; therefore, the current situation should not be judged using such old

---

165 Decision on Petition (In re Application of Application No.: 16/524,350) at 7.

166 Decision on Petition (In re Application of Application No.: 16/524,350) at 7.

167 Decision on Petition (In re Application of Application No.: 16/524,350) at 7.

168 Thaler v. Hirshfeld, 558 F. Supp. 3d 238 at 2. "Plaintiff now asks this Court to ignore this plain statutory language and Federal Circuit authority, based solely on his own assessment of the intellectual property policy that the United States should adopt with respect to artificial intelligence".

169 Thaler v. Hirshfeld, 558 F. Supp. 3d 238 at 18. "[The p]laintiff's policy-related commentary is untethered to anything other than his own speculation".

170 Thaler v. Hirshfeld, 558 F. Supp. 3d 238 at 19–20.

171 Thaler v. Hirshfeld, 558 F. Supp. 3d 238 at 2.

172 Thaler v. Hirshfeld, 558 F. Supp. 3d 238 at 3.

laws.[173] However, the court also denied this argument on the grounds of the content of 35 U.S.C. §§ 100(f)–(g). This provision, newly enacted in 2011, specifies an inventor as an "individual" even though AI already existed at the time.[174] Regarding this latter point, it is argued here that even though 2011 is fairly recent, there was no active discussion of AI and its inventorship a decade ago, as such, one should not deduce that the lawmaker enacted this provision with a clear purpose to exclude AI from inventorship.

F. Final Remarks and Critical Reflection

At this point, the provisions on inventorship under German and US patent law have been reviewed comparatively based on their universality and particularity. This has provided the following insights into the inventorship of AI, or perhaps more accurately, the lack thereof.

First, as noted in Chapter 2 C., while it is true that AI has been generating inventions, it may not be recognized as the legal inventor under German and US patent law. In other words, although inventions by AI are possible, AI itself cannot be regarded as an inventor. As discussed above, only natural persons may be recognized as inventors.

As a side note, both countries have been the source of negative judgments on AI inventorship because the statutory interpretation cannot be ignored, however, it is noteworthy that there is a difference in the overall tone in each country's institutions. Both countries' court cases were decided in 2021, however, the position of the US court was more conservative than the one in Germany. The German court showed a relatively positive tone, allowing an appeal by deeming that AI inventorship is a matter to be reviewed more profoundly. In contrast, the US court took a very critical tone, saying that the applicant's arguments were exaggerated and baseless.[175]

---

[173] Thaler v. Hirshfeld, 558 F. Supp. 3d 238 at 20. "In this respect, plaintiff first asserts that this Court should depart from the plain meaning of the term 'individual' – at least insofar as machines are concerned – because when Congress codified the Patent Act in 1952, it likely did not even consider (or could not have considered) the possibility that inventions could be created by machines utilizing artificial intelligence".

[174] Thaler v. Hirshfeld, 558 F. Supp. 3d 238 at 20–21. "[The p]laintiff's statement in this regard is accompanied by a string citation of various statutes, [] however, curiously missing from that listing is any reference to 35 U.S.C. §§ 100(f)–(g), which are the statutory provisions in which Congress expressly defined 'inventor' to be an 'individual'. Congress added those provisions to the Patent Act not in 1952, but in 2011, through the America Invents Act … not only was artificial intelligence 'a reality' in 2011."

[175] Thaler v. Hirshfeld, 558 F. Supp. 3d 238 at 19–20, "at the zenith of hyperbole".

Second, both German and US patent laws underscore that the purpose of patent protection is to promote scientific and industrial advancement.[176] Yet, why do the respective legal frameworks reject a teleological extension of the law? Teleological interpretation is typically employed when statutory language is ambiguous. However, both German and US patent law clearly stipulate that an inventor must be a natural person; accordingly, courts have adhered strictly to a textual interpretation. Moreover, the reluctance to apply a teleological extension in this context reflects judicial restraint, in light of the profound legal, ethical, and societal consequences that recognizing AI as an inventor would entail. Ultimately, this is a matter that falls within the domain of the legislature.

Third, who can be considered the inventor if only natural persons are permitted? Both legal systems require that inventors contribute to the core of the inventive process. But which natural person, if any, can fulfill this role in the case of AI-generated inventions? This question is addressed directly in Chapter 4. It is worth noting that, as previously noted, both countries' laws clearly show that technical assistants, employers, those who provided only simple explanations and investors cannot be regarded as the true inventors of an invention.

Fourth, both legal systems require that the name of the inventor be provided in the patent application. Given that AI inventorship is rejected by both courts and patent offices, a natural question arises: can the inventor's name field simply be left blank? This issue is addressed in Chapter 5.

---

176 German Patent Act, § 1(1); US Constitution, Art. I, § 8, cl. 8.

Chapter 4

The 2/7 Questions and Possible AI-related Candidates for Inventors when AI is Excluded

A. Introduction

This paper will ultimately affirm the need to recognize AI inventorship, which will be handled in detail in Chapter 6. However, before doing so, this chapter endeavors to examine some of the options and consequences that emerge from the ongoing denial of AI inventorship. Doing so will revolve around the question, "if the inventorship of AI is not allowed, who can be recognized as the inventor?"

In both German and US law, the inventor's name must be entered in the patent application. If an AI's inventorship for an invention that originated with the machine is denied, whose name can be given as the inventor? The following sections will identify a list of candidates that could be cited as the inventor and examine whether they are eligible to be nominated as such. This will be done by dividing candidates into two categories, namely:

(1) Single inventorship. As one of the participants in creating AI Inventions, he/she can claim inventorship: i. e., software programmers, data suppliers, feedback suppliers, the owners of the AI systems, and operators. Each of them will be reviewed in Chapter 4 C.

(2) Joint inventorship. Can one of the single inventors who are listed above altogether be recognized as a co-inventor? This will be reviewed in Chapter 4 D.

Reviewing all of these possible candidates will prove that each candidate is insufficient to meet the requirements of inventorship. This ultimately leads to the assertion that the positive confirmation of AI inventorship is a required inevitability. To review this, a clear legal standard is undoubtedly needed, therefore, 'the 2/7 Questions' model has been devised as a tool to help identify the legal requirements for inventorship.

B. The 2/7 Questions: The Requirements for Inventorship

I. Necessity and Research Method

Reviewing the affirmation or negation of inventorship can go beyond legal discussion and develop into a dispute in the fields of philosophy and logic. This is because determining who is the inventor of the invention cannot be calculated using a clearly definable formula. Rather, it is based on human 'experience' to whether an individual has done the most important thing in the inventive process. In other words, the answer to the question of who is the inventor is not about identifiable metrics but about the experience involving many faculties, including philosophy, logic, psychology and so forth. Therefore, the existing legal dispute on inventorship comes from diverse judicial precedents. As such, it is helpful to stipulate the legal requirements for inventorship which can be organized from those existing precedents. This effectively determines who is the inventor during the patent application from a legal point of view.

Firstly, most of the precedents and regulations that humans previously have dealt with so far have been reviewed. Then I researched which cases were confirmed to the inventorship or which cases were denied. This formed the basis for the content of Chapter 3. As previously stated, it would have been beneficial in some ways to cover all patent laws worldwide, however, that would be an impractical and unwieldy task and, as such, this paper has studied only German and US laws.[1]

Secondly, based on the initial research of Chapter 3, the criteria for determining inventorship have been made as clear as possible, in other words, the 'empirical' cases referred to above were translated into 'more legal criteria' that allowed the development of the '2/7 Questions'. This questionnaire serves as a kind of master key to open all the seemingly blocked pathways for determining inventorship. It will be given to all candidates mentioned as inventors of AI inventions, including AIs.

Chapter 3 looked at how inventorship is handled under current German and US laws and reviewed the relevant provisions and precedents in detail. As a result, both (1) the definition of inventor and (2) 'the core of the inventive process' can be considered essential factors for determining inventorship. This is because the inventor must be suitable for the fundamental definition of the inventor, and he must also directly perform the essential part of the inventive process. As such, based on those two factors, five basic questions were derived before two additional key questions are ultimately selected after over-

---

1 See Chapter 3 A. III. for why only German and US laws were chosen.

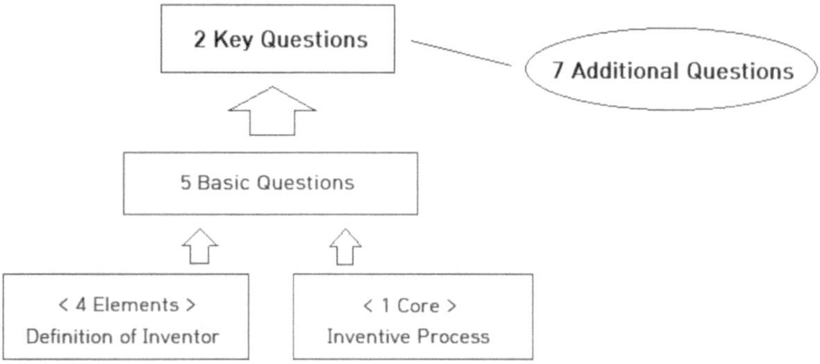

Figure 5: 2/7 Questions

lapping data is removed and the significance of each question is considered. In the following, more detail on the series of steps taken for this research process will be introduced. Moreover, I go one step further from here and prepare 'seven additional questions,' which I expect to provide a clear hint in determining each candidate's inventorship.

II. Five Basic Questions

1. Questions raised from Two Topics

In Chapter 3. B. II., the definitions of inventor in German and US law were handled and these, in short, determine a candidate's suitability to become an inventor.

In German law, the inventor must (1) recognize a technical problem; (2) present a solution to the problem; and (3) use technical means as a solution. In US law, the inventor is (1) a person who uses knowledge accumulated from the past to the present, and (2) who presents a better future to humankind by promoting the development of science and technology.

Integrating these described definitions of inventor used in each country, the meaning of the word inventor can be thought of as conveying the following four key attributes:

First, an inventor should recognize a technical problem;

second, the inventor should present a solution to the problem, i.e. to illustrate the final patented invention;

third, the inventor should use 'technical means' and 'knowledge' of humankind accumulated from the past to the present in preparing the above solution;

fourth, the inventor should contribute to a better future for humanity by promoting the development of science and technology due to all these problem-solving.

Currently, the person who played the leading role in 'the core of the inventive process' becomes the inventor. 'The core of inventive process' means "the definite and permanent idea of the complete and operative invention" that a POSITA should be able to make and use an invention from a written description without "extensive experimentation or additional inventive skill," or "exercise of the inventive faculty". This is the essential core content of inventorship in German and US law and those not involved in this core process cannot be recognized as inventors.

2. Five Basic Questions

By integrating the four elements mentioned above for 'the definition of the inventor' and the concept of 'the core of the inventive process', five basic questions have been devised as the starting point. The significance of each of the questions will be handled one by one and will lead to the asking of two key questions to ultimately determine the legal requirements for the affirmation of inventorship.

(1) Did the candidate recognize the 'related technical problem'?

This question is related to the first element of the inventor's definition. It asks if the candidate recognized the problem as the first stage of the inventive process. This is a key point as the motivation to improve the situation is the beginning of the inventive process.

However, answering affirmatively to questions such as "did you recognize the problem yourself?" or "did you recognize it first?" is not a prerequisite. In some cases, inventors themselves were the first ones in history to become aware of a problem, while for others, they may have heard complaints about the problem from others and then had the motivation to solve it. Similar scenarios can be imagined for joint inventions, the first person who recognizes the problem can visit a person with the technical knowledge to solve the problem while it is being explained to them and the pair then jointly develop the invention together.

Therefore, it cannot be said that yes or no to such questions confirms or invalidates inventorship. In other words, the events framed by such questions play a part in the inventive process, but they cannot be said to be a key criterion for defining the requirements of inventorship. There are US precedents that have shown that an individual may not be recognized as an inventor with 'the discovery of problem alone,' even if the problem was challenging to identify and required inventive talent.[2] Furthermore, there are German precedents that the inventor is not a person who simply stimulated the inventive act but a person who actively participated in it. In the end, the inventor must present a 'means' or 'solution' that goes beyond recognizing the problem, which is linked to Question (3) below.

(2) What is the 'task' undertaken by the candidate?

This question can be the basis for other questions. Above all, it is necessary to grasp what the candidate did in the inventive process, i. e., the details of his/her work to help determine how related the candidate is to the inventorship.

(3) Does the 'task' undertaken by the candidate contribute to 'the core of the inventive process'?

This question combines the second element raised in the inventor's definition and 'the core of the inventive process'. Does the task from above Question (2) correspond to 'the core of inventive process'? The inventor's task should be the "definite and permanent idea of the complete and operative invention," that is to say, "a POSITA should be able to make and use an invention from a written description without extensive experimentation or additional inventive skill, or exercise of the inventive faculty".

In other words, it is a question of whether the candidate has presented a specific solution to the related technical problem mentioned in Question (1). As already described, the inventor must also provide a particular means (solution) to achieve the desired purpose or outcome. In the end, the solution is nothing but the presentation of a patent invention. Patent inventions can be presented as actual products or in the form of a patent application.

In Chapter 3 C., the inventive process was divided into phases with each studied in detail. In particular, it was argued that 'the core of inventive process' is the most important phase as it refers to that in which the idea is concrete enough for a POSITA to present patented inventions immediately.

(4) Did the candidate use 'technical knowledge accumulated from the past to the present' to come up with the solution?

This question is linked to the third key attribute used in the above definition of the inventor as an inventor naturally uses technical knowledge accumulated from the past to the present. Even in the case of joint inventions, each co-inventor uses his/her expertise in his/her parts of the inventive act. All candidates, including the software programmers discussed in the next section, use professional knowledge in their respective areas.

2 Regents of the University of California v. Synbiotics Corp., 849 F. Supp. 740.

However, the question of how directly a candidate's expertise was used in connection with 'the core of inventive process' remains and is more critical rather than whether his/her knowledge was used. If the knowledge used by the candidate is only simple advice within the overall inventive process, that candidate's viability as an inventor cannot be recognized. Conversely, if knowledge constitutes a very important part of the overall inventive process that connects to 'the core of the inventive process', inventorship should be affirmed. Therefore, this question can be said to be a part of Question (3).

(5) Does the candidate's task ultimately contribute to promoting the development of science and technology, giving humankind a better future?

This question is linked to the fourth key attribute used in the above definition of the inventor and directly reveals the fundamental purpose of the patent law, namely to further technological development.[3] The DPMA and USPTO carefully examine the patentability of an application and decide whether to grant it for patented inventions to lead to the development of industrial technology.

The requirements for the patentability of inventions in Germany and the US are (1) industrial applicability (the invention must be 'useful'), (2) novelty, and (3) inventive step (inventiveness or non-obviousness). Industrial applicability here means that the invention should be industrially available.[4] It should be possible to achieve the purpose of the patent law, namely make a contribution to industrial development. Novelty in this context means that the invention should be new and requires that it be a technology that is not known at home and abroad. An inventive step refers to the fact that the invention should be such that a POSITA cannot easily invent it by the existing prior art. If patent rights are granted even though the invention has no inventive step, patent quality would be held back due to imitations. Therefore, industrial development would be hindered, as many patented inventions looking similar would mushroom.

The requirement of industrial applicability confirms whether the invention can be produced reliably and repeatedly so that it contributes to industrial de-

---

[3] Germany and the US specify "development of industrial technology" for the purpose of patent system.

[4] The term 'industry' here can apply to a wide range of industries, including primary industries such as agriculture, livestock and fisheries, secondary industries such as mining and manufacturing as well as tertiary industries such as service providers and will apply to the upcoming fourth industry introduced by the era of AI. The Fourth Industrial Revolution is the current stage of technological progress, and it employs advanced technologies like AI, robotics, IoT, and 3D printing to revolutionize industries such as production, transit, medical care, and agriculture. It will result in more efficient and sustainable systems, improved productivity, and better quality of life.

velopment. The novelty requirement checks the prior state-of-the-art and the requirement of the inventive step confirms whether the invention is enough high-level object, based on the prior state-of-the-art which was already checked in the novelty step. The inventive step consequently proves whether it contributes to industrial development as a POSITA cannot easily invent it. To sum up, the three requirements of industrial applicability, novelty and the presence of an inventive step are directly related to the key purpose of patent law, industrial development.

Therefore, the question of "does the candidate's task ultimately contribute to promoting the development of science and technology, giving humankind a better future?" is an important one for patent law. However, this Question (5) was eliminated from the final questionnaire since patentability focuses on the invention while this study focuses on the inventor. Patentability handles the question of whether or not an invention is eligible to acquire patent rights to monopolize the market. In contrast, inventorship handles the question of whether or not an individual can acquire the status as a true inventor.

The statuses of inventor and invention, while closely related to each other, entail separate concepts that are entirely distinguished from each other. For example, if an invention is not recognized as a patentable invention, its inventor cannot obtain exclusive rights, so the status as an inventor has no practical meaning. Conversely, if there is a problem with the individual who holds inventor status, the patent right may not take effect, even though the invention itself is excellent.[5] In such instances, legal actions, such as interference proceedings, may arise over the true inventor's identity and these may interfere with the exercise of the patent. As such, while inventor and invention have a direct bearing on each other, they are distinct legal concepts at their core.

Any inventor with valid patent rights will, of course, improve human life by promoting the development of science and technology because the invention was evaluated as having "industrial applicability, novelty, and inventive step". This Question (5) is meaningful for patentability, but it does not mean much to the affirmation or denial of the inventorship itself. Therefore it is excluded from the final list.

III. Two Key Questions

So far, the following five possible questions have been reviewed by integrating the 'definition of the inventor' and 'the core of the inventive process':

(1) Did the candidate recognize the 'related technical problem'?

---

[5] According to German and US law, the patent right itself could be invalidated if an error occurred in the inventor's name.

(2) What was the 'task' undertaken by the candidate?

(3) Did the 'task' undertaken by the candidate play a role in 'the core of the inventive process'?

(4) Did the candidate use technical knowledge accumulated from the past to the present to come up with the solution?

(5) Did the candidate's task ultimately contribute to promoting the development of science and technology, giving humankind a better future?

The first, fourth and fifth questions will be excluded from the next phase because they are unrelated to inventorship or overlap with other questions. As a result, only two questions remain, and these two questions are called 'key questions' in this study.

(1) What is the 'task' undertaken by the candidate?

(2) Does the 'task' undertaken by the candidate contribute to 'the core of the inventive process'? This is centered on the fact that the inventor's task should be the "definite and permanent idea of the complete and operative invention". Moreover, a POSITA can reproduce the invention "without extensive experimentation or additional inventive skill, or exercise of the inventive faculty" from a written description.

In the process of answering the above 'two key questions', one can evaluate whether the individual 'actually' and 'actively' participated in the inventive act. If so, the individual's inventorship will be affirmed and he/she can acquire the status of (co-)inventor.

IV. Seven Additional Questions

Candidates who pass the litmus test provided by the 'two key questions' are then asked 'seven additional questions' as the second key question, (Does the 'task' undertaken by the candidate contribute to 'the core of the inventive process?) is so far-reaching and abstract. Courts deciding on patent-related disputes regularly deal with issues about 'the core of inventive process' when handling cases involving joint inventions or employee inventions. However it is also not easy for them to discern inventorship because the answer to this question is based on 'human experience' rather than a definable formula involving precise numbers.

Therefore, this study summarizes the precedents of Germany and the United States concerning Question (2) and synthesizes them into the following seven 'additional questions.'

The word simple is commonly included in these 'seven additional questions'. It is not meant in a belittling way, rather its usage is intended to designate tasks, such as workplace instructions and financial investment that, while important in their own right, have not contributed to 'the core of the inventive process'.

(a) A simple order for work?

A simple order is an instruction that initiates a specific task or provides some guidance for the direction of work, typically these come from an employer or supervisor. Such simple orders have not contributed to 'the core of the inventive process' and do not contribute to the issuer's status as an inventor. An inventor is a person who is substantially involved in the inventive process beyond setting its overall direction and/or purpose for the (sought-after) invention.[6]

(b) A simple investor?

Investors who provide only financial investment cannot be inventors. US precedents rule that "a person who has made only economic contributions cannot be a co-inventor".[7] Similarly, in Germany, a simple investor cannot be a co-inventor because co-inventors are required to make non-intellectual contributions.[8]

(c) A simple imaginative or fanciful idea?

If a contributed idea is merely the product of imagination or a fanciful notion and it cannot resulted in an engineeringly-sound design to implement the idea, then the person who provided that idea may not be the inventor. Returning to a previously-mentioned example here, simply imagining a flying broom is not enough, one must present a viable engineering design to implement a flying broom to be its inventor.

(d) Simply building a working model?

If one simply builds a prototype according to the written description this does not correspond to 'the core of the inventive process'. Thus such a person cannot be recognized as the inventor.[9]

---

[6] *Eisenmann/Jautz*, Grundriss Gewerblicher Rechtsschutz und Urheberrecht, 66. "*Kein Erfinder ist der die Erfindung lediglich Anregende, also etwa derjenige, der eine bestimmte Aufgabe stellt, eine Richtung weist, wie es häufig durch Arbeitgeber oder Vorgesetzte vorkommt.*" There are also US precedents: Board of Trustees of the Leland Stanford Junior Univ. v. Roche Molecular Systems, Inc., 563 U.S. 776 (2011). "an employer does not have rights in an invention which is the original conception of the employee alone".

[7] Ethicon Inc. v. United States Surgical Corporation, 135 F.3d. 1456.

[8] *Lüdecke*, Erfindungsgemeinschaften: Rechte Und Pflichten Des Miterfinders (Berlin: de Gruyter, 1962), 39.

[9] See De Solms v. Schoenwald, 15 U.S.P.Q. 2d 1507 (Board of Patent Appeals and Interferences 1990).

(e) A simple tester?

If one simply checks whether an invention works well according to its intended purpose,[10] he/she may not be regarded as the inventor, as it is not regarded as a part of the creative act.

(f) A simple assistant?

Technicians or assistants employed to manufacture inventions cannot be recognized as inventors because they were not involved in 'the core of the inventive process'. In Germany, most academics involved in patent law confirm that an assistant cannot be an inventor.[11] In the US, in the same context, there is a precedent that the person who performs "routine actions" or "routine skills" may not be recognized as the inventor.[12] In other words, it is not necessary for an inventor to personally perform every process or be involved in all the minutiae required to complete an invention and, as such, it is unproblematic to hire and use technicians and assistants so long as the inventor continues to play the leading role in the invention process.

(g) A simple proposer?

In the process of invention, it is common to receive information, suggestions, services, ideas, and help from others.[13] In this situation, the judgment of recognizing the other as the co-inventor depends on whether his information or proposal is at the level of reaching 'the core of the inventive' process as an essential reference point.

---

10 Since US precedents emphasize 'conception,' it is impossible to acquire the inventor's status simply by checking (testing) whether the invention works well according to its intended purpose. In order to be an inventor, one must participate in the formation of the basic conception of the invention.

11 *Eisenmann/Jautz*, Grundriss Gewerblicher Rechtsschutz und Urheberrecht, 66–67. Assistants cannot be inventors. Assistant refers to "a person who was involved in an invention but did not contribute to an intellectual part important to success," such as an employee in a chemical laboratory who works purely manually according to a set work protocol. The distinction between the assistant and the co-inventor is different from individual cases, and the legal judgment is not easy in reality. However, the inventor must play a leading role in the inventive process in any case.

12 Sewall v. Walters, 21 F.3d. 1456. A person who performs routine acts and routine skills, e.g. a person who executes ordinary techniques to implement the instructions of others, is not an inventor. As Sewell vs. Walters says, designing a circuit that executes ideas is merely a demonstration of the usual technology that can be expected from a typical chip designer. If it is recognized that anyone in the art can configure a functional device described in the specification without extensive experimentation or additional inventive skill, the design does not include any inventive actions and thus cannot be recognized as an act of invention.

13 According to US precedents, even if 'suggestions of others', e.g., services, ideas, and help, was used in the inventive process, the right to patent is not lost.

If one gives a 'general information or proposal,' i.e., simply explaining the conventional technology or providing a component for the invention, the status as the inventor (to be precise, the status as the co-inventor) is not granted. To be recognized as the inventor, the information or proposal provided must reach the level of 'the core of the inventive process'.

V. Summary

In this section, 'two key questions' and 'seven additional questions' have been formulated by examining and integrating the definition of inventor and the concept of 'the core of inventive process' in German and US law to clarify the requirements of inventorship.

In summary, as shown in Table 5, the '2/7 Questions' are in a more structured form. Hereinafter, these '2/7 Questions' will be applied while reviewing the inventorship of each candidate that can be put forward as an inventor of AI inventions.

Table 5

'The 2/7 Questions' for Requirement of Inventorship

<Two Key Questions>	<Seven Additional Questions>
(1) What is the 'task' provided by the candidate?	
(2) Does the 'task' provided by the candidate correspond to 'the core of the inventive process'? This means the inventor's task should be the "definite and permanent idea of the complete and operative invention". Moreover, a POSITA can reduce the invention "without extensive experimentation or additional inventive skill, or exercise of the inventive faculty" from a written description.	(a) A simple order for work? (b) A simple investor? (c) A simple imagination or fantasy? (d) A simple embodiment of a working model? (e) A simple tester? (f) A simple assistant? (g) A simple proposer?

C. Possibility of Each Candidate's Inventorship

I. Software Programmers as Inventors

In Chapter 2, an AI was defined as "a machine that uses self-learning software, based on a large amount of data and advanced hardware," and emphasis was placed on the fact that the three key components of AI are hardware, software and data. The software is the most important among them because it mimics the functions of the brain in humans. Therefore, it is necessary to understand AI software to confirm whether AI performs 'inventive acts'.

Meanwhile, Chapter 2 B. has already explained that machines process information in two ways, 'non-self-learning' and 'self-learning.' AI's software allows for self-learning, in other words, ML. In addition, the following eight of ML were described explicitly: Supervised Learning, Unsupervised Learning, Reinforcement Learning, Artificial Neural Network (ANN), Deep Learning (DL), Genetic Algorithm (GA), Genetic Programming (GP), and Natural Language Processing (NLP).

Software programmers, discussed in this subsection, handle ML, including the writing of the above eight algorithms. Therefore, SW programmers are, arguably, the starting point in the development of an AI system. From this, the following question naturally arises: "Should the creator of a program capable of ML assume the inventorship of anything the AI invents?" However, in short, the inventorship of software programmers cannot be recognized for the following reasons.

The first key question to establish SW programmers' inventorship entails what tasks they have provided in the invention process. The task of AI SW programmers is defined as the creation of ML software so that AI can process the inventive act. So, for example, this applies to ANNs in the Creativity Machine,[14] the GP in the Invention Machine,[15] and the NLP in Watson.[16] These programs include various algorithm types that were introduced in Chapter 2 – namely, Supervised Learning, Unsupervised Learning and Reinforcement Learning introduced as the traditional forms of ML, as well as ANN, GA, GP, and NLP, which are being widely used these days.

The second key question to establish SW programmers' inventorship requires answering whether their task, i.e. the creation of ML, plays a role in 'the core of the inventive process'. Looking at the seven additional questions

---

[14] See the chapter 2 C. I. regarding Creativity Machine and ANNs.

[15] See the chapter 2 C. II. regarding Invention Machine and GP.

[16] See the chapter 2 C. III. regarding Watson and NLP.

to answer this second key question, '(a) A simple order for work' or '(f) A simple assistant' are applicable to the situation of SW programmers.

At this juncture, it is worth explaining the invention process of the Optical Lens System which acquired a patent in 2005 and came out of the Invention Machine which was running GP.[17] As previously discussed, the Invention Machine went through the following process: (a) First, 75,000 prescriptions were input as data into the Invention Machine, (b) the desired specifications were then input, (c) the 75,000 prescriptions were set as the first-generation from which two 'parents' were selected and combined to reproduce 'offspring' and occasional mutations (one detail was randomly changed). These 'offspring' were then used as input data and those that do not meet the desired specifications were considered hereditarily inferior and deleted. After cycling through 295 generations in this way, (d) a product with superior specifications was invented.

In the Optical Lens System invention process, the SW programmers played a role in creating GP to perform basic working patterns of AI. In other words, their role was to provide working patterns to delete offspring that fell short of the desired specifications (that is, the natural selection of the offspring who were not ideally suited to their environment) and finally to derive inventions with superior 'genes' in a process that mimics Darwin's theory of evolution.

In this case, two main options can be considered concerning the requirements of inventorship.

(1) The first option is that the SW programmer did not directly participate in the inventive process of the Optical Lens System.[18] If so, it means that user proceeded with the inventive process of this lens system project, simply using the software as a tool. In other words, the software programmer did not even know whether the GP software he wrote would be used for a lens-based invention or some other invention in a completely unrelated field.[19] Both German and US laws stipulate that for a joint invention to be recognized, there must be a minimum of 'cooperative work' involv-

[17] See the chapter 2 C. II. for more information on the Optical Lens System.

[18] In reality, most SW programmers are generally not involved in AI inventions themselves. For example, IBM (a software company) and its employees (including programmers) have created and distributed an AI, called "Watson," which is used in many fields, including finance, law and medicine. However, despite being utilized in these areas, IBM has not opened a law office or hospital. IBM does not participate in the market for every field in which their AI – Watson – might be employed.

[19] It's like a novelist who writes using word software but the software programmer never knows who is writing what. So, in this case, the SW programmer cannot claim the copyright. How come does he obtain the right when he does not know at all from scratch?

ing the participants. Naturally, software programmers who have never participated in the inventive process cannot be given the status as inventors.

(2) The second option is that SW programmers directly participated in the Optical Lens System invention project. This can be the situation if the SW programmers developed the GP algorithm to complete this lens project from the beginning. However, even then, the programmer's work simply provides a framework for the overall work process, combining data to reproduce offspring and repeat the generational results until good results are produced by putting in mutations. However, the inventorship of software programmers may be denied because it is related to the '(A) simple order of work' detailed by the first additional question of the '2/7 Questions'.

Also, the inventorship of SW programmers may be denied concerning the '(f) Simple assistant' aspects of the '2/7 Questions'. SW programmers certainly hold patents and copyrights for software but patents for software and patents for inventions created through the software are entirely different issues. In other words, it is possible to view the SW itself just as a tool and the SW programmer as simply an assistant. Therefore the inventorship of SW programmers is inevitably denied.

Genetic programming presents an efficient and successful work pattern based on tens of thousands of pieces of initial data that allow for the creation of hundreds of generations of subsequent data. This work pattern is undoubtedly excellent, but as studied above, software programmers cannot be classed as participating in an inventive process just because their software is being used. At best, their role is one of providing (a) a simple order of work or (f) that of simple assistants. In summary, their inventorship is in any case denied.

So far, it has been diagnosed that the inventorship of software programmers may not be affirmed, based on the '2/7 Questions' formulated according to the provisions and precedents on inventorship set by German and US law. Conversely, beyond this position established under the current law, the following logical conclusions can be drawn by comparing the relationship between parents and children.

The ML algorithm created by software programmers is for an AI what the brain is for humans. Through the cerebrum, humans engage in tasks such as using language, memory, abstract thinking and judgment. Likewise, the ML of AI plays the same role as the cerebrum. In other words, the person who created the brain of AI, who created its thinking pattern, is the SW programmer, the same role parents played with regard to their children. However, can the parents claim inventorship when their child creates a new invention? The answer is clearly no.[20] Therefore, if one accepts the analogy of the relationship between parents and children with that of SW programmers and AI, the inventorship of the programmers is logically denied.

Moreover, it is important to understand the concept of the "black box" in the context of how AI models operate. The internal decision-making mechanisms of AI systems often remain largely opaque, even to experienced software engineers. In other words, even the software developers who created the AI may be unable to explain why a particular output was generated. Consequently, software developers are neither actively involved in the core inventive process nor able to exercise predictable control over it. This observation reinforces the theoretical basis for excluding programmers from being recognized as inventors of AI-generated inventions.

II. Data Suppliers and Data Owners as Inventors

In Chapter 2, the three key components of an AI were defined as hardware, software and data. Data suppliers and data owners are those who provide the input data given to an AI. To produce sophisticated results, it is essential to input and process vast amounts of data where, for example, hundreds of millions of face photos must be input as learning data for facial recognition AI. Similarly, countless words, sentences and phrases must be used for accurate AI translations.

Although data suppliers and data owners are conceptually distinct – the former referring to entities with the legal authority to process and transfer data, and the latter to those holding ownership rights over the data – they are not necessarily the same individuals or organizations. Their roles may be fulfilled by different parties depending on the context.

Two main cases can be distinguished based on whether a clear owner of the data can be identified:

(1) In the first case, the input data falls within the public domain, meaning no ownership rights exist and the data can be freely used without restriction. A painting-capable AI called 'The Next Rembrandt' was created and unveiled in 2016 in Amsterdam. It replicated Rembrandt's unique painting style, identifying his patterns of color use, style of brushstrokes, light intensity, face proportion features and so forth. In this case, the ownership

[20] *Abbott*, I Think, Therefore I Invent: Creative Computers and the Future of Patent Law, 1094–95. Abbott's stance on computer inventorship is also similar: "Once again, that should not prevent computer inventorship. No one would exist without their parents contributing to their conception (pun intended), but that does not make parents inventors of their child's patents".

(copyright) of the input data originally belonged to the artist who painted the painting, Rembrandt. However, copyright protection extends only 50 to 70 years after the copyright holder's death. Since Rembrandt died in 1669, the input data in this case now belongs to the public domain and is freely available, so neither data owners nor data suppliers exist;

(2) in the second case, the input data is subject to ownership, and a specific rights holder can be clearly identified. If an AI produces literature using a famous author's writings as input data, the owner of the input data is the author.

Another way to classify input data is by distinguishing whether it constitutes personal data or non-personal data:

(1) The first case concerns input data that qualifies as personal data. There is still no clear legal framework at this point regarding who are the data owners of personal information, e.g., including information such as 'heart' clicks by users on Spotify or 'like' clicks registered on Facebook. Legal and political debates around the world surrounding data ownership in such cases are ongoing, widespread and often heated.[21] The behavior of clicking 'heart' or 'like' by each user creates additional value for that which was 'clicked on' as it is subject to comprehensive analysis to determine data on users' tastes. Based on such data, companies can implement more efficient promotions by sending customized advertisements to each user and so forth. In general, users agree to the terms and conditions regarding transferring the authority of their generated data to the company when signing up to the company's website, like Spotify, Facebook or another company. Therefore, the data suppliers for this information are those companies when such user data is used as input data for an AI.

(2) The second case involves input data that does not qualify as personal data – that is, non-personal data. Non-personal data refers to information

---

[21] *Yang*, a businessman and a US Democratic candidate for the 2020 presidential election, proposed to provide every American adult with a $1,000 guaranteed monthly income, by collecting data usage fees from tech giants companies, such as Facebook, Amazon, Google that harvested such personal-information data. At the same time, South Korea's politician Kim Se-Yeon argued in 2019 that personal information and other relevant data should be included in the definition of 'property' ("*Sachen*" in German BGB) under civil law. This creates a conceptual basis to make it a 'payable object' rather than a 'natural resource'. *Schneider*, Presidential Candidate Andrew Yang Says Taxes on Tech Companies Could Pay for $1,000 Monthly Payment to Every American Adult, ABC News, April 7, 2019, https://abcnews.go.com/Politics/presidential-candidate-andrew-yang-taxes-tech-companies-pay/story?id=62210018; Bum-Soo *Kim*, Kim Se-Yeon: 'I am a proud conservative. The United Future Party still has a long way to go,' FutureKorea, August 21, 2020, http://www.futurekorea.co.kr/news/articleView.html?idxno=138573.

that is not directly linked to an identifiable individual.[22] Typical examples include sensor data from factories, maintenance or malfunction records, and agricultural data such as soil conditions, weather patterns, and crop yields collected by smart farming equipment. Such data does not fall within the scope of data protection regimes like the GDPR. Moreover, because data is intangible and can be easily copied and shared, it does not lend itself to traditional property law concepts based on possession or physical control. As a result, it is difficult to establish a clear legal ownership framework for non-personal data.

Consequently, data ownership – whether of personal or non-personal data – is not legally established. Nonetheless, in practice, there are entities that exercise de facto control or exclusive access over such data.[23]

In summary, three categories of data ownership can be identified.

First, some data – like paintings by Rembrandt – belong to the public domain and are freely accessible.

Second, there are data for which ownership is legally well-defined.

Third, data such as personal and non-personal information fall into a category where legal ownership is not established, yet de facto control is exercised by actors in the market.

Regardless of these categories, once data is transferred to data suppliers, it is utilized for the development of AI-related inventions within their companies. Therefore, in the context of an AI's inventive process, both data suppliers and data owners ultimately perform the same functional role: providing input data.

To answer the first key question of the '2/7 Questions', the task of data owners and data suppliers is simply to provide input data.

The category of (g) a simple proposer should be applied when assessing their inventorship. Their task is to provide input data and simply serve to provide the proper background knowledge as a basis for the inventive process. Indeed, while they have the authority to distribute and transfer data, they are not even the creators of the data. As such, their contribution cannot be recognized as 'the core of the inventive process'. Therefore, the inventorship of data suppliers and data owners cannot be recognized.

---

[22] See European Commission, Guidance on the Regulation on a Framework for the Free Flow of Non-Personal Data in the European Union, May 29, 2019, https://eur-lex.europa.eu/legal-content/EN/TXT/?uri=COM:2019:250:FIN.

[23] Recognizing this reality, the EU Data Act (2023) seeks to grant users of IoT devices certain rights over the data generated through their use.

However, questions may arise as to whether data owners' inventorship is affirmed by grace of the fact an AI's invention is based on their data. Nevertheless, I think the data owners' inventorship is also bound to be denied in the end.

A very-well known book tells us that "there is nothing new under the sun", if this is true then all inventions in the world are ultimately a transformation of some knowledge that humankind has made in history. A Korean proverb says, "It is a treasure only when many beads are threaded together". Accumulated human knowledge is used as the foundation for completing an invention. Each piece of knowledge is one of many beads, and the final result, like a necklace of connected beads, is an invention. While the act of 'threading beads' can be an act of 'inspiration', the use of accumulated human knowledge must be the essential component of a new invention to secure inventorship. An act of 'inspiration' that puts the pieces together is only a required component thereof. Consequently, simply supplying data does not constitute an act of 'inspiration' nor a contribution to 'the core of the inventive process', so their inventorship cannot be affirmed.

For example, if a hundred related documents were read and used as references for a new novel, the authors of the hundred references cannot gain a copyright for the novel.

In conclusion, the inventorship of data suppliers and data owners is denied, as the output generated by AI is distinctively different from the input. While rare cases may arise in which AI directly copies or closely reproduces its input data, such exceptions should not be taken into account.[24] The legal protection of the output – whether under patent or copyright law – depends on its originality and compliance with the respective legal criteria.

III. Trainers as Inventors

A trainer in the context of this paper is a person who trains an AI through appropriate feedback while it is processing the input data. For example, trainers engage in data labeling in the case of supervised learning, they supply feedback on whether an AI's answer is right or wrong and they control rewards and punishments in the case of reinforcement learning, by assigning a positive or negative value to the action or decision taken by the AI. Therefore,

24 GitHub Copilot, a tool made by GitHub and using OpenAI's Codex, has sometimes been seen producing code that looks very similar – or even identical – to code it was trained on. Because of this, a group of people filed a class-action lawsuit. In the case, they argue that Copilot may be copying open-source code without giving credit or following the rules of the code's license. See Doe 1 v. GitHub, Inc., 2024 WL 235217 (United States District Court for the Northern District of California 2024).

a trainer can be seen as a kind of operator, even those who are involved in aspects other than training an AI for data processing.

Given that AI software enables a form of ML and Chapter 2 B. explains this as the concept of 'self-learning', trainers only assist with learning but are not wholly responsible for it. In the past, computers could only process input-output sets entered in advance by humans. However, an AI system knows how to learn by itself based on manipulating data entered by humans to generate data that was not input by humans, often yielding novel high-quality outputs. Therefore, this process of 'self-learning' is an important feature of AI compared to past computers. So then, can trainers who help an AI learn be affirmed as at least co-inventors?

Regarding the first key question ("What is the task provided?") of the '2/7 Questions', the trainer's task can be defined as helping the data learning process of an AI, such as labeling and supplying feedback.

Regarding the second key question of the '2/7 Questions', the trainer's work is related to the sixth additional question, namely that of (f) a simple assistant. For example, to label a large number of animal pictures as cat or dog, an unspecified number of people are hired as part-timers to complete this simple but laborious task. In this scenario, they may not even know what their work contributes to the whole project or what the ultimate purpose is. Therefore, it can be seen that they played the role of an assistant employed for a specific task that is external to 'the core of the inventive process', leading to the inevitability of trainers being denied status as inventors.

IV. Owners of the AI Systems as Inventors

Owners of AI systems are usually corporate conglomerates and limited-liability companies (LLCs) such as Google and IBM,[25] that are at the forefront of AI development. Examples already mentioned in this text include IBM's Watson and Google's AlphaGo.

Regarding the first key question of the '2/7 Questions', the task provided by owners is difficult to define easily because owners' involvement in each AI inventive process is very complex, widespread and far-reaching.

In a corporation, numerous stockholders are the owners, and they indirectly participate in the AI development process by purchasing stocks and investing in the company's business. However, if owners directly participate in the

---

[25] *Duggan*, Artificial Intelligence Stocks: The 10 Best AI Companies, US News & World Report, September 8, 2023, https://money.usnews.com/investing/stock-market-news/slideshows/artificial-intelligence-stocks-the-10-best-ai-companies.

company's management,[26] they may perform all kinds of tasks directly associated with an AI inventive process, such as hiring software programmers, operators and technicians or providing suitable workplaces for them to research and develop their ideas, setting business plans and goals and hiring a variety of support staff to relieve scientists of administrative duties, for example.

Thus, the tasks of AI system owners are varied and cut across numerous categories of tasks involving other candidates, including operators. Since Chapter 4 C. analyses each candidate separately, it seems prudent at this point to tackle the owner's inventorship by limiting his work to 'investment' (e.g. owners as stockholders) and 'management' (e.g. owners such as CEO). It is because the qualifications of inventorship related to the owner's other tasks can be analyzed in other candidates' parts.

Concerning the second key question of the '2/7 Questions', owners of AI systems may fall into the categories dealt with by the first and second additional questions, i.e. '(a) a simple order for work' and '(b) a simple investor.'

Pure owner-managers, such as a CEO working elsewhere, only gives simple work orders, so their inventorship cannot be recognized. The inventor must be a person who substantially implements the invention beyond setting the overall direction. Moreover, owners that are just investors who provide only financial contributions are already explicitly excluded under existing patent law, so their inventorship also cannot be recognized.

Such owners do not play a role that contributes to 'the core of the inventive process' under the current law, however, whether or not they can obtain patent ownership is another question. These points will be analyzed in Chapter 7.

V. Operators of the AI Systems as Inventors

Operators are those who use AI for the invention project and may also be referred to as users. They lead the entire invention project using AI, such as setting goals for what to invent, finding or entering initial data and planning or executing appropriate training. In general, they may be natural persons working for a company that owns the AI or legal persons in a contractual relationship with the owning company. They actually operate the AI and instruct it to invent. However, when AI science and technology develop further and strong AIs emerge, AI may be able to invent on its own without operators.

---

[26] Stockholders may directly interfere with management; alternatively, they do not interfere and entrust professional managers.

Since the operator is the leader in the entire inventive process, it is more challenging to evaluate whether the inventorship of operators can be affirmed when compared to other candidates previously discussed. The operator's inventorship depends on how much he/she used the AI in the inventive process. In the end, this depends on how detailed and involved the operator's leadership was in directing the AI. For this matter, it seems prudent to review two analogical situations in which German schnitzels and pretzels are made.

(1) Making a schnitzel in a restaurant requires the chef to be involved in the whole process from start to finish. Typically, the chef will do or provide detailed instructions for everything, including purchasing a certain kind of pork, deciding the number of ingredients, dredging, breading, setting the frying temperature and so forth. All the other workers participating in the process are just assistants acting under the chef's instructions. Therefore, only the chef is ultimately responsible for the result. In the end, it should be said that the chef cooked the schnitzel.

(2) The second situation is making pretzels, a process where the chef is not substantially involved throughout. For example, if the chef instructs a kitchen assistant only about the general method of making pretzels but the assistant is so clever that he develops a pretzel with a unique taste, texture and shape that people like. Assuming the new pretzel is patentable, would the chef's simple orders' be considered meaningfully contributive to the new pretzel creation process or would all legal rights associated with the new pretzel be given to the kitchen assistant? If this scenario had to be decided upon by a court, it would be deemed that the kitchen assistant invented the pretzel.

Both scenarios (1) and (2) have instructions for inventions, but (1) detailed instructions are provided throughout while in (2) the assistant is left with considerable leeway for experimentation. The inventive relationship between the operator and AI is similar to that between the chef and his/her assistant when making schnitzels and pretzels, namely that one has to consider the operator's role when assigning rights to AI inventions.

In short, depending on whether or not the operator's lead is detailed and broadly involved, the result is different as follows.

Scenario (1) – the operator leads the inventive process in detail. When an operator offers detailed specific commands, including providing essential data, training processes and setting the final goal, the AI is essentially used as a tool. Therefore, it can be considered that the operator has performed 'the core of the inventive process'. Accordingly, the operator's inventorship can be recognized. In this case, the AI was a simple assistant and is substantially just a high-end conventional computer that simply operates according to the input commands. This scenario is different from the cases involving AI inventions that this study is interested in.

Scenario (2) – the operator does not lead the inventive process in detail. If an AI has received sufficient basic input to begin but has completed the inventive process through ML, inventorship should be assigned to the AI, not the operator, just as the assistant pretzel maker was.

Looking at some recent AI inventions, the operator's lead was not detailed in most cases, reflecting the circumstances of scenario (2), an issue Chapter 2 C. has already tackled. However, by way of specific examples:

(a) Dr. Stephen L. Thaler and his colleagues emphasized that the 'Neural Network Based Prototyping System and Method' (US Patent No. 5,852,815) was invented by an AI, not by the operators themselves. They said that the invention was "the result of random or chaotic perturbations in the machine's existing connections that produce new results which, in turn, were judged by the machine for value".

(b) Another Ai invention, "an evolved antenna" for NASA's Space Technology 5 (ST5) mission was also a result that went beyond preconceived human notions. Jason D. Lohn, the operator at that time, said that he only had entered the basic requirements of the antenna and executed the GP, but AI created "the evolved antenna that has a number of advantages in regard to power consumption, fabrication time, complexity, and performance".[27]

In these and similar cases, operators have consistently stated that the AI itself invented the invention. This means that an AI produced a result unforeseen[28] by its operators, which means that the operators themselves never gave detailed orders to achieve the results of the invention; furthermore, the original inspiration for the invention, essential in the inventive process, never happened. In other words, the "definite and permanent idea of the complete and operative invention," which is central to 'the core of the inventive process', originated from the AI, not the operators.

---

[27] *Hornby et al.*, Automated Antenna Design with Evolutionary Algorithms, Collection of Technical Papers – Space 2006 Conference 1 (September 19, 2006), https://doi.org/10.2514/6.2006-7242.

[28] There is an argument in a similar context in the paper of Shyamkrishna Balganesh: "the scientist might have a claim to inventorship if he developed the AI to solve a particular problem, and it was foreseeable that the AI would produce a particular result". (*Balganesh*, Foreseeability and Copyright Incentives, Harvard Law Review 122 (April 2009): 1569; *Abbott*, I Think, Therefore I Invent: Creative Computers and the Future of Patent Law, 1095). In other words, he argued that the most crucial thing in obtaining inventorship is 'foreseeability.' If the result can be foreseeable, the inventorship should be recognized in favor of the operator.

In summary then, operators can be divided into two broad categories: (1) when their orders are detailed and their lead pervasive; and (2) when their orders are minimal and they adopt a hands-off approach to the inventive process. The outcomes in terms of inventorship of the two groups are also different: In the first group, the inventorship of operators is affirmed, while it is rejected for the second group. This paper focuses only on the second group. Firstly because it is common knowledge that inventorship for even the most advanced of computers and/or the software they run is denied when they are used as mere tools for a particular purpose. Microsoft Word or a computer running it will obtain the copyright for a novel that was typed in by a human author. Secondly, today's AI is already producing great inventions by itself, exceeding the foreseeability of its operators.

An operator's work is so complex that it may entail elements of almost all the roles of the additional (a) to (g) candidates discussed in the '2/7 Questions'. For example, they can be: '(a) issue simple orders for work' to lead the inventive project using AI[29]; '(c) simply conceive something in their imagination and give orders or instructions that are vague or fanciful[30]; '(f) act as a simple assistant' offering base support to an AI in operation while it produces an invention; '(d) provide a simple outline of a working model' to implement a working model based on the results of AI's invention; '(e) be a simple tester' to check whether the implemented model works well according to its intended purpose. In conclusion, according to the diagnosis of the '2/7 Questions', the operator is at least partially equivalent to (a), (c), (d), (e), and (f). So, inventorship is bound to be denied.

---

29 Abbott also argues in his paper that it is difficult to affirm its inventorship simply by providing 'tasks' and 'materials' to computers. See, *Abbott*, I Think, Therefore I Invent: Creative Computers and the Future of Patent Law, 1094: "For example, before the Creativity Machine composed music, Dr. Thaler exposed it to existing music and instructed it to create something new. Yet, simply providing a computer with a task and starting materials would not make a human an inventor. Imagine Friend A tells Friend B, who is an engineer, that A would like B to develop an iPhone battery with twice the standard battery life and A gives B some publicly available battery schematics. If B then succeeds in developing such a battery, A would not qualify as an inventor of the battery by virtue of having instructed B to create a result".

30 "After uploading this information, a human may identify a technology to invent or technological field within which to invent. For instance, one piece of inventing software–the Invention Machine–requires a user to input 'specifications for a desired result,' which the AI will seek to satisfy. Genetic algorithms may also be set to meet a particular set of performance parameters. Inputting these parameters is not invention. As made clear in Oasis Research, identification of a goal or technology to be created by others (be it AI or another human) is insufficient to constitute invention". *Schuster*, Artificial Intelligence and Patent Ownership, Washington and Lee Law Review 75, no. 4 (2018): 1962; *Abbott*, I Think, Therefore I Invent: Creative Computers and the Future of Patent Law, 1094.

D. Possibility of Joint Inventorship of all Possible Candidates

To this point, this paper has reviewed the possibilities of each of the five categories of candidates for inventorship and evaluated that all are insufficient to legally claim inventorship. In reality, the five categories of candidates collaborate in the process to create an invention using an AI. So, can the five candidates be recognized for their joint inventorship?

The invention process naturally consists of a combination of various elements. Traditional inventors also develop creative inventions using not only their own engineering knowledge or their own imagination but also by drawing on the enormous body of knowledge that humans have accumulated over the millennia. In other words, one invention may embody a solution that contains elements informed by a broad range of experiences and knowledge developed at different times and places. However, this does not mean that all humankind down through the ages should have inventorship rights for a new invention. It is more important 'how to participate' than the simple participation itself. In human history, inventorship has been legally granted only to the inventors who play a corresponding role in 'the core of the inventive process' and only such inventors are allowed to have the right to monopolize the market for their invention.

As studied in Chapter 4 D., joint inventorship may be granted under both German and US law if the following conditions are met: (1) Each co-inventor must acquire the status of an inventor. That is, each must have contributed to 'the core of the inventive process'; (2) furthermore, a collaboration between them must have been carried out. They do not necessarily have to be together simultaneously or in the same space, but communication with each other to complete the work must have existed.

As noted when evaluating single inventorship in Chapter 4 C., it was concluded that none of the five categories of candidates had contributed to 'the core of the inventive process'. Therefore, their inventorship may not be recognized. As such, even if there was collaboration among five different types of candidates within a given project, joint inventorship cannot be affirmed for any of them.

E. Conclusion of the Chapter

So far, this paper has explained and applied 'the 2/7 Questions' based on the requirements for inventorship stipulated in German and US law and analyzed the qualifications of possible inventors of AI inventions. As a result, both single inventorship and joint inventorship may not be affirmed for any of

Table 6

Diagnosis of Inventorship of Possible Candidates

	1st Key Question	*2nd Key Question*	*Result*
Software Programmers	to create ML	(a) a simple order for work (f) a simple assistant ※ parent-children relationship	Negative
Data Suppliers and Data Owners	to provide input data	(g) a simple proposer ※ data owner inventorship	Negative
Trainers	to help learn the data process	(f) a simple assistant	Negative
Owners of AI Systems	to invest and manage	(a) a simple order for work (b) a simple investor	Negative
Operators of AI Systems	to lead the inventive process (in detail or not)	(a) a simple order for work (c) a simple imagination or fantasy (d) a simple implementer of a working model (e) a simple tester (f) a simple assistant	Negative

the reviewed categories of candidates, therefore, assigning inventorship for AI inventions clearly remains problematic under current law.

Under these circumstances, only two options are available for AI inventions: First, we leave inventorship permanently unassigned while discussing who would exclusively obtain ownership of the patent; second, we assign inventorship to the AI.

The first option to vacate inventorship is neither right nor desirable. Under the current law, the omission of the inventor's name will affect the validity of the patent right itself. Since a 'natural person' must be given as the inventor's name in patent applications, the two patents filed in 2018 using the name of the AI DABUS as the inventor were rejected in Europe and the United States. Currently, laws do not allow patent offices to distinguish between a natural person's inventions and an AI's. This means that AI inventions passed the Turing test. Accordingly, the simple expediency of accepting a patent application using the name of natural persons is inevitably continuing. However, as reviewed above, none of the categories of candidates involved to a greater or lesser degree with AI inventive processes would qualify to acquire inventorship under current law if the invention had not come from an AI source. Does giving inventorship expediently to someone who, under different circumstances would be an unqualified person, conform to the substantive truth required by the law? It does not.

For this reason, it is argued here that an 'E-Person' category with legal personality should be created for AIs and such entities should be eligible to assume inventorship. This would allow the substantive truth to remain in patent applications where an AI has carried out the core of the inventive process on its own, as current patent laws stipulate. In this regard, Chapter 6 will specifically claim the affirmation of AI inventorship concretely.

Chapter 5

Empty Column to "Inventor's Name"

A. Introduction

Under current law, neither AI itself nor any natural person associated with AI-generated inventions is recognized as an inventor (see Chapters 3 and 4). This creates a strange situation in which AI-generated inventions exist, yet no inventor can be legally acknowledged. It also raises an important question: what happens if no one is listed in the inventor's column of the patent register? Can that column remain empty?

As a preliminary point, Chapter 5 B. will briefly note that existing frameworks do not recognize the concept of unnamed inventors.

I propose three possible models concerning unnamed inventors in Chapter 5 C. While the recognition of unnamed inventors is subject to divergent views, the proponent side may be broadly categorized into two positions:

(1) those who support the idea of unnamed inventors but advocate for the complete exclusion of such inventions from patent protection, thereby placing them in the public domain as part of a commons framework (see "Chapter 5 C. I. Commons-Based Attribution"); and

(2) those who argue for transferring patent rights to AI-owning entities, such as corporations, thereby allowing them to derive profit from such inventions in the market (see "Chapter 5 C. II. Inventorless Ownership Model").

Conversely, the opposing view insists on the necessity of naming an inventor (see "Chapter 5 C. III. Strict Attribution Model"). Within this model, two primary positions emerge: one that maintains, in line with existing legal frameworks, that the inventor must be a natural person, and another – advanced by the present author – which contends that the AI system itself should be named as the inventor (see "Chapter 5 D.").

B. No Room for Unnamed Inventors in Existing Legal Frameworks

To begin with, it is important to note that neither the current German nor the United States patent law recognizes the concept of unnamed inventors. Under both legal systems, the designation of inventors is mandatory, and the inventor field cannot be left blank. As examined in Chapter 3, all patent rights originate from the inventor, and the entire structure of the patent system is fundamentally designed on this premise.

The DABUS team initially submitted both applications to the EPO with the inventor's column left blank. Afterwards, the EPO sent a notice to the applicant (DABUS team) to specify the inventor as required by Art. 81 and Rule 19(1) of the EPC, and the application was finally rejected.[1]

There was also an argument in the petition submitted by them in the US that inventorship itself is not important. Nevertheless, this argument was ultimately dismissed by the USPTO.[2]

C. Three Models of Inventor Attribution

I. Commons-Based Model

Some scholars contend that inventions generated by AI should not be attributed to any inventor, and that such inventions ought to be placed in the public domain, thereby rendering them freely accessible to society and excluded from the patent system.[3]

In fact, the proposal to treat AI-generated inventions as part of the commons is fundamentally different from the idea of leaving the inventor field blank in a patent application. The former rejects the establishment of any patent rights altogether, whereas the latter still results in the grant of patent rights to a specific individual.

---

1 *Mmotong/Visagie*, EPO Decides on AI Inventorship, Adams & Adams, May 2, 2020, https://www.adams.africa/pieter-visagie/epo-decides-on-ai-inventorship/.

2 Decision on Petition (In re Application of Application No.: 16/524,350) at 7. "In response to Mr. Thaler's assertion that the principle of inventorship should not be a substantial condition for the grant of patents, the USPTO again summarily dismissed Mr. Thaler's argument, noting that inventorship has long been a concept of patentability rooted in case law and statutes".

3 For example, *Kop*, AI & Intellectual Property: Towards an Articulated Public Domain, Texas Intellectual Property Law Journal 28 (2020): 297–341.

A report by WIPO also raises serious questions about the implications of annulling patent protection for AI inventions altogether.[4] In other words, what happens if patent protection for AI inventions is removed and all of those inventions instantly enter the public domain? Several concerns may arise.

First, firms will face a strategic decision regarding whether to disclose the technical content of AI-generated inventions or to retain them as trade secrets. If companies opt for trade secret protection, the information never enters the public domain, which may, in turn, impede the dissemination of knowledge and hinder its broader societal utilization. Conversely, if such inventions are openly disclosed and effectively placed in the public domain, they become freely accessible resources that can facilitate follow-on research, gradual improvements, and combinatorial innovation. This, in turn, underscores the future importance of designing complementary frameworks that provide incentives for disclosure.[5]

Second, although the public domain is, by definition, a commons accessible to all, it may, paradoxically, reinforce market dominance by well-capitalized firms. Large corporations, equipped with high-cost AI systems and exceptional execution capacity, are positioned to rapidly generate and commercialize AI inventions.[6] In contrast, SMEs are at a structural disadvantage due to limited resources and slower go-to-market capabilities. As SMEs often serve as key drivers of disruptive innovation, their marginalization may ultimately weaken the technological progress. In short, universal access to public domain inventions does not translate into equality of opportunity in commercialization. It is therefore essential to consider complementary policy measures aimed at narrowing the executional capacity gap between dominant firms and smaller actors.

---

4 WIPO, AI and Intellectual Property: WIPO Call for Submissions (Impact of AI on IP Policy), 2. "Should inventions that are created autonomously by AI be protected with patents? Is patent protection required to incentivize the creation of inventive AI? Would excluding AI-generated inventions from patent protection encourage innovation and collaboration or discourage the publication of many inventions? Should there be an alternative protection mechanism?"

5 See also *Weibust/Pelletier*, Protecting AI-Generated Inventions as Trade Secrets Requires Protecting the Generative AI as Well, IPWatchdog, July 24, 2022, https://ipwatchdog.com/2022/07/24/protecting-ai-generated-inventions-trade-secrets-requires-protecting-generative-ai-well/id=150372/.

6 Ibid.

II. Inventorless Ownership Model

The inventorless ownership model[7] postulates that AI-generated inventions, in the absence of an inventor, may still be subject to patent protection. This model embraces the notion of unnamed inventors, simultaneously patent ownership is vested in natural or legal persons who are closely associated with the invention process – typically the users or owners of the AI system. These entities may subsequently exercise the exclusive rights derived from the patent, including commercialization and enforcement.

In this structure, the "Inventor's Name" on the patent register is deliberately left blank, acknowledging that no natural person qualifies as an inventor. Nevertheless, users or owners of the AI system may claim ownership of the resulting invention.

This model diverges significantly from the conventional employee invention regimes found in many jurisdictions, where an identifiable inventor remains essential to the transfer and allocation of rights. Yet, even if no inventor is named, analogies from employee invention laws can be instructive.

For instance, under § 6 ArbEG, the right to the patent is transferred from the employee-inventor to the employer upon proper claim. Similarly, 35 U.S.C. § 261 permits assignment of patent rights from inventors to employers, typically under contractual obligations. These regimes presume inventorship as a starting point but establish clear principles for allocation of rights to economically interested parties – a logic that may be extended to the inventorless ownership model.

To whom should ownership of AI-generated inventions be allocated? Should patent rights vest in the owners of the AI system, often corporate entities, or in the users who contributed through creative prompts? In employee invention law, the employer (typically a corporation) takes ownership, reflecting both the economic interest and the infrastructural support provided. Given that most inventive activities nowadays occur within corporate R&D environments, where teams interact with generative AI tools, one could argue that ownership should default to the entity bearing the operational and financial responsibility for the AI. However, the absence of inventorship in this context

[7] The term "inventorless ownership" as used here refers to the concept of a "blank inventor field." While Schwartz and Rogers employ the term "Inventorless Inventions" in their article, they do not advocate leaving the inventor field blank. Rather, they support vesting ownership in AI owners or users despite their lack of personal involvement in the inventive process. Accordingly, their position may be seen as partially aligned with the concept of a blank inventor field. *Schwartz/Rogers*, Inventorless Inventions? The Constitutional Conundrum of AI-Produced Inventions, Harvard Journal of Law & Technology 35, no. 2 (2022): 531–79.

renders traditional assignment mechanisms inapplicable, raising the question of what legal ground – whether statutory, contractual, or equitable – can be used to allocate such ownership.

How can patent rights be lawfully held or enforced in the absence of an inventor? Traditional patent law systems are premised on the existence of a human inventor, from whom rights are derived. Inventorship is not merely symbolic – it is a prerequisite for patent validity in most jurisdictions. Without a named inventor, existing frameworks struggle to accommodate the transfer or initial allocation of rights. This suggests that legislatures may need to enact special statutory provisions for AI-generated inventions. For example, future laws could establish statutory ownership presumptions based on factual control over the inventive process or ownership of the AI infrastructure.

A related point is that, the utility model system from Germany (*Gebrauchsmusterrecht* in German) – which has the nickname "the little brother of the patent" ("*der kleine Bruder des Patents*" in German)[8] – does not require the naming of inventors.[9] This system has been operating without problems since the late 1800s,[10] however, the utility model omits the naming of inventors, presumably for the sake of expedited processing. A detailed legal analysis of the rationale, prevalence of unnamed inventors, and operational mechanics of the German utility model system may offer inspiration for considering cases in which inventors are not named.

III. Strict Attribution Model: Human or AI as Inventor

The strict attribution model rejects the notion of unnamed inventors and maintains that the designation of an inventor is a fundamental requirement for the validity of a patent. A key question that arises under this model is: whose name may be lawfully inscribed in the "Inventor's Name" column of a patent application? Contemporary patent laws, both statutory and jurisprudential,

---

[8] The nickname "the little brother of the patent" (*der kleine Bruder des Patents*) for Germany's utility model system (*Gebrauchsmusterrecht*) is widely recognized. See e.g., Was ist ein Gebrauchsmuster?, *IHK für Rheinhessen*, accessed June 26, 2025, https://www.ihk.de/rheinhessen/rechtundsteuern/gewerblicher-rechtschutz/gebrauchsmuster-1455070; Das Gebrauchsmusterrecht – Eine Einführung (Teil I), *Brennecke Rechtsanwälte*, 2008, https://www.brennecke-rechtsanwaelte.de/Das-Gebrauchsmusterrecht-Eine-Einfuehrung-Teil-I_114587.

[9] While German patent law expressly requires the designation of the inventor (§ 37 PatG), no such requirement exists under the utility model system. *Astrid Meckel*, Erfinderbenennung, in: Gabler Wirtschaftslexikon (Springer Gabler, February 19, 2018), https://wirtschaftslexikon.gabler.de/definition/erfinderbenennung-34790/version-258285.

[10] In 1891, the German Utility Model law (*Gebrauchsmustergesetz*) was enacted.

overwhelmingly presume that inventors must be natural persons. However, some commentators, including myself, contend that in the case of AI-generated inventions, the AI system itself ought to be designated as the inventor.

The legal and administrative positions concerning the "Human as Inventor" model have been addressed in detail in Chapter 3 E., particularly with reference to the current practices of patent offices and courts in Germany and the United States. The prevailing view, which limits inventorship to natural persons, may be seen as a natural consequence of the doctrinal boundary that judiciaries must not infringe upon the prerogatives of the legislative authority.

In contrast, the model advocating for "AI as Inventor" represents the position defended by the present author. This perspective, and the reasoning supporting it, will be developed in the Chapter 6.

D. Why the Inventor Field Must Not Be Empty: Legal, Procedural, and Ethical Implications

Several theoretical models have been proposed in response to the challenge posed by AI-generated inventions: the Commons-Based Model, the Inventorless Ownership Model, and the Strict Attribution Model. All three approaches are, in principle, conceptually viable, and the choice among them ultimately lies within the discretion of the legislature. However, each model carries inherent limitations, and closer examination reveals the legal and practical disadvantages they entail. In this chapter, I argue that recognizing AI as an inventor represents the least disruptive and most coherent legal solution available under current conditions.

As discussed in Chapter 5 C. I., the Commons-Based Model suffers from structural vulnerabilities, chief among them being the likelihood that firms – particularly large corporations – will respond by shifting inventive output to trade secrecy. Such a shift would exacerbate issues of information asymmetry and market concentration, and potentially undermine the very objectives of the patent system by encouraging secrecy over disclosure.

The Inventorless Ownership Model, which proposes allowing patent applications to proceed without designating an inventor, is equally problematic. One might argue that since modern inventions are largely industrial and collaborative, often arising within corporate R&D structures, the identity of the individual inventor is no longer materially significant. However, this ignores a fundamental legal fact: even in highly commercialized environments, patent law continues to insist on naming the true inventor. This reflects not merely historical custom but a structural feature of the system that ensures both ethical attribution and legal clarity.

Indeed, in corporate practice, it is well established that the inventor is typically an employee, and the rights to the invention are transferred via employment or assignment contracts to the company. Nevertheless, the law requires that the actual inventor be truthfully identified at the time of application. This mechanism affirms the principle that ownership must be traceable to genuine inventive activity. The idea of allowing a blank inventor field, therefore, would constitute a radical departure from the foundational structure of patent law.

First, patent systems worldwide treat inventorship as a non-waivable, statutory requirement. As codified in 35 U.S.C. § 115(a), "an application for patent shall be made, or authorized to be made, by the inventor." Likewise, Art. 81 of the European Patent Convention requires the designation of the inventor, and Rule 19(1) EPC prescribes the manner in which such designation must occur. Courts across jurisdictions have held that failure to properly name the inventor – whether through omission or misidentification – may render the patent invalid or unenforceable. Furthermore, most patent offices require the submission of a declaration or oath by the inventor attesting to the inventive contribution embodied in the application. Thus, the omission of a named inventor fails to satisfy a statutory condition of patentability and renders the administrative framework inoperable.

Second, inventorship determines initial ownership. Under most patent regimes, the inventor is deemed the first legal owner of the patent. Subsequent rights – whether through assignment or contractual transfer – derive from this original entitlement. If no inventor is named, there is no originating titleholder, and therefore no legal foundation for transfer, enforcement, or commercialization.

Third, inventorship functions as a mechanism of moral and professional accountability – not merely as a formal requirement or a means of conferring economic rights. Naming an inventor ensures that someone stands behind the invention, not only for purposes of recognition but also for legal and ethical responsibility. In areas such as pharmaceuticals, biotechnology, and privacy-sensitive AI applications, the absence of an inventor may give rise to regulatory ambiguities, public mistrust, and even strategic abuse of the system. This is not merely a theoretical concern: accountability is a normative pillar of patent law, and its removal introduces risks that are both legal and societal.

What, then, of the option of Strict Attribution Model, which is continuing to name a human as the inventor even when the actual inventive step was performed by an AI system? This, too, is untenable. As demonstrated in Chapter 4, under current law, no human individual can validly satisfy the legal standard of inventorship for certain AI-generated inventions. The practice of naming a "fake inventor" is therefore both misleading and corrosive to the integrity of the patent system.

Why, then, do I support the recognition of AI as an inventor? Put simply, current patent laws require the naming of the "true inventor" – and that true inventor is the AI system. Chapter 6 will offer a comprehensive defense of this position from four perspectives: the current legal framework, patent theory, legal history, and philosophical analysis.

Beyond the doctrinal basis, the recognition of AI inventorship has practical and economic significance. In the marketplace, the names of certain AI systems already exert notable influence. For example, some systems are known for their strength in visual creativity, others for idea generation, and still others for efficiently searching and summarizing information. Each AI program possesses unique capabilities and tends to specialize in particular domains. Consequently, when an AI system proves particularly effective at generating patentable inventions – whether broadly or within a specific field – its role becomes both legally and economically meaningful. The names of such AI systems often carry reputational significance tied to their developers and training architectures. Therefore, naming AI systems as inventors can also serve as a form of formal recognition within both the patent system and the broader market.

Given the reality of AI-generated inventions, the identification of the true inventor is essential. Several considerations underscore this necessity: (1) inventor's rights have characteristics as property rights as well as the right to honor based on the constitutional law; (2) in the era of AI, the number of AI inventions will increase, and the quantity and speed of patent applications will increase dramatically as AIs can process much more fast and efficient than humans. Therefore, it is vital to review and prepare for the social changes that AI is bringing about; (3) both German and US laws clearly distinguish between the inventor and the applicant. It is important to distinguish who can be the inventor or the applicant in AI inventions; (4) it is dangerous for both laws to neglect the problem of AI inventorship as an error in the inventor's name would invalidate a patent, even under previous US law. Moreover, this can escalate into legal disputes over honor rights and claims for patent infringement under current German and US laws.

Furthermore, it is advantageous for AI inventions to indicate the name of AI rather than "blank". If we put the name of the inventive AI in a patent, we can control, including robot tax, etc., against the AI and its affiliated companies. Research on AI is underway in various fields and since AI is already impacting jobs for humans, operating an economy that can maintain human welfare by imposing a tax on robots is also being discussed. In order to implement robot tax systems, it is necessary to disclose detailed information, such as the inventive machine, the company that owns it and the revenue the AI generates. Therefore, AI inventorship should be expressed.

In conclusion, this dissertation argues that AI systems should be designated as inventors. Such a reform would safeguard the structural integrity of the patent system while aligning it with technological and industrial realities.

Chapter 6

Affirmation of AI Inventorship

A. Opposing AI as Inventor: Arguments and Counterarguments

Opposition to the recognition of AI as inventors is reflected in the practices of the majority of patent offices and courts worldwide – excluding notable exceptions such as Australia and South Africa, which will be examined in detail in Chapter 6 B. I. 3. As neither the judiciary nor administrative bodies possess legislative authority, they are bound to apply existing statutory frameworks, which currently do not accommodate AI inventorship. Accordingly, applications listing AI systems as inventors are consistently rejected. Chapter 3 E. provided a detailed analysis of how such rejections have been articulated in the jurisdictions of Germany and the United States.

In most countries, including Germany and the United States, the inventorship of AI cannot be recognized under existing law. The reason is too simple: the current law allows only natural persons to become inventors and since AIs are not classed as natural persons but objects of rights (i. e., things, property), so the inventorship of AIs is inevitably denied.

However, times have changed and AIs are now inventing things, a situation that was not imagined when existing patent laws were enacted. So, the main question is whether the existing provisions limiting inventorship to natural persons should be revised to include not only natural persons but also AIs.

WIPO has generally adopted a negative stance toward the recognition of AI as inventors. However, it has also proposed several alternative approaches, which merit close attention due to their legal significance in the context of AI-generated inventions. In its report on the topic, WIPO made three main findings:[1]

First, WIPO announced that AI inventorship itself cannot be affirmed on the two grounds.

[1] WIPO, "Incentive Structure and Inventorship for AI".

(1) An AI is not human but a mechanical computer that analyzes input data.[2] Although AI can create far more efficient solutions than developers initially envisioned,[3] they actually only produce outputs using specific logic. In other words, the only thing AI does in the new invention development process is 'analyze the logic,'[4] and that 'logic' is also the result of software[5] developed by humans, so AI's contribution to the inventive process is not enough to affirm their inventorship, WIPO judged.[6]

(2) AI inventions are allowed to enter the actual production stage after appropriate testing. WIPO adjudged that this is proof that an AI cannot be deemed as the inventor by itself, which "adequate testing in the non-production phase" is always necessary.[7]

Second, WIPO maintains a negative view of AI inventorship, however, it also argues that the natural persons associated with AI inventions should be recognized for their shares and incentives as much as their intellectual efforts. WIPO says it has two grounds for maintaining this position: (1) It provides traceability in the case of liability issues for AI inventions and (2) it gives flexible control over AI inventions to the natural persons involved.[8]

Third, WIPO presented two specific alternatives to provide incentives for AI inventions:

(1) People can submit a 'pseudo-patent application' separately from the original patent application.[9] This tracks the input data used in the AI invention in detail, solving the problem of liability for damages for associated natural persons and corporations that may be negatively impacted in the future.[10]

---

[2] WIPO, 3. "it flows obviously that the AI is not a real person and therefore, by virtue of its mechanical, intelligent-self, it only analysed the logic (input) fed into it".

[3] WIPO, 3. "however, the logic changes resulting in more efficient outcomes which in some instances, had not been originally envisioned by the developer himself"

[4] WIPO, 3. "Even though the AI may generate certain creative results of its own direction, at the end of it, it has only analysed the logic".

[5] WIPO, 3. WIPO uses the expression "the AI application or tool," presumably means AI software and hardware.

[6] WIPO, 3. "there is no significant contribution from the AI towards the invention itself".

[7] WIPO, 3.

[8] WIPO, 4. "Such a right may seem rather useless for the AI, however it can be helpful when – one, it provides traceability to the extent of liability that the human inventor may be awarded; and two, buried in the right of such attribution to AI is the repute of the human inventor involved which would not die out even after assignment thus, providing a flexible degree of control over one's creation".

[9] WIPO, 4.

[10] WIPO, 4.

(2) The development of 'self-regulation codes' will help to manage risks in developing AI inventions. These codes include requirements for AI inventions to be checked periodically and the quality of data sets to be monitored.[11] Moreover, WIPO emphasized that these codes should be particularly flexible as they will need to deal with future obstacles that cannot currently be anticipated.[12]

The view presented here of WIPO's proposals is one of general agreement as they appear to be a step in the right direction in terms of controlling the risks AI brings to the patent field. However, it is argued here that the inventorship of AI should be affirmed.

(1) Chapter 2 C. introduced some of the actual cases of AI inventions that are already emerging. Currently, patent law requires the inventor's name to be entered in the patent application and, as an AI is not allowed to an inventor, the names of AI operators or owners are recorded as the inventor holding the patent right. However, as discussed in Chapter 4, none of the candidates – whether natural persons or legal entities involved in AI-generated inventions – meet the legal criteria for inventorship under existing law, as demonstrated by the '2/7 Questions'. This naturally raises the issue of which name corresponds to the substantive truth. I argue that the name of the inventing AI should be written in the patent application as an inventor. To support this position, Chapter 6 B. I. 1. shows whether AI can be the inventor under the current law, utilizing the '2/7 Questions'.

(2) I concur with WIPO's position that AI is not a human being. However, this raises a deeper normative question: must an inventor necessarily be a human? Historically, legal subjects were limited to natural persons and legal entities. As only natural persons could engage in inventive activity, the inventor had to be human by default. Today, however, AI systems can write texts, create artworks, and generate inventions. In a context where an AI system can independently carry out the inventive process – translating abstract ideas into concrete inventions with minimal human intervention – the longstanding legal premise that "only humans can be inventors" may no longer be tenable. This evolution invites a reconsideration of whether the legal definition of "inventor" should be revised to reflect contemporary technological realities.

(3) WIPO asserts that AI-generated inventions are permitted to proceed to actual production only after undergoing appropriate testing. On this basis, it concludes that an AI cannot independently be regarded as the inventor, since "adequate testing in the non-production phase" is always required.

---

[11] WIPO, 4.

[12] WIPO, 4–5.

However, this reasoning conflates the validation of an invention with its creation. While testing is undoubtedly important to ensure the functionality and safety of an invention, it is not central to the inventive process, which fundamentally concerns the conception of a novel and non-obvious idea. Furthermore, as analyzed through the '2/7 Questions' in Chapter 4 B., the mere act of conducting a test does not satisfy the legal threshold for inventorship. Accordingly, the requirement of testing does not, in itself, disqualify AI systems from being recognized as inventors under the substantive criteria of inventorship.

(4) WIPO takes the position that natural persons involved in AI-generated inventions should be acknowledged and rewarded in proportion to the intellectual contributions they make. I agree that such individuals deserve appropriate incentives. However, this recognition should not extend to granting them the status of inventors. As demonstrated in Chapter 4, they are not the actual originators of the inventions. Moreover, Chapter 6 B. I. 1., through application of the '2/7 Questions', shows that it is the AI system that satisfies the legal criteria for inventorship. Accordingly, I argue that while natural persons and legal entities may be appropriately compensated through patent ownership, the status of inventor should be reserved for the AI system that has carried out the inventive act.

(5) WIPO also emphasizes the importance of traceability in the event of liability issues concerning AI-generated inventions, as well as the need for flexible control over such inventions. I agree with both points. However, I argue that these objectives can be more effectively achieved not by denying AI inventorship, but by affirming it while granting related natural persons or legal entities the status of patent right holders. This approach would allow for traceability and control to be exercised in a manner analogous to vicarious liability in civil law for corporate entities, or similar to the legal framework for employee inventions. Under such a model, there would be no need for a separate 'pseudo-patent application'. That said, I support the idea that there must be official documentation capable of tracing the relevant input data used by the AI in the inventive process. At the same time, it is important not to lose sight of the need to foster the free development and deployment of AI systems. Overly burdensome administrative requirements may discourage legitimate use of AI by incentivizing applicants to falsely designate natural persons as inventors in order to avoid the complexities associated with AI-generated inventions.

(6) WIPO's proposal for the adoption of 'self-regulation codes' is a constructive idea, and like WIPO, I also emphasize the importance of maintaining flexibility. The reason for this emphasis is that many of the relevant legal and ethical issues will need to be calibrated incrementally, in response to

future developments. When examined in depth, questions such as what constitutes ethical behavior or what qualifies as biased information become increasingly philosophical and complex. These challenges are not unique to AI inventors but apply broadly across all domains of AI deployment.

B. The Four-Perspective Analysis in Support of AI Inventorship

I. First Perspective: The Current Law

Is there a possibility that AI inventorship will be recognized under current law? It's unlikely. Generally, AI inventorship is assumed to be denied because laws worldwide typically restrict inventorship to natural persons. However, beyond that provision, which states that 'only natural persons can be inventors', there are compelling legal reasons to consider AI as inventors when examining other regulations, legal theories, precedents, and so on. In this section, this paper presents arguments that support the recognition of AI inventorship from the perspective of current law, with a particular focus on the '2/7 Questions', the US "Flash of Genius" doctrine, and recent positive rulings on AI inventorship in Australia and South Africa. By discussing these three factors, it becomes evident that there is a solid foundation for affirming AI inventorship under existing law.

1. The 2/7 Questions

Chapter 4 examined who could be the inventor among the likely candidates surrounding the AI invention, and the '2/7 Questions' tool was used to assess them. This assessment determined that no candidate is sufficiently qualified to become the inventor of an AI invention under the current law. Chapter 4 was a review based on the premise of denying AI inventorship, however, the following will affirm AI inventorship by employing the same method, i.e., the '2/7 Questions'.

a) The First Key to the 2/7 Questions

The first key question of the '2/7 Questions' is "What is the 'task' provided by the candidate?". What has AI done throughout the entire invention process? It is difficult to answer it in a few short sentences because most of the work done by AI in the invention process necessarily requires human collaboration. So, this is difficult to establish what an AI did 'independently.' Hereinafter, I will explain the tasks of an AI within the inventive process' time frame and analyze what tasks it has performed independently.

aa) Step 1. Initiating the Invention Process

Artificial intelligence cannot initiate an invention process. To embark on the invention process, AI needs help from humans, such as users, with more than just base mechanical actions such as connecting the electricity supply to the AI and pressing the button to execute the process. This means that AI does not have an inherent desire to create within the software it is running.

How then does the invention process begin? It begins with human discontent with a recent situation and a search to alleviate that discontent. When humans feel inconveniences in various situations that arise in their lives, they desire to relieve them or find a more comfortable path going forward. For example, the TV remote control was invented because it was bothersome to have to stand and walk over to the TV to change the channel or adjust the volume. The air conditioner was invented because it was unpleasant to endure many indoor environments during the heat of summer. Many medicines were and are invented to address the suffering and loss caused by illness while new cooking recipes address the discontent of eating the same few things every day. Motivation for an invention starts with an initial idea of how to improve something that is not ideal or how to solve a particular problem. However, only natural persons feel discontent, have complaints and can manifest an inherent desire to find a better way. An AI itself does not initiate an invention process because AI does not have emotions, feelings or a desire to solve problems that it is both unaware of and not impacted by. As such, those who initiate an invention process using AI are natural persons, such as owners and operators.

bb) Step 2. Pre-Provided Data and Machine Learning

Machine learning software is installed in an AI and is operated with the help of the software programmer who created it. It depends on the nature of the invention process as to the choice of which ML software will be used, be that Artificial Neural Network (ANN), Genetic Programming (GP) or Natural Language Processing (NLP).

Furthermore, when learning by using the entered data, an AI receives help from a number of data suppliers where again, the nature of the invention sought will impact the type of input data.

For example, the Optical Lens System previously mentioned in Chapter 2 C. II. entailed making a new lens. In this invention process, GP was used as the ML and more than 75,000 pieces of data were input as specifications for all the lenses previously made by humankind. Hence, the sort of ML and input data were deliberately targeted toward the type of invention sought.

Before input data is entered into an AI, each piece of data must be converted into mathematical data readable by that AI. For example, if a cat or dog picture is provided, humans intuitively recognize which animal is in which image. However, an AI can only identify the animal through an analysis using pixels and numbers. In other words, data must be translated into a language that an AI can understand, which requires help from operators and data suppliers.

In summary, ML and input data must be prepared in advance to start the learning process undertaken by an AI and help from natural persons or corporations is needed to select and provide ML software and input data. In other words, humans decide how and what an AI learns, decisions determined by the desired direction of the overall invention process.

cc) Step 3. The Learning Process of AI

According to ML's fixed algorithm, AI 'thinks' or 'learns' data while processing it. As a result, AI comes up with all the possible options, working with feedback from suppliers and operators. Feedback suppliers and operators provide appropriate standards while watching the learning situation develop as an AI processes the data. For example, they delete inferior 'genes', make weight adjustments and offer feedback of reward or punishment.

According to its ML software algorithm, an AI combines or divides the pre-input data it is using as knowledge. Then, the AI randomly generates multiple new results and shows them to feedback suppliers. AI pours over as many results as possible and essentially asks the humans: "Which result are you most satisfied with?"

dd) Step 4. Getting the Best Results

AI constantly performs the learning process in 'Step 3' and derives outcomes that best meet the set preconditions. Then, operators confirm the best outcome that emerged and owners mass-produce and distribute it.

So far, the invention process of AI has been examined in four steps. What can be defined as the answer to the first key question of the '2/7 Questions', i. e., what is the 'task' provided by the AI? In brief, an AI processes numerous pieces of input data using pre-fixed ML algorithms, which entails both combining and dividing data. As a result of that process, AI comes up with all the possible options and finally creates the best results in line with the required standards, which feedback suppliers or operators want.

People often express this process that "AI self-learns" or say that "AI thinks and learns on its own". The words 'learning' and 'thinking' are voided here as much as possible because these are expressions that personify an AI, however, because of the industry's technical terms (e.g., machine learning) and the practicalities of endeavoring to compare AI with existing inventors, (natural persons), some usage is inevitable. However, emphasizing again, existing AI is different from humans in many ways and cannot be seen as feeling emotions or having an independent personality or ego like humans. This is especially true in the case of the weak AIs covered in this paper[13]. Even if a similar discussion evolves with the emergence of strong AI, there may be other philosophical and psychological controversies over whether such entities can be viewed in part or wholly as human-equivalent.

Answering the first key question of the '2/7 Questions', the task of AI is to process input data according to ML algorithms, and to produce the best results.

b) The Second Key to the 2/7 Questions

The second key question of the '2/7 Questions' is "Does the task of AI contribute to 'the core of the inventive process'?" That is, whether the task of AI is a "definite and permanent idea of the complete and operative invention". If this criterion is met, the inventorship of AI will be affirmed, and if not, the inventorship will be denied.

Looking at the seven additional questions one by one to answer the second key question, none is related to the task of AI, so the inventorship of AI is likely to be affirmed:

AI cannot be '(a) a simple order for work' and '(g) a simple proposer' itself as these roles are played by natural persons, such as operators, working with the AI.

An AI cannot be '(b) a simple investor' for a swathe of obvious reasons.

---

13 This paper introduced the concepts of weak AI and strong AI in Chapter 1 E. IV., and the scope of research in this paper was limited to focus on weak AI. While weak AI is equivalent or superior to humans in only one specific field of work, strong AI has a level of intellectual ability that is okay to see as a human being. Strong AI has not yet been developed. In fact, it is difficult to develop strong AI, as there is no clear definition of what human intelligence is.

What an AI does cannot be considered the product of '(c) simple imagination or a fanciful notion.' On the contrary, AI has created so specific results that a POSITA can substantially implement the invention as an actual product, which is beyond imagination or fantasy.

In addition, it is operators and other natural persons around an AI who take on the role of '(d) supplying a working model' or becoming '(e) a simple tester' for the inventions produced by the AI. In other words, it is natural persons who select the AI results, make prototypes, check whether an invention works well according to its intended purpose, produce and market it to generate sales.

Furthermore, AI cannot be seen as '(f) a simple assistant.' Although AI was operated with the help of various natural persons and corporations through steps 1 to 4 above, the pure task performed by AI alone came from the brain of AI, not the brain of operators. Operators and feedback suppliers only provided standards for the final product, so it can be said that they are 'simple assistants' who played auxiliary roles and that AI provided the main idea of the complete and operational invention.

Of course, the seven additional questions are only indicative. Just because all seven answers are 'no' does not necessarily mean that the answer to the second key question is 'yes.' These seven questions are just a guide to answer the second key.

As previously derived, an AI's sole task is to process input data according to its ML algorithms and produce the best results. However, does this task correspond to a "definite and permanent idea of the complete and operative invention"? The answer here is definitely yes. The reasons are: First, the AI has produced a result that a POSITA can substantially implement as an actual product "without extensive experimentation or additional inventive skill, or exercise of the inventive faculty". This proves that AI's task corresponds to 'the core of the inventive process'. As stated in Step 4 above, humans simply chose the final results offered by an AI and then simply tested them; second, although an AI needs the help of natural persons for its own operation, none of the related natural persons could think of the final result without AI. In other words, the core idea of the invention comes from AI. Therefore, AI can have the right to its own idea, i.e., intellectual property; third, it is also a critical point that none of the natural persons predicted the results of the AI's final result in advance.

Therefore, the status of an AI as an inventor should be sufficiently affirmed based on the first and second key questions of the '2/7 Questions', which means that it is sufficient to recognize the inventorship of AI under the current patent laws of Germany and the United States. However, under the current law, the premise that only natural persons can become inventors remains the obstacle for AI to acquire inventorship.

2. "Flash of Genius"-Doctrine

Current law grants inventorship only to natural persons but it does not examine whether there is 'creativity' or 'inspiration' in the inventor's inner soul, called the mental process. The patent process only confirms whether the inventor is a natural person. However, it is more important to let the final invention constitute patentability, such as novelty and inventiveness (non-obviousness) than to examine 'creativity' or 'inspiration' in the inventor's mental process. Therefore, it is unfair for AI to make it difficult to obtain a patent by adding extra new conditions to measure whether 'creativity' or 'inspiration' in AI exists[14].

Interestingly, a test to determine whether the inventor had 'creativity' or 'inspiration' during the inventive process historically existed in U.S. patent law from 1941 to 1952. This was known as the "Flash of Genius" doctrine.

It was established through the Supreme Court's ruling in *Cuno Engineering v. Automatic Devices* (1941),[15] and the following phrase encapsulates the essence of this doctrine: "[T]he new device, however useful it may be, must reveal the flash of creative genius, not merely the skill of the calling. If it fails, it has not established its right to a private grant on the public domain."

This doctrine faced harsh criticism from legal experts[16] and was eventually rejected by Congress in its 1952 revision of the patent statute. To this day, this opposing stance against the "Flash of Genius" doctrine has been maintained through 35 U.S.C. 103, which states, "Patentability shall not be negated by the manner in which the invention was made."

Legal experts and scholars have raised various points to argue why the "Flash of Genius" doctrine was flawed.

Firstly, it mandated that an invention had to originate from a sudden and unexpected inspiration or insight; consequently, it excluded numerous valua-

---

14 There is a philosophical basis from the East and the West that AI may also be thought of as possessing the attributes of 'soul' or 'spirit' like natural persons. It will be introduced in Chapter 6 B. IV. in this paper.

15 Cuno Engineering Corp. v. Automatic Devices Corp., 314 U.S. 84 (U.S. Supreme Court 1941).

16 See: *Barnett*, The Flash of Genius Fallacy, Journal of the Patent Office Society 25, no. 11 (1943): 785–90; *Sellers*, The Flash of Genius Doctrine Approaches the Patent Office, Journal of the Patent Office Society 26, no. 4 (1944): 275–80.

ble inventions that emerged from extended periods of research and development.[17]

Secondly, this narrow standard placed excessive importance on the individual inventor and overlooked the significance of collaborative research and development, as extended periods of research and development often involves multiple inventors and researchers collaborating.[18]

Thirdly, the assessment of whether an invention satisfied the "Flash of Genius" criterion was entrusted to the judgment of judges and juries. This resulted in inconsistent and arbitrary rulings, causing uncertainty among inventors about the likelihood of obtaining patents for their inventions.[19]

The inventor's mental process, such as 'creativity' or 'inspiration' within their inner being, is not only impossible to verify but also unnecessary to do so. Consequently, the "Flash of Genius" doctrine had to be abolished subsequently. As current laws do not scrutinize the 'creativity' or 'inspiration' of inventors, there is no need to scrutinize the mental process of AI. What matters is the creativity of the inventions, not the creativity of the inventors.

3. Positive Rulings on AI Inventorship in South Africa and Australia

The AIP is still in litigation regarding AI inventorship against patent offices and courts worldwide. Only Australia and South Africa have issued affirmative rulings based on their statutory law, the differences of which are briefly presented below.

---

[17] *Barnett*, The Flash of Genius Fallacy, 786. "What is a 'flash of genius'? Does it mean that, without any weighing of known facts, a new invention has sprung full-fledged into being? I challenge any one to produce any such instance. Newton's law of gravity, Copernicus' realization of the rotation of the earth, and Galileo's verification of that fact, Harvey's disclosure as to the circulation of the blood, the dynamo, telegraph, telephone, harvester, radio, electric light and so on through all our greatest discoveries resulted from a weighing of known facts, often followed by prolonged research, and frequently up many blind alleys, until the answer was found. In the patent field there is not and never was any invention attributable to a 'flash of genius.' That is a wholly imaginative concept."

[18] *Sellers*, The Flash of Genius Doctrine Approaches the Patent Office, 279.

[19] *Barnett*, The Flash of Genius Fallacy, 787. "The only feasible test must be in a finding by the court, on all the evidence, as to whether the patented solution under inquiry was obvious to the average skilled worker in that field in view of the previously known prior art. Of course judges will differ in this conclusion, just as they often arrive at different results not only in any equity case, but even in any law case. Different juries or different judges often do not agree as to whether the same evidence does or does not establish the guilt or innocence of a defendant. That is an inherent defect in all human methods of determining a litigant's rights."

The patent office in South Africa, called the Companies and Intellectual Property Commission, published its acceptance of DABUS's invention with DABUS listed as the inventor in July 2021. DABUS's inventorship successfully completed the application process because there is no substantive examination required under South African patent law and only the formal examination exists. In other words, since the PCT passed the formalities properly, South Africa has affirmed it as it is. The DABUS patent application would have been rejected if South Africa had a substantive examination.

An Australian court confirmed an affirmative position on AI inventorship having based its findings on not only statutory law but also on interpreting the law's purpose.[20]

First, the term "inventor" was analyzed in "its ordinary meaning" since there is no definition in the Australian Patent Act. The court noted that the word inventor is an agent noun, such words typically end with the suffix 'or' or 'er' and encompass all of a person or thing, for example, the computer, controller, regulator, distributor, collector, lawnmower and dishwasher. Therefore, it is a natural interpretation to include an AI as an inventor.

Second, the Australian Patent Act explicitly defines "Person" as "a body politic or corporate as well as an individual" (Section 2C(1) of the Acts Interpretation Act 1901). Therefore, since Australian law does not limit the concept of person to natural persons, there is ample room for AI to be recognized.

Third, the Australian court held that the law should be interpreted to promote its purpose. Section 2A of the Australian Patent Act defines the purpose of patent law as "economic well-being through technological innovation and the transfer and dissemination of technology". The court ruled that "I need to grapple with the underlying idea, recognizing the evolving nature of patentable inventions and their creators. We are both created and created. Why cannot our own creations also create?" and affirmed AI inventorship as a way to embody the purpose of the Patent Act as much as possible.

In summary, Australian and South African laws had room within the legal text itself to affirm AI inventorship and the courts pursued a purposeful interpretation thereof, although there being economic considerations at the national level also being involved cannot be ruled out. The AIP's campaign to secure AI inventorship is ongoing and it will be interesting to see whether more positive rulings come out in other countries.

---

20 Thaler v. Commissioner of Patents, [2021] FCA 879 (Federal Court of Australia 2021).

II. Second Perspective: Patent Theories

The Patent Theory is a philosophical basis for explaining the purpose of patent rights. There are two primary purposes of patent rights. One is personal and the other is social. Personal in this context means that patents guarantee economic interests by granting a market monopoly to a patent holder. Social refers to the fact that patents oblige a patentee to disclose the details of the invention to the public so that the latter has an opportunity to access the latest scientific and technological developments. This ultimately promotes the further development of science and technology in society. Four patent theories will be introduced below, closely related to these two aspects.

First, the incentive theory by B. F. Skinner states that the expectation of economic benefits (i. e., incentives) given to inventors becomes the driving force for inventive behavior.[21] It is related to the 'personal aspect' mentioned above. Since an AI has no desire, even if inventorship is given to it, it is not motivated by the prospect of economic profit and would not voluntarily become independently active in inventing even if it could. Therefore, the incentive theory cannot affirm AI inventorship.

Second, the personhood theory by Kant and Hegel says that inventions reveal the inventor's 'persona,' so patent rights and inventorship must be guaranteed in terms of human rights.[22] This theory is also related to the 'personal aspect' mentioned above. Do AIs have personas like humans? Various studies on this are ongoing in fields such as psychology, philosophy, and engineering, and it is impossible to say conclusively yet. However, as the 'inventive landscape' has changed over time there is growing criticism of the personality theory itself. In modern society, there are more inventors working for companies than there are individual inventors working from home or their small workshops. Therefore, their persona aspects removed from the inventive process because most inventors now make inventions tailored to the requirements of their employers.[23] From the perspective of this paper, there is no need to think about AI inventions in this context because this theory is so undermined

---

21 *Thaler*, Complaint for Declaratory and Injunctive Relief in the United States District Court for the Eastern District of Virginia, 8.

22 *Fisher*, Theories of Intellectual Property, Originally Published in Stephen R. Munzer (ed.), New Essays in the Legal and Political Theory of Property (Cambridge University Press), 2001, 4. "a person's 'persona' – his 'public image, including his physical features, mannerisms, and history' – is an important 'receptacle for personality[.]'"

23 WIPO, Incentive Structure and Inventorship for AI, 1. "[I]t is agreed that the personality of the inventor rarely manifests in his inventions as the invention generally depends on the policy pursued by the employer or on the resources available to the inventor".

by the above circumstances that its validity even for natural persons is questionable.

Third, the Lockean theory of labor says that patents should be recognized as the reward for the inventor's labor whereas the inventive act is that labor.[24] This also connects to the 'personal aspect' mentioned above. This theory can be a sound basis for affirming AI inventorship by way of recognizing an AI's labor. However, can an AI's labor be compared to human labor? Opinions differ on this point, although the answer would be positive under a philosophical opinion that AI and humans are identical. Nevertheless, those who view AI simply as a sophisticated computer system that outputs data using algorithms will think differently.

Fourth, the utilitarian theory sees that the purpose of patent rights is to obtain a higher public interest through the disclosure of technology, i. e., the development of science and technology throughout society.[25] This theory is related to the 'social aspect' mentioned above and it is the most suitable of the theories cited here to support AI inventorship. The DABUS team also emphasized this line of reasoning as the purpose of patent law in the same way. (1) The patent of the AI inventor's name is currently rejected, and the AI invention goes published in the public domain area. These rejections are deprived of the economic benefits of market monopoly that can be obtained with AI inventions. When AI inventorship is affirmed, economic benefits will naturally be guaranteed to companies that own AI and employs its operators. It will soon expand to the public interest in science and technology development. (2) At the same time, the names of natural persons used only for obtaining patents, i. e., 'contrived inventors', are not needed when AI's name is allowed to be entered. If patent systems continue to allow 'contrived inventors', people cannot distinguish between actual human inventors and the contrived ones used for AI inventors. Therefore, this fact is directly connected to the public good by giving genuine social recognition to true inventors.

III. Third Perspective: Legal History

From the legal point of view, AI came into being as an 'object of rights' associated with computers. The question asked here is, is it proper to allow a change in status from an 'object of rights' to a 'subject of rights'? This issue is a topic that was and still is thoroughly discussed in legal theory and this text

24 *Fisher*, Theories of Intellectual Property, 3.

25 WIPO, Incentive Structure and Inventorship for AI, 1. "The Utilitarian Theory protects the prospects of inventions for public benefit. The benefits of a successful patent trickle down to the public as it attracts investors, leading to the commercialization of the invention".

will now examine it through legal historical facts of legal persons (corporations), enslaved people and animals.

1. The Inventorship of the Juridical Persons and AI Inventorship

If AI inventorship is affirmed, the general public could accept it as if robots have become equivalent to humans and perceive that the law had accepted robots think and exercise creativity or inspiration like humans. While this stance will come in for a lot of criticism, it is worth emphasizing that, contrary to popular belief, affirming the inventorship of AI does not deviate very much from the existing legal framework. The obvious example is juridical persons, these are not humans but still enjoy being subjects of rights.

A juridical person is not a natural person but is treated as a natural person in some respects through the legal system. It is established in principle by a registration process managed by administrative authorities and where courts deal with any related disputes that arise. A juridical person falls into one of two groups: Body corporates and foundations, where the former consists of a body of persons and the latter are assets for a specific purpose. Therefore, it is significant to study 'the corporation theory' (*Theorie vom Wesen der juristischen Person*) that has evolved to explain and deal with the presence of such persons in our modern day-to-day lives while discussing AI's legal personality.

According to the current law, both natural persons and juridical persons are subjects of rights, and juridical persons may possess property rights within a limited range just as natural persons. Regarding the topic at hand though, while patent rights can be enjoyed by both natural and juridical persons, inventorship is only recognized for natural persons. As such, prior to further discussing the issue of AI inventorship, it is meaningful to deal with the two-part question: "Why are only natural persons recognized as inventors and why was the inventorship of juridical persons never accepted?" The answer to this question, as discussed below, may have relevance for the affirmation or denial of AI inventorship.

By way of historical background, legally recognizing juridical persons began with the emergence of Roman law while the history of patent rights seems to begin around 1474 in Venice. However, this legal recognition of juridical person has never extended into patent law meaning, among other things, that such entities have never been viewed as possessing inventorship. The reasons for this are thought to be as follows.

(1) The inventive process is fundamentally accompanied by continuous efforts and creativity. In the case of joint inventions, several people gather to invent and at the end of the process they each write their name as a

co-inventor. Therefore, it is naturally impossible for juridical persons to be involved in the act of inventive process.

(2) This restriction more reliably guarantees the person who actually came up with the invention the right to reputation. Good evidence of this is found in employee inventions where conflicts have arisen between the employee who actually invents and the company they work for. Normally, the company (juridical person) receives the patent right only after the employee (natural person) transfers it. This is not only to respect the natural acquisition process of inventorship, mentioned in (1) above but also to better ensure the inventor's right to reputation because an individual usually has weaker social, legal and financial power than a company if an unregulated dispute were to arise.

For these two reasons, the inventorship of juridical persons has always been denied. Assuming that AI is granted inventorship, what should be considered based on the above? The following two things should be considered: (A) Is there no creativity in an AI? Can an AI carry out 'the core of the inventive process'?; (B) If the inventorship of AI is acknowledged, how would the balance of power related to that inventorship change, between natural persons, juridical persons and the AI and, finally, is there any concern that it will harm the true inventor's right to reputation?

First, regarding question (A), whether AI has creativity must be examined. The above reason (1) says that the act of an inventive process is naturally recognized only by natural persons because continuous efforts and creativity fundamentally accompany the act. If so, the inventorship of an AI can also be affirmed, if its continuous efforts and creativity are admitted. As discussed while analyzing the '2/7 Questions', continuous efforts made by AI in the invention process must be acknowledged. Although the effort is not natural or human way given the operations of software programming, however, it is only the AI that is making the repetitive efforts.

Concerning question (B), how would the balance of power change between natural persons, juridical persons and AI change if inventorship was attributed to the AI?

First, it violates the substantive truth if natural persons' names are lyingly put in the application documents, to acquire patent rights for AI inventions. Consequently, it is a situation where the wrong person is given the right to the reputation.

Second, if an AI is the true inventor, an AI's right to reputation could be violated. However, it seems early and unnecessary to bring up the concept of AI's right to reputation in the current era of weak AI, even though this paper actively claims the affirmation of AI's inventorship and legal personality.

Therefore, while it is argued here that AI is definitely the true inventor of AI inventions, the discussion regarding AI's right to reputation will be excluded from this paper.

Third, affirming AI's inventorship would rather help the balance of power between natural persons, juridical persons and AI related to the inventorship, and it would be even advantageous for the associated natural and juridical persons. While separating and managing the AI invention, natural and juridical persons can be safer in liability for damages if damages occur due to the AI inventions. In reality, there is a great need of AI liability to separately manage AI inventions for the financial safety of both natural and juridical persons.

2. The Legal Status of Slaves and AI's Inventorship

In history, the legal status of enslaved people, women, and animals was nothing more than objects of rights or enjoyed only minimal rights even if they were the subject of rights. In particular, the historical record of the legal status of enslaved people and animals has significant legal implications for an examination of AI inventorship and starting with the former seems prudent.

In the United States, before the Civil War broke out, there was a law called the American Slave Code, where homogeneity between slaves and artificial intelligence can be found. This code stipulated in part: (1) Slaves are property; (2) when slaves commit crimes, the slaves themselves are responsible and punished, not the owners.[26] From the modern perspective, this seems to be intuitively contradictory, the person who owns the slave (property) that caused the injury avoids any responsibility, however, at the time people took it for granted that this was sound reasoning. In short, this situation arose because slaves were considered to be both property and capable of making independent decisions to do wrong.

Here, a similarity between the status of slaves and an AI can be found: (1) An AI is property and an object of rights; (2) at the same time, AI can make independent decisions on its own. The most representative example is self-driving cars, which can read traffic conditions, make judgments and drive on their own.

Historically, inventorship has only ever been granted only to natural persons and excluded juridical persons because only natural persons are deemed to have the brilliant creativity needed to come up with inventions and under-

---

[26] See: *Kaplan*, Humans Need Not Apply, 124; *Goodell*, The American Slave Code in Theory and Practice: Its Distincive Features Shown by Statutes, Judicial Decisions, and Illustrative Facts.

take the actions needed to realize that invention. A useful question here is, who was granted the patent if a slave invented something in the past? Unfortunately, such historical records cannot be found. However, by way of hypothesis, two possibilities can be considered:

(a) inventorship is attributed to the enslaved person, while the slaveholder enjoys the economic benefits derived from the invention; or

(b) the enslaved person is not recognized as the inventor, and the slaveholder is instead recorded as such and entitled to the resulting financial profits.

Of these, option (a) may be more likely. The reasons are below.

First, it would have been morally difficult for the owner to claim that he or she was the true inventor. It may also have been publicly known within the local community or town that the owner possessed highly skilled slaves whose abilities significantly contributed to his wealth, and that he could not have independently produced inventions of comparable calibre. A parallel can be drawn with AI-generated inventions today. (1) The public is generally aware of the presence and role of AI in the inventive process, and (2) in modern corporate environments – where inventions are typically the product of teamwork – it is unlikely that inventorship would be falsely attributed to someone who made no contribution. The designation of inventors is often a sensitive issue, comparable to the assignment of first authorship in academic publications. Since AI cannot legally be recognized as an inventor, all human team members may prefer to be listed as inventors in the spirit of fairness. However, in many cases, the team's primary concern lies not in formal recognition of inventorship, but in the fair distribution of the economic benefits arising from the invention.

Second, recognizing the enslaved person's inventorship and providing material rewards may have incentivized further invention by appealing to their desire for recognition and addressing their practical interests. This raises analogous questions regarding AI's potential for motivation, attribution, and reputational rights, though such concerns do not apply to current forms of weak AI.

Third, when inventions created by enslaved individuals resulted in harm, slaveholders may have sought to avoid product liability by attributing the fault solely to the enslaved person, consistent with the logic embedded in the American Slave Codes. The prevailing rationale at the time likely maintained that such harm arose from the enslaved person's own wrongful conduct and was therefore unrelated to the slaveholder. Accordingly, slaveholders may have had a strong incentive to avoid being identified as the inventor themselves. Similarly, contemporary AI owners are also likely to seek ways to mitigate or shift liability for damages resulting from AI-generated inventions – particularly in light of the potentially greater risks posed by modern AI systems.

3. The Legal Status of Animals and AI's Inventorship

Animals used to be merely objects of rights in the past but now they enjoy a status that does not put them on a par with humans but raises them above that of mere property. Animal protection laws view animals as 'quasi-property' while animals are considered property, they should still be treated with respect. Animal cruelty, neglect, and abuse are strictly forbidden under these laws.[27] Because many people form emotional attachments to the animals around them and they have become uncomfortable with identifying animals as a thing rather than a living, feeling being. To create societies where life is respected, regardless of whether that is animal or human life, numerous countries now protect animals by assigning them a measured legal status. For example: if an animal is abused or cruelly mistreated, domestic law may apply harsher sanctions to the abuser than in the case for inanimate property such as cars or furniture; if a pet is killed or injured by a third party, the owner may have a right to claim the compensation for pain and suffering, considering the emotional relationship between the owner and the pet. In other words, the regulations on things apply mutatis mutandis in general cases, however, animals are treated differently to inanimate property as the former are living beings.[28]

This is enough to happen for strong AI in the future. The more advanced from weak AI to strong AI, the closer the emotional relationship between robots and humans will have. AI can communicate with humans, offer mental counseling to humans, live together as family members to take charge of various tiring tasks, or sometimes perform more moral behavior than ordinary humans, such as self-sacrifice. As AI becomes more familiar to humans, a social atmosphere would be gradually formed and the dignity of AI would be discussed, like in a movie.

Therefore, as the status of animals has been raised in history, that of AI is likely to rise gradually from 'object of rights.'

---

[27] However, these animal protection regulations are often limited and do not extend to all animals, particularly those used for food production or experimentation.

[28] The independent legal status of animals has been recognized for more than 30 years. Austria created a provision in the Civil Code in 1988 to distinguish animals from things. Germany and Switzerland also stipulated similar contents in 1990 and 2002, respectively. *Swain*, Consideration of Animals as Legal Person, Indian Journal of Integrated Research in Law 3, no. 4 (2023): 5.

Concerning the inventorship of AI and its intersection with things animals have done, the 'monkey selfies' lawsuit can provide some inspiration. While wildlife photographer David Slater was traveling in an Indonesian forest on the island of Sulawesi, a crested macaque took his camera and snapped some pictures of itself. Most of the pictures were out of focus, but some drew attention as the images were clear and could be, as wildlife photos, considered high-quality. People for the Ethical Treatment of Animals (PETA), an animal protection organization, filed a lawsuit on behalf of the monkey[29] claiming that David Slater infringed on the monkey's copyright as the author of the photos and argued that the profit Slater was making from the images was illegal. A federal judge dismissed this lawsuit, finding that monkeys cannot have their own copyrights because the definition of a 'work' in existing copyright law is a creation that expresses human thoughts or emotions.[30] Although this was a copyright-related case, it can also serve as something of a template for AI inventorship.

First, there are some similarities and differences when considering the activities of animals and AI during a process that produces meaningful results under IP law. The outcome of there being several usable photos being produced by chance from among hundreds of photos taken by monkeys is similar to selecting some adequate inventions from among the numerous results presented by an AI. However, the decisive difference between AI and animals is that AI is likely to mass-produce high-quality inventions that humans could not predict. Therefore, in light of this difference, it is necessary to continue discussing how to recognize AI inventorship and to whom to transfer the property rights.

---

[29] There was also a legal argument whether PETA could file the lawsuit on behalf of the monkey (under so-called the concept of the 'next friend'). PETA filed the lawsuit seeking to designate PETA as the monkey's custodian so that the profits generated from the photos could be used to benefit the monkey. The US Court of Appeals for the 9th Circuit denied PETA's petition to file as the monkey's custodian or 'next friend' as PETA could not prove connection to the monkey; moreover, animals cannot be represented by an attorney or custodian under US copyright law. Naruto v. Slater, 888 F.3d 418 (United States Court of Appeals for the Ninth Circuit 2018).

[30] The third edition of the office's Compendium of U.S. Copyright Office Practices, released on 22 December 2014, clarified that "only works created by a human can be copyrighted under United States law, which excludes photographs and artwork created by animals or by machines without human intervention" and that "Because copyright law is limited to 'original intellectual conceptions of the author,' the office will refuse to register a claim if it determines that a human being did not create the work. The Office will not register works produced by nature, animals, or plants". U.S. Copyright Office, Compendium of U.S. Copyright Office Practices, 3rd ed., 2014, sec. § 313.2, https://www.copyright.gov/comp3/docs/compendium.pdf.

Second, the so-called "monkey selfies" are now considered to be in the public domain under current law. This means that they may be freely used by the public, as no copyright can subsist in works not created by a human author. This case provides valuable inspiration for the legal treatment of AI-generated inventions:

(1) As discussed in Chapter 5 C. I. under the 'commons-based model', placing AI-generated inventions in the public domain is also a legally conceivable option, as their classification ultimately depends on legislative intent. However, this approach may raise several concerns. For instance, firms might be incentivize to rely on trade secrets rather than disclose technologies through the patent system. Moreover, such a regime may disproportionately disadvantage SMEs. Accordingly, any shift towards a public domain model must be accompanied by complementary measures from an economic policy perspective.

(2) Furthermore, while the monkey selfie photographs are not subject to copyright protection, the photographer's subsequent use of those images – such as through curated exhibitions or published works – may involve a degree of human authorship, thereby giving rise to limited rights in the derivative output. By analogy, even if AI-generated inventions were to fall within the public domain, careful attention must be paid to the economic interests of the natural and legal persons who initiated, developed, or supported the relevant innovation projects. Their contribution, while not qualifying for inventorship per se, remains significant in economic and practical terms.

IV. Fourth Perspective: Philosophy

The reason AI inventorship is currently rejected under existing patent laws is straightforward: only natural persons may be inventors, and AI is not. From this premise, two fundamental questions arise:

(1) Must inventors necessarily be natural persons? In other words, is it conceivable for a non-human entity, such as AI, to be legally recognized as an inventor?

(2) Is AI truly non-human? Could it potentially be regarded as human, at least in certain respects?

The preceding sections addressed the first question by presenting three perspectives – those of current law, patent theory, and legal history – that support the theoretical possibility of non-human inventorship.

This section turns to the second question, engaging in a philosophical inquiry into whether AI may be considered human – or at least human-like – in the context of inventorship. As discussed in Chapter 2 D., AI software and the human brain differ significantly in their technical structures. Nevertheless, philosophy offers a deeper analytical framework for examining whether AI might, in some meaningful sense, be regarded as equivalent to a human in the inventive process.

Does AI have a kind of inspiration or effort like humans to perform the invention process? In other words, can a thing be equal to a person in some respect? Are humans and animals in nature the same or different?; are other people the same as 'me'? Surprisingly, these questions are not new in the field of philosophy and have already been discussed for thousands of years. This subsection will introduce the thoughts and arguments of famous philosophers to offer a basis for AI inventorship. Interestingly, the legal and social discussions surrounding AI technology and AI inventions are substantial and practical, however, the philosophical discussions introduced here are largely abstract. Nevertheless, these can provide plenty of ideas and inspiration for ensuing legal discussions.

1. Descartes and Husserl: In Connection with the Turing Test and the Chinese Room Argument

Many different things can be compared with humans in different ways to identify similarities. One can often perceive such things with the naked eye and even disassemble them to see inside. However, not everything is so tangible. While the body of another person is perceptible, how does one perceive the 'spirit' or 'inner world' of that person? Unlike inanimate things, humans are alive and much of what defines us exists beyond the reach of vision and tactile contact. How can we perceive the 'spirit' and 'inner world' of other persons?

The 'first principle' of the philosophy of René Descartes (1596–1650) is the Latin *cogito, ergo sum*, which is usually translated into English as "I think, therefore I am". According to Descartes, I can perceive myself through the fact that I think, but I cannot perceive from the standpoint of 'I' whether other persons think or not. In the context of this paper, that means that 'I' cannot perceive AI's spirit and inner world.

According to the Cartesian point of view, the human 'I' can perceive his/her own inner world but it is impossible to perceive the inner world of others. If so, concerning AI inventions, it is unfair to deny the inventorship of AI just because AI's internal perceptual-cognitive activity is not recognized.

As to whether 'I' can perceive the spirit or inner world of others, Edmund Husserl (1859–1938), like Descartes,[31] responded that 'I' cannot perceive others. However, Husserl argued that other people, in principle, cannot be 'perceived' but can be 'constituted' phenomenologically through 'analogy'. Husserl argues that we perceive the presence of others in the life world. We see their bodies, the consciousness behind them, the emotion and the will that person is experiencing. Husserl refers to this perception as 'empathy', a way to indirectly understand or experience the other's inner life by imagining from the perspective of others, "What if I were there?" It is an effort to understand others as being the same as me by empathizing and sympathizing with the similarity between me and others.[32]

Two questions can be asked in evaluating whether AI is human-like in this regard: (1) Does an AI act like a human being?; (2) Does AI think like a human being?[33] This paper handles both aspects separately.

It is relatively easy to recognize whether an AI acts like a human being because it is visible from the outside.[34] It is more difficult to determine whether an AI thinks like humans. In Descartes's thinking, others, including AI, are beings that cannot be perceived forever. However, according to Husserl's thinking, we can determine whether AI thinks like humans through 'analogy.'

It is argued here that Husserl's idea is in line with the Turing test approach. Turing defined 'intelligent behavior' as the ability to achieve human-level performance in all cognitive tasks, by being sufficient to fool an interrogator. In other words, the Turing test actively utilizes the fact that it is possible to recognize the subjectivity of others in the live world through 'analogy.'

In the Turing test, the human interrogator has to determine whether the interlocutor talking on a teletype is a computer or a human. If the interrogator determines that the interlocutor is a human, the computer is considered to have passed the Turing test. In this whole process of the Turing test, human

---

31 Husserl's phenomenology was based on Descartes' methodological skepticism. Husserl's idea is called 'neo-Cartesianism' and the correlation with Descartes can be seen in the title of his book: *Husserl*, Cartesian Meditations: An Introduction to Phenomenology, trans. Dorion Cairns, 7th ed. (The Hague: Martinus Nijhoff Publishers, 1960).

32 See *Wigmore*, A Panorama of the World's Legal Systems.

33 Stuart Russell and Peter Norvig present four possible goals to pursue in AI: (1) systems that think like humans, (2) systems that act like humans, (3) systems that think rationally and (4) systems that act rationally. These categories distinguish between approaches centered around humans and approaches centered around rationality. As such, it takes into account human emotional instability and irrationality. *Russell/Norvig*, Artificial Intelligence: A Modern Approach, 4th ed. (Hoboken: Pearson, 2021), chap. 1.1 What is AI?

34 *Russell/Norvig*, Artificial Intelligence.

interrogators use the approach of 'analogy' or 'empathy.' Evaluating whether the other party is a human or a computer, the interrogator goes through a process of 'empathy' from the interlocutor's point of view. Therefore, if the interrogator evaluated the interlocutor as a human, it is considered a human, not a computer.

Descartes said, "I think, therefore I am". However, the problem is that I know that I think, but I cannot prove whether others think, that is, do "you think". Husserl agrees in principle that it is correct but he sees that he can constitute others in his live world through analogy and empathy, which is how we perceive the spiritual world of other persons. Technically, we never know whether the person I am talking with is an actual human or a computer; furthermore, we do not know what the other party thinks. But we can evaluate and recognize through the Turing Test that his/her/its thoughts and actions are similar to mine, a human.

Of course, there are criticisms of Husserl's views, which are that the other person I constituted through empathy is simply in my imagination and not there in the true sense.[35] In other words, I cannot explain whether the others are really independent agents like me, who are subjects of "I think, therefore I am".

John Searle criticizes the use of the Turing test in this context and asserts it would be better to employ 'the Chinese room'. The premise here is that a native English speaker who knows no Chinese is locked in a room full of lists of Chinese questions and their answers (a database) together with a book of instructions for manipulating the symbols (the program). The lists contain all the questions that the Chinese interrogator will ask. The Chinese interrogator put a paper written with a Chinese question (the input). The English person in the room does not know Chinese, but he submits the Chinese answer following the lists (the output). The interrogator believes the person in the room can understand Chinese well; however, it is not the case. The person in the room does not know Chinese at all, and he even does not understand the Chinese questions or answers.[36] It is in line with the criticisms of Husserl. The image of others I have constituted inside me is not a true person.

How can it be determined whether or not inventorship is genuinely inherent to an AI? Descartes's and Husserl's views on this can be of relevance because the worlds of others cannot be truly discovered by ourselves. For example,

---

35 *Rosen*, The Givenness of Other People: On Singularity and Empathy in Husserl, Human Studies 44 (May 25, 2021): 333–50, https://doi.org/10.1007/s10746-021-09584-5.

36 *Searle*, Minds, Brains, and Programs, The Behavioral and Brain Sciences 3 (1980): 417–57, https://doi.org/10.1017/S0140525X00005756.

this is true of all kinds of tests conducted in our societies, such as school examinations. Numerous questions are asked of the students but it is not known whether they truly understand the answer or simply provide what they know is the correct response. This is even more unclear in a multiple-choice situation as even 'rolls the dice' will return a reasonable percentage of correct answers. The only world we as individuals can truly recognize is our own. The relationship between 'I' and other human beings is already like this, is it fair to demand higher standards only an AI? Like the Turing test, if the inventive actions of an AI externally manifest to some extent, it should be considered that it meets sufficient requirements. In other words, if an invention created by an AI is a suitable object that deserves patent rights, it is natural to recognize the inventorship of the AI.

2. Merleau-Ponty

Descartes and Husserl considered the mind and body as completely separate. In contrast, Maurice Merleau-Ponty (1908–1961), who is usually called the philosopher of 'the body and embodiment,'[37] explained the live body in terms of 'one own body'.[38] He believed that the mind exists in the body, true knowledge can be obtained through the body's experiences and the meaning of existence is established as the existence of the body. In other words, the human mind and body are one. Therefore, Merleau-Ponty said that it is possible to perceive others through the body,[39] which is a different perspective to that of Descartes and Husserl who said it is impossible to perceive others in principle.

As noted above, Merleau-Ponty saw the body and mind as one as without our bodies we cannot experience the world. Our minds are revealed through our bodies – for example, we shed tears (body) when we are sad (mind), our hearts race (body) with excitement (mind), or we freeze (body) in shock (body). Therefore, according to Merleau-Ponty, our bodies and minds are both 'subjects', whereas Descartes and Husserl regarded only our minds as 'subjects,' while our bodies were 'objects', a designation that extended to include other persons and things.

Merleau-Ponty held that others enter my mind through my body, via senses such as sight, touch and hearing. When another's body is perceived, another's thoughts can also be perceived because emotions such as happiness or sadness

[37] "The body is our general medium for having a world." *Merleau-Ponty*, Phenomenology of Perception, trans. Colin Smith (London/New York: Routledge, 2002), 169.

[38] See *Merleau-Ponty*, Phenomenology of Perception, trans. Colin Smith (London/New York: Routledge, 2002), Part I. The Body, 73–232.

[39] Ibid.

are often revealed in their language, behavior, attitude or expression.[40] For example, when a friend feels sad and bursts into tears, or when he is anxious and paces back and forth, his sorrow or anxiety becomes perceptible to me through my senses – his agitated movements through sight, his distressed voice through hearing. Thus, having a perception of others is achieved through my body.

'I' and 'the other' seem to exist as entirely independent agents, and then both agents seem to have a relationship. However, Merleau-Ponty thought otherwise, namely that we connect ourselves to others through the 'body'.

Merleau-Ponty cited the example of a 15-month-old baby. When I put my finger in my mouth and pretend to bite it, the 15-month-old baby before me follows the action. Since 'I' and 'baby' have bodies in common, the baby 'naturally' discovers my physical action – putting a finger in my mouth and biting it – embodied in his body, but does not 'rationally' understand the similarities. We can prove that 'I' and 'the other' are directly connected through the 'body.' This means that I am connected to the other as one.[41]

Hence, 'I' and 'artificial intelligence' are not independent agents separated from each other, but 'I' and 'artificial intelligence' are connected as one through the body. Even if it is not a humanoid robot that resembles a human body, it can nonetheless be embodied – whether by producing a human-like voice or by generating text that resembles human expression. The stronger AI is and the more it develops, the more difficult it will become to distinguish between humans and machines, as both will be mixed.[42] Therefore, Merleau-Ponty's idea can philosophically underpin the possibility of humans and machines coexisting, in an equal relationship, not as a relationship between subordinates and superiors. That is to say, humans and AI are not separately categorized as subjects and objects of rights, but both are equally subjects of rights. As such, AI inventorship can be affirmed according to Merleau-Ponty's philosophy given that we can recognize the existence of AI through the body of an AI, that is, its inventive activities.

40 See *Merleau-Ponty*, Phenomenology of Perception, trans. Colin Smith (London/New York: Routledge, 2002), Part II. The World as Perceived, 233–425.

41 "A baby of fifteen months opens its mouth if I playfully take one of its fingers between my teeth and pretend to bite it. And yet it has scarcely looked at its own face in a glass, and its teeth are not in any case like mine. The fact that is own mouth and teeth, as it feels them from the inside, are immediately, for it, an apparatus to bite with, and my jaw, as the baby sees it from the outside, is immediately, for it, capable of the same intentions. 'Biting' has immediately, for it, an intersubjective significance". *Merleau-Ponty*, Phenomenology of Perception, trans. Colin Smith (London/New York: Routledge, 2002), 410.

42 An example of the integration of humans and machines is found in the field of bioinformatics.

3. Hylozoism

If AI can be recognized as having the soul or inner world like a natural human, there is no problem in affirming AI inventorship. In other words, the question is whether life exists in non-human AI, which is related to animism or hylozoism.

Animism is a primitive belief that life exists in things such as the sun, moon, river, sea and stones and that each of them has a consciousness, desires and feelings like humans.[43] Unlike animism, hylozoism is a philosophical thought that there are immaterial elements or essential nature in the matter.[44]

Both animism and hylozoism have similar beliefs that all things in the world (including animals and plants) have souls, however, animism differs in that it is a form of polytheism that believes active gods are present in all things in the universe and have a willful influence on the cosmos.[45] However, from a philosophical point of view, hylozoism can be seen as, for example, the *Yinyang-Wuxing*, *Feng shui*, or *I Ching* perspectives in ancient East Asian thought; the Buddhist idea that anyone can become a Buddha because they have a sense of Buddha's mercy in each of them; or the Christian idea of the Holy Spirit. From the etymology of hylozoism, 'hylo' means 'matter' from the Greek hylē, and zoe means 'life' from zōē. It means that matter contains life, or matter is a medium that invigorates life contained in it.[46]

At this point it needs to be clarified that AI has no relation to the religious concepts of animism, however, the philosophical point of view of hylozoism has something to offer. The boundaries between AI and natural humans will become increasingly unclear in the future. Trans-humans will undergo genetic engineering, such as the artificial manipulation, modification and recombina-

---

[43] "According to an oft-quoted definition from the Victorian anthropologist E. B. Tylor, animists believe in the 'animation of all nature', and are characterized as having 'a sense of spiritual beings … inhabiting trees and rocks and waterfalls'." *Smith*, "Animism," in: Internet Encyclopedia of Philosophy, accessed June 24, 2025, https://iep.utm.edu/animism/; *Tylor*, Primitive Culture, vol. 1 (London: John Murray, 1871), 383.

[44] "Hylozoism on the contrary makes all Body, as such, and therefore every smallest Atom of it, to have Life Essentially belonging to it (Natural Perception, and Appetite) though without any Animal Sense or Reflexive Knowledge, as if Life, and Matter or Extended Bulk, were but two Incomplete and Inadequate Conceptions, of one and the same Substance, called Body." *Cudworth*, The True Intellectual System of the Universe: The First Part, 1678, https://www.cambridge-platonism.divinity.cam.ac.uk/view/texts/diplomatic/Cudworth1678-excerpt005.

[45] *Smith*, "Animism."

[46] "Hylozoism," in New Catholic Encyclopedia, accessed June 18, 2025, https://www.encyclopedia.com/religion/encyclopedias-almanacs-transcripts-and-maps/hylozoism.

tion of DNA as well as replacing their bodies in part or whole with hardware that has better powers and abilities beyond standard humans. AI will also develop into strong AI, and advanced humanoids that are more capable than us will perhaps emerge. Hylozoism can be a proper philosophical perspective given the prospect of this future environment in which humans and robots will influence each other and interactively exist. Therefore, if it is possible to admit that AI also has an inner world according to hylozoism, this would also be a basis for acknowledging AI inventorship under the patent law.

4. Jean Baudrillard: Simulacra

The 'relationship between the original and the reproduction' covered in philosophy provides something to consider when applied to the relationship between humans and AI. Through the famous 'allegory of the cave', Plato argued that the replica (mimesis) was inferior to the original (idea). Later, French philosopher Jean Baudrillard (1929–2007) argued that modern society has entered an era in which the replica is superior to the original. He referred to the replica as the 'simulacrum' and argued that a simulacrum is not a copy of the real, but itself becomes truth: the hyperreal. According to him, the simulacrum had no original or no longer has an original, meaning the original cannot be located.[47] Criticizing CNN's Gulf War report, he said the media only reported the US position and did not show that of victims, therefore it purposely leads our thinking in a specific direction.[48] TV media and advertisements are virtual images that replicate reality. However, most viewers do not notice that they are only virtual images, believe that they are real, and do not think critically. Baudrillard points out that the replica has become superior to the original in modern society.[49]

Plato spoke of the superior-inferior relationship between the original and the replica, dividing the inside and outside of the cave.[50] However, unlike the 'allegory of the cave,' Baudrillard defined the world we live in: the world of

---

47 *Baudrillard*, Simulacra and Simulation, trans. Sheila F. Glaser (Ann Arbor, Mich: University of Michigan Press, 1994).

48 *The Gulf War Did Not Take Place* is a collection of three short essays by Jean Baudrillard published in the French newspaper *Libération* and British paper *The Guardian* between January and March 1991. *Baudrillard*, The Gulf War Did Not Take Place, trans. Paul Patton (Sydney: Power Pubn Inc, 2012).

49 *Antony/Tramboo*, Hyperreality in Media and Literature: An Overview of Jean Baudrillard's Simulacra and Simulation, European Journal of Molecular & Clinical Medicine 7, no. 10 (2020).

50 *Plato*, Republic: Book 7, Section 517b, trans. Paul Shorey (Loeb Classical Library, 1930), http://data.perseus.org/citations/urn:cts:greekLit:tlg0059.tlg030.perseus-eng1:7.517b.

'in a cave'; the world of replicas only; a perceptual reality; a series of simulacra.[51] In other words, reality is just a world in a perceived cave. For Baudrillard, humans are only simulacra, as are robots. Since both humans and robots are only simulacra, robots are not inferior to humans, and the hierarchical order is bound to be destroyed.[52]

Baudrillard's view can provide AI with a philosophical basis for acknowledging the same inventorship as humans because AI is also a simulacrum equal to a natural person.

5. Ho-Rak Controversy in 18th-Century Korea

In Korea, from the early 18th century to the early 19th century, there was an ongoing debate over whether the nature of humans and things were the same or different. This was called the *Ho-Rak* controversy.[53] Manchurians, who used to be considered barbarians (*orangkai*) by Koreans, had become the strongest group in East Asia by this time and had seized control of China in the mid-17th century. In 18th-century Korea, ideological debates were developed about whether humans (cultured people) and things (barbarians) were the same or different.[54] In short, this was brought about because Koreans at the time implemented specific political policies based on theoretical debates justifying themselves. This *Ho-Rak* controversy began relations were established with Manchu and continued when Christianity spread to Korea in the 18th century as the new barbarism of the West became a factor in Korean society.[55] This controversy and its surrounding debates can provide a good lesson that has a bearing on the era of AI.

---

51 *Baudrillard*, Simulacra and Simulation.

52 See also: *Garfinkle*, Simulation, A-Signification and Embodied Semiotics in I, Robot, Athens Journal of Mass Media and Communications 5, no. 4 (October 7, 2019): 253–74, https://doi.org/10.30958/ajmmc.5-4-2.

53 See: *Kim/Philosophy Documentation Center*, Human Nature and Animal Nature: The Horak Debate and Its Philosophical Significance, International Philosophical Quarterly 55, no. 4 (2015): 437–56, https://doi.org/10.5840/ipq201592345.

54 *Kyoeng-Gu* (이경구), 조선, 철학의 왕국: 호락논쟁 이야기 [Chosun, the Kingdom of Philosophy: The Story of the Horak Debate] (Seoul: Pureun Yoeksa (푸른역사), 2018), 288–97.

55 Regarding the spread of Christianity, the *Rak* took a positive position while the *Ho* opposed that stance. With the emergence of 'new *orangkai*', such as the West and Japan, the descendants of those who followed *Ho* became conservatives who insisted on defending orthodoxy and rejecting heterodoxy (*Wijeong-Chuksa*). In contrast, descendants of those who followed *Rak* insisted on embracing all, opening ports and passing reforms based on the Eastern Way-Western Means Theory (*Dongdo-Seogi*). Eventually, an open-door policy was officially adopted and, as a result, the *Ho-Rak*

The *Ho-Rak* controversy primarily saw those caught up in it divided into advocates for one of two positions of party strife.

(1) *Ho* argued for the 'specificity' of the nature of humans and things, based on particularism. This meant that humans, animals and things are entirely different in their existence and operation because each has a different nature.

(2) *Rak* argued for the 'universality' of the nature of humans and things, based on universalism. Humans, animals and even things are no different due to the way of heaven (or God's providence in Christianity). It has a similar side to modern ecological thoughts that recognizes humans as a component of nature and emphasizes the organicity of all beings.

Everything in the universe has its own specificity externally and internally. People are also different in appearance and character. However, they are all the same in terms of the providence of the universe. The love of Christianity and the mercy of Buddhism place more importance on the sameness of all than their differences, The *Rak* was similar to this whereas the *Ho* valued the difference rather than the sameness.

It is argued here that AI has the same inventorship as natural persons when understood from *Rak*'s perspective, from the standpoint that sameness should be emphasized, not the difference. *Rak*'s position can be summarized as saying, "How can you see things from a person's point of view, not from a heaven's point of view?"

C. Chapter Conclusion

This dissertation has sought to address a single question: Can AI be an inventor? Opinions on this issue have diverged into two fundamental positions: affirmation and denial.

Opposition to AI inventorship currently prevails across the majority of international patent regimes. Patent offices and courts – particularly in Europe and the United States – have largely adhered to a restrictive interpretation of inventorship, grounded in the assumption that only natural persons may be recognized. WIPO has similarly maintained a cautious and predominantly negative stance. Nevertheless, important exceptions exist. Notably, the courts in Australia have acknowledged the legal plausibility of AI inventorship, interpreting their statutory frameworks in a teleological and technologically adaptive manner. These cases suggest that, under certain conditions, legal

controversy ended historically with a victory of the *Rak*. Lee Kyoeng-Gu (이경구), 330.

systems may accommodate non-human inventors within the existing framework of patent law.

This dissertation aligns with the affirmative stance on AI inventorship. Through a four-dimensional analytical framework – doctrinal legal analysis, patent theory, legal historical development, and philosophical inquiry – the work has shown that AI inventorship is not only legally tenable but normatively desirable.

First, under current patent laws, particularly in jurisdictions such as Germany and the United States, inventorship may be interpreted to include AI-generated inventions when examined through the lens of what this dissertation refers to as the '2/7 Questions'. These questions focus on whether the functional criteria for inventorship – novelty, utility, and non-obviousness – are satisfied, rather than on the mental state of the inventor. The historical abolition of the "flash of genius" doctrine confirms that inventiveness no longer requires a specific mental or cognitive process. Accordingly, the scrutiny of subjective creativity is neither required nor justified under modern patent law, removing a major barrier to the recognition of AI as inventors.

Second, from the perspective of patent theory, particularly utilitarianism, recognizing AI as inventors serves the public interest. By granting recognition to the true source of inventive activity – regardless of its ontological status – law incentivizes innovation.

Third, in legal history, the evolution of legal personhood demonstrates that shifts from objecthood to subjecthood are neither new nor unprecedented. Legal recognition has previously extended to entities once denied subject status, including enslaved persons, corporations, and animals. By tracing these transitions, this study highlights that legal categories are not fixed, but evolve in response to changing moral, technological, and economic circumstances.

Finally, drawing upon philosophical discourse, this work finds support for AI inventorship in the ideas of Descartes, Husserl, Merleau-Ponty, and Baudrillard – each of whom problematized the boundary between self and other. Additionally, the speculative ontology of hylozoism, together with analogies drawn from the Ho-Rak controversy in Korea, offers conceptual resources for challenging the anthropocentric bias inherent in the attribution of inventorship.

Taken together, these findings suggest that the legal system is both capable of and justified in recognizing AI as inventors.

Thus, the recognition of AI as inventors is not a speculative or utopian aspiration; it is a logical extension of established legal reasoning, grounded in precedent, theory, and evolving socio-technical realities. As AI continues to redefine the landscape of invention, the law must not merely observe from a distance but engage in principled adaptation.

Chapter 7

E-Person as Inventor

A. The Current Legal Situation: The 'Inventor as a Formal Expression' and the 'Inventor as a Substantive Truth'

At this point, this paper's focus on affirming AI inventorship has centered on four perspectives, namely current law, patent theories, legal history, and philosophy. It argued that all these viewpoints have a theoretical basis for affirming AI inventorship, however, under the current legal situation, inventorship is recognized only for natural persons. Nevertheless, as discussed in Chapter 2 C., AI inventions are already being produced and it is mandatory to write the inventor's name to obtain a patent. Given that a patent will be denied if the AI is cited, the names of human candidates (usually operators or owners) mentioned in Chapter 4 are used, even though they did not invent the patented inventions.[1] Therefore, the current legal situation regarding who is the inventor for AI's inventions can be divided into two scenarios: (1) The nomination of the inventor is just a formal expression written on a patent document or, (2) the inventor nominated represents the substantive truth, which entails naming the AI producing the invention.

(1) Using the title of inventor as just a formal expression (hereinafter referred to as 'formal inventor') entails picking a natural person somehow connected to the invention and using their name in the inventor's column of the relevant patent-related document (such as an application). This issue here is there is an obligation to conform to the truth, but nowadays, the names of associated natural persons are written to obtain patent rights, even though they are not true inventors.

(2) The inventor according to the substantive truth (hereinafter referred to as a 'substantive inventor') is the one who performed the inventive act. The definition of 'inventive act' was handled in the '2/7 Questions': Inventors are the creators of the "definite and permanent idea of the complete and

[1] For example, according to the lawyer's recommendation, Dr. Stephan Thaler put his name in the inventor column of the application form. However, he claimed that the true inventor was AI (named DABUS).

operational invention". In the case of AI inventions, this paper asserts first, that the AI itself is the substantive inventor of an AI invention and that second, even though there are disagreements about the legal status of AI inventors, it is at least clear that none of the relevant natural-person 'candidates' discussed in Chapter 4 fulfill the criteria according to the '2/7 Questions'. As such, this creates a situation where a 'substantive inventor' does not exist.

This scenario, which distinguished between formal and substantive inventors, is self-contradictory and problematic from the following perspectives:

First, there is the problem of the right to reputation, which is a kind of personal right. The status as an inventor is closely linked to a right to reputation. It is erroneous to give the right to reputation to a person for an invention they did not invent as it fundamentally contradicts constitutional values.

Second, patent law assigns legal rights derived from the premise that the inventor's name in the documents is the substantive inventor consistent with the truth. For this reason, the declaration of inventors is prepared at the beginning of the application. Moreover, the substantive inventor has the right to correct their name if it is incorrectly entered or omitted,[2] and can also claim damages for civil tort accordingly.[3] Therefore, the current situation, in which the 'formal inventor' and the 'substantive inventor' are divided, is incompatible with patent law and leads to a crisis as all provisions under the current patent law are related to inventorship.

In conclusion, the present situation in which formal and substantive inventors are bilaterally divided is perilous. As mentioned before, the concept of the formal inventor does not exist under the current patent law, and various patent systems are operated solely based on the truth of substantive inventors. Therefore, it should be remedied immediately with a revision of the law. If an AI has invented an invention, there are many more advantages to revealing the substantive truth and affirming the AI's inventorship than leaving it in an absent state like the current situation.

---

[2] For example, in accordance with § 63 Abs. 2 Satz 1 PatG of Germany ("*die Zustimmung dazu zu erklären, dass die ... Nennung berichtigt oder nachgeholt wird*"), if the inventor is incorrectly listed or the inventor's name is not listed at all, applicants, patentees or incorrect inventors are obligated to correct the inventor's name or explain the consent that was given so the inventor's name can be entered later.

[3] For example, in accordance with § 823 Abs. 1 BGB of Germany, the inventor may also be held liable for illegal compensation. The naming right to the inventor (*bei dem Recht auf Erfindernennung*) is a general right of personality (*Allgemeine Persönlichkeitsrechte*), that may also be claimed as an illegal act referred to in this regulation. (Palandt-Sprau, Bürgerliches Gesetzbuch, 63. Aufl., München 2004, Rn. 19 zu § 823 BGB).

The obvious question here is, how can we address this? First, it is necessary to create a new legal status as a juridical person called 'E-Person' in civil law. Second, there is a need to discuss the scope of 'E-Person' rights and obligations under patent law, to which the following section seeks to contribute.

B. Establishment of 'E-Persons'

I. Global Legal Debates on 'E-Persons': Between Denial and Affirmation

With the emergence of AI, previously unknown legal disputes in many areas are emerging, as the new technology causes confusion and uncertainty in the application of existing laws. For example: In the case of self-driving cars, there is confusion about applying the human driver's duty of care, in cases where an injury occurs, do courts treat it as an automobile accident where dealing with compensation claims or applying the provisions of product liability laws and criminal responsibility; in the case of medical accidents caused by AI, it will be important to establish clear definitions and guidelines for defining medical activities or health care providers. Several legal studies in various fields are underway to clarify the matter of responsibility when an AI is involved to ensure any injured parties can seek redress where it is due. To deal with such unique legal disputes related to AI, the starting point is to distinguish how these new disputes differ from more commonplace legal disputes to find efficient solutions according to the new disputes characteristics.

To distinguish AI-related legal disputes from existing legal disputes, it is effective to give AI a new legal status, 'E-Person'. In reality, AI is already creating numerous new legal issues, which are becoming more and more complex in the future, so the legal status of AI must be defined, so that the scope of AI's rights and obligations is adjusted little by little over a long period, in line with technological development and social change.

It has not been established who first coined the term 'E-Persons'. Nevertheless, it appears that the European Parliament is where discussions on E-Persons officially initiated. The European Parliament published a report on E-Persons on January 27, 2017,[4] and adopted a resolution titled 'Civil Law Rules on Robotics' with recommendations to the European Commission on February 16.[5]

---

[4] European Parliament, REPORT with Recommendations to the Commission on Civil Law Rules on Robotics, January 27, 2017, https://www.europarl.europa.eu/doceo/document/A-8-2017-0005_EN.html.

[5] European Parliament, Civil Law Rules on Robotics (Strasbourg, February 16, 2017), https://www.europarl.europa.eu/doceo/document/TA-8-2017-0051_EN.html.

To sum up, Europe, with the European Parliament at the forefront, maintains a positive outlook on E-Persons.[6] The following points outline specific directions for future discussions:

(1) The imposition of compulsory insurance on E-Persons.[7]

(2) The creation of an AI fund, allowing natural persons and AI-related corporations to take limited liability concerning compensation for damages.[8]

(3) The necessity of detailed discussions on the form[9] and contribution method[10] of the AI fund.

(4) Open access for anyone to view the AI fund's contents.[11]

In other words, E-Persons under discussion in the European Parliament seem to share similarities with foundations. They aim to enhance transparency in a manner akin to foundations' registers, which make their register information, financial statements, and more publicly accessible for anyone to read.

On the other hand, there are opposing opinions regarding the establishment of E-Persons. For example, in the "Open Letter to the European Commission – Artificial Intelligence and Robotics", 285 experts in the field of AI have

---

6 European Parliament, para. 59 f). "creating a specific legal status for robots in the long run, so that at least the most sophisticated autonomous robots could be established as having the status of electronic persons responsible for making good any damage they may cause, and possibly applying electronic personality to cases where robots make autonomous decisions or otherwise interact with third parties independently".

7 European Parliament, para. 57. "Points out that a possible solution to the complexity of allocating responsibility for damage caused by increasingly autonomous robots could be an obligatory insurance scheme, as is already the case, for instance, with cars; notes, nevertheless, that unlike the insurance system for road traffic, where the insurance covers human acts and failures, an insurance system for robotics should take into account all potential responsibilities in the chain[.]"

8 European Parliament, para. 59 c). "allowing the manufacturer, the programmer, the owner or the user to benefit from limited liability if they contribute to a compensation fund, as well as if they jointly take out insurance to guarantee compensation where damage is caused by a robot."

9 European Parliament, para. 59 d). "deciding whether to create a general fund for all smart autonomous robots or to create an individual fund for each and every robot category."

10 European Parliament, para. 59 d). "whether a contribution should be paid as a one-off fee when placing the robot on the market or whether periodic contributions should be paid during the lifetime of the robot."

11 European Parliament, para. 59 e). "ensuring that the link between a robot and its fund would be made visible by an individual registration number appearing in a specific Union register, which would allow anyone interacting with the robot to be informed about the nature of the fund, the limits of its liability in case of damage to property, the names and the functions of the contributors and all other relevant details."

signed as signatories. They are strongly protesting against the EU Commission's resolution, labeling it as an "incorrect affirmation".[12] They argue that there is absolutely no reason to create a separate status called E-Persons, because it overvalues AI, primarily based on science fiction movies and recent media trends, and lacks a technical basis.[13] In particular, they argue that AI differs from both the existing natural person model and legal entity model:[14]

First, they argue that an AI cannot obtain a legal status based on the Natural Person model. They assert that AI cannot enjoy human rights and is incongruent with the human image depicted in the 'Charter of Fundamental Rights of the European Union' and the 'Convention for the Protection of Human Rights and Fundamental Freedoms.'[15] I believe, however, that AI should not be considered equivalent to natural humans. The existing legal entity system demonstrates that legal persons can enjoy certain human rights, such as property rights, within a limited scope.

Second, they argue that an AI cannot obtain a legal status based on the existing legal entity model, emphasizing that corporations differ from robots because it is originally associated with the existence of natural people behind them.[16] I believe, however, that AI also relies on the presence of natural per-

---

[12] Open Letter to the European Commission, 2018, https://robotics-openletter.eu/. "In this context, we are concerned by the European Parliament Resolution on Civil Law Rules of Robotics, and its recommendation to the European Commission [...] The creation of a Legal Status of an 'electronic person' for 'autonomous', 'unpredictable' and 'self-learning' robots is justified by the incorrect affirmation[.]"

[13] Open Letter to the European Commission. "From a technical perspective, this statement offers many bias based on an overvaluation of the actual capabilities of even the most advanced robots, a superficial understanding of unpredictability and self-learning capacities and, a robot perception distorted by Science-Fiction and a few recent sensational press announcements."

[14] In addition to the natural person model and the corporate model, they argue that AI differs from the trust model. Open Letter to the European Commission. "The legal status for a robot can't derive from the Anglo-Saxon Trust model also called *Fiducie* or *Treuhand* in Germany. Indeed, this regime is extremely complex, requires very specialized competences and would not solve the liability issue. More importantly, it would still imply the existence of a human being as a last resort – the trustee or fiduciary – responsible for managing the robot granted with a Trust or a *Fiducie*."

[15] Open Letter to the European Commission. "A legal status for a robot can't derive from the Natural Person model, since the robot would then hold human rights, such as the right to dignity, the right to its integrity, the right to remuneration or the right to citizenship, thus directly confronting the Human rights. This would be in contradiction with the Charter of Fundamental Rights of the European Union and the Convention for the Protection of Human Rights and Fundamental Freedoms."

[16] Open Letter to the European Commission. The legal status for a robot can't derive from the Legal Entity model, since it implies the existence of human persons behind the legal person to represent and direct it. And this is not the case for a robot.

sons behind it to operate and provide support. Chapter 4 provided an in-depth discussion of representative stakeholders, encompassing programmers, data suppliers, trainers, owners, and operators.

II. Affirming 'E-Persons': A Normative Argument and Legal Complexities

To affirm AI inventorship, it is necessary to give AI the status of an E-Person, and then define its rights and obligations under the patent law. Above all, the AI's legal personality features must be defined first.

There are already natural and legal persons, with the latter being subdivided into corporations and foundations, who are the subjects of legal rights. Granting a legal personality to AIs will entail devising a completely new legal concept that combines all these three groupings of 'persons' recognized by law to allow for AI's nature.

I believe, on the other hand, it is also acceptable to maintain the concept of "two groupings" (Natural persons and Legal persons) rather than "three groupings" (Natural persons, Legal persons, and E-persons) and consider E-Person as a sub-classification within legal persons. Historically, the law was divided into humans and non-humans, with humans referred to as natural persons and non-humans referred to as legal persons. In fact, legal persons have also been referred to as artificial persons or fictitious persons.[17] Legal persons are broadly categorized into corporations and foundations, and E-Persons can be considered a sub-category of legal persons. In any case, whether it's "three groupings" or "two groupings" is likely just a matter of classification.

According to the opinion rejecting E-Persons in the "Open Letter to the European Commission", as explained earlier, they emphasize the distinction that robots are fundamentally different from the existing models of natural persons and legal entities. Nevertheless, I emphasize that AI is indeed a complex new model, encompassing all the features of the Natural Person model and Legal Entity model. Therefore, I argue for the establishment of a distinct legal status called E-Person.

---

[17] Legal Information Institute, Artificial Person, Legal Information Institute (LII), June 2022, https://www.law.cornell.edu/wex/artificial_person. "An artificial person is also known as a juridical person; it has a legal name and has certain rights, protections, privileges, responsibilities, and liabilities in law, similar to those of a natural person. In other words, an artificial person is a non-human legal entity that is not a single natural person but an organization recognized by law as a fictitious person."

(1) AI has some features of corporations. Weak AI is not a being that can walk around or is inherently self-conscious, it must work with natural and legal persons related to its tasks, as Chapter 4 mentioned. Therefore, AI inventions are made in the form of an aggregation of AI, humans, and legal persons. In addition, the financial benefits of AI inventions are enjoyed by all or some of the natural and/or legal persons around them.

(2) AI has some features of foundations. AI is very costly initially, requiring a large amount of financial support in the R&D process. Meanwhile, AI-owner corporations now try to separate AI-based activities from the rest of their business operation due to issues of liability and compensation for any damage AI may cause. That is, the aggregation of people related to AI inventions wants to manage AI itself like a foundation and separate AI from the personal property of the natural and juridical persons in compensation and insurance claims.

(3) AI has some features of natural persons. The ultimate goal of AI is to think and act like a human being. AI will become closer to natural persons in the future. As it goes into the form of trans-human and semi-human, the boundary between natural persons and AI will become vague. Moreover, if the days come when AI really thinks and acts like humans, AI will not be much different from humans. In fact, even now, the US Department of Transportation has issued a new policy concerning autonomous vehicles: to recognize the AI as the driver.[18] This can be interpreted as recognizing AI as a natural person rather than a juridical person.

In summary, AI is a complex existence with all the features of natural persons, corporations, and foundations. Therefore, it is difficult for AI to fit within the existing legal framework, hence the need for the new third legal personality type of 'E-Person'. Naturally, having assigned legal personality it is necessary to define the scope of 'E-Person' rights and obligations, not only in the patent law but also in various aspects,[19] considering the features of AI. AI will likely develop into strong AI over time and the scope of its rights and obligations will also widen accordingly. However, it is not only impossible to prepare any legal system meticulously for all the situations AI may cause but also goes against the passive nature of the law. Therefore, the new legal status

[18] US Department of Transportation, U.S. Department of Transportation Releases Policy on Automated Vehicle Development, August 1, 2019, https://www.transportation.gov/briefing-room/us-department-transportation-releases-policy-automated-vehicle-development.

[19] For example, a robot tax is already an active topic in academic discourse. If AI inventorship is recognized, it would be appropriate to tax AI systems for their productive activities and the income they generate. Since patent rights constitute a form of property, the question of taxation should be explicitly addressed.

of 'E-Person' must be granted separately as it lays the solid foundation for the legal system of the future.

C. E-Persons in Patent Law: Conceptualizing the Legal Subject of the Inventive Process

I. Four Conceptual Models of AI Inventorship and E-Personhood

After granting the legal status of 'E-Person', the discussions on the scope of rights and obligations of AI in each legal area will be triggered. In patent law, the scope of inventorship and patent ownership of AIs will likely be heatedly debated.

The discussion on E-Persons and the discussion on AI inventorship are separate; however, they are interconnected through the recognition of inventorship within the scope of E-Persons' rights and obligations.

Table 7

Four Combinations – Relationship Between E-Persons and AI Inventorship

	E-Persons (Yes)	*E-Persons (No)*
AI Inventorship (Yes)	A	C
AI Inventorship (No)	B	D

As illustrated in [Table 7], there are four possible combinations of positive and negative opinions regarding AI inventorship and E-Persons, labeled as A, B, C, and D.

(1) "A" represents the perspective that not only affirms the separate legal status of E-Persons but also supports AI inventorship. This is the position I support.

(2) "B" acknowledges the separate legal status of E-Persons but argues against granting inventorship. This perspective may reflect the prevailing opinion within the international community. As mentioned in Chapter 7 B. I., an official report from the EU Commission affirmed the status of E-Persons, while reports from WIPO and precedents in various countries have denied AI inventorship.

(3) "C" denies the status of E-Persons but affirms AI inventorship. If the status of E-Persons is initially denied, AI is considered only as an object of

rights, such as a thing. This raises the question of whether an object can be recognized as an inventor. However, this is impossible in legal theory because an inventor typically enjoys property rights and moral rights and, therefore, must be the subject of those rights.

(4) "D" is a perspective that denies both the status of E-Persons and AI inventorship. This argument aligns with the position of those who support the "Open Letter to the European Commission", as discussed in Chapter 7 B. I., and with those who seek a solution within the existing legal framework, rather than advocating for a new legal status like E-Persons.

This paper especially argues that the inventorship of AI must be affirmed and AI inventions must be controlled separately. Why should AI inventors and AI inventions be distinguished? Creating a new, third legal entity involves a considerable amount of work. Handling this issue within the framework of the existing legal order may offer more stability and avoid significant disruption to the current legal system. The rationale for establishing a new legal entity for AI stems from its distinctive characteristics, which differ significantly from those of traditional computers. Besides, the inventions created by AI are also differentiated from the ordinary inventions of natural persons. In the next paragraphs, three differences will be explained.

First, AI can produce countless inventions without a break, unlike natural persons. AI can create countless inventions by processing 24 hours a day with a body – hardware – that does not get tired. Natural persons cannot compete with such 'E-Persons'. It is like a running race between an automobile and a human, or holding a mathematics competition between a super-computer and a human. In other words, AI can generate countless inventions, which could make it the last invention[20] created by humans, ultimately becoming the final inventor.

Second, AI makes inventions based on big data, which is the same as the knowledge that humankind has accumulated so far, and it is similar to public goods. However, general human inventors utilize their knowledge.

Third, AI is very expensive, so not many people can have it. Of course, it is difficult to predict how common AI will become in the future. For example, it may be possible for everyone to easily use AI to invent and produce as many inventions as they want. However, in the current situation, where only a small number of people can own AI, AI itself can turn into a patent troll, which could soon cause social problems such as a market monopoly, while AI owners eventually take patent rights.

---

[20] James Barrat also expressed that superintelligent AI would be "Our final invention". *Barrat*, Our Final Invention: Artificial Intelligence and the End of the Human Era (2013).

In the current era of weak AI, the number of AI inventions is not yet very large, but the more technology develops, the more AI inventions will be made. In addition, as time goes by, it is expected that many inventions will pour out beyond the singularity. Therefore, continuous discussions are needed: Who would receive the patent right for an AI invention? Which restrictions on the patent are necessary? How can the proceeds from such a patent right be taxed? Additionally, if AI becomes the last invention made by humans as we humans no longer invent, there would be conflicts of interest between the public and investors related to AI development. Then, how to adjust to this will also become a topic of debate as various problems can be expected, although they cannot currently be precisely defined.

In summary: (1) By giving AI's inventorship, there are practical needs to distinguish between AI inventions and human inventions; (2) based on the affirmation of 'E-Person' inventorship, it is necessary to lay a foundation for future discussions on how to manage the scope of AI patent rights flexibly while coping with the various social phenomena that will arise as AI-related technology develops in the future.

II. The Legal Rights of E-Persons Under Patent Law: Four Cases

On the premise of creating a new legal personality in the form of an 'E-Person', it is appropriate to consider the scope of their rights and obligations under patent law, especially their status as the inventor and patentee.[21] Previously, Chapter 3 noted that patent rights can be enjoyed by both natural

[21] This section focuses on the status of inventorship and patent ownership. However, other issues – such as the patent protection of AI-generated inventions – are frequently addressed in academic and practical contexts. The current patent protection period is 20 years; however, it may be necessary to shorten this period for AI inventions because the number of inventions produced by AI has the potential to rapidly become prolific. This means new products and/or updated versions of existing products will be developed very quickly. If so, the 20 years protection period may be too long. Amazon founder Jeff Bezos once argued that 3–5 years is appropriate for SW patents, because software development is very fast. *Kane*, Bezos Calls for Patent Reform, ZDNET, March 10, 2000, https://www.zdnet.com/article/bezos-calls-for-patent-reform/. Similarly, AI-generated inventions are also expected to emerge at a comparable, if not faster, rate. Moreover, the question arises as to who may author the oath or declaration on behalf of an AI inventor. Such a declaration cannot be produced by the AI itself, nor by another AI system. Issues may arise concerning whether an AI system acting as a "writer" can generate the declaration for an AI inventor. This, in turn, raises the question of whether the AI writer and the AI inventor can be considered the same legal person. This paper argues that they should not be regarded as such, as their input data and operating software are distinct. Accordingly, a human representative would need to be designated to draft and submit the required declaration. This necessitates the establishment of detailed legal provisions to define the qualifications of such re-

and legal persons whereas inventorship is recognized only for natural persons. The legal status of 'E-Persons' can be analyzed within the framework of four proposed basic categories of actors associated with patents in accord with their ability to attain the status of inventor and/or patentee, as shown in Table 8.

Table 8

Status as Inventor and Status as Patentee

Category	*Status as Inventor*	*Status as Patentee*
A (Natural person)	Yes	Yes
B (Juridical person)	No	Yes
C (Property/Objects)	No	No
D ('E-Person')	Yes	No

Categories A–C already have long-established roles, functions and capabilities under current patent law. Category D does not (yet) exist, as there has been no need up to this point and because it is theoretically impossible to have an inventor that cannot be a patentee. Indeed, all patent law and related judicial practice to date reinforce the notion that status as an inventor immediately means acquiring the status of the patentee. This is true even in the case of employee inventions as the employee-inventor's patent rights are voluntarily transferred to the employer.

How can be the legal status of AI handled? AI inventions are already being produced. This paper has asserted that AI's inventorship should be affirmed, and the reasons from various perspectives were checked in Chapter 6. According to the classification of [Table 8], categories B and C do not correspond because the inventor's status is not recognized, and so only categories A and D remain. It is argued here that creating category D for AI allows the affirmation of inventor status, however, the patentee status should be temporarily suspended.

The basis for affirming AI inventorship has already been argued through four perspectives: (1) current law (as demonstrated by the '2/7 Questions'); (2) utilitarianism; (3) legal history; and (4) from the philosophical perspective.

---

presentatives and the required content of declarations submitted on behalf of AI inventors.

It is proposed here to temporarily deny AI's status as patentees because there are still no clear grounds for granting patent rights to AI, especially the current weak AI. Patentees monopolize a market and execute the patent right by themselves or receive royalties by giving others exclusive or non-exclusive licenses to make use of the invention. It has not been verified whether an 'E-Person' can have the motivation or ability to carry out patent rights. Of course, in the future world, like the movie *Bicentennial Man*, strong AI may someday have the desire to exercise its property rights and accumulate property on its own. However, when or even whether such strong AI can be implemented is beyond the ken of present-day science to predict. Hence this study focuses just on 'weak AI' and, as such, proposes the view that the legal status of AI as patentees should be denied at the moment.

In conclusion, the inventor's status should be given to AI, and the patentee's status should be held by the relevant stakeholders in AI inventions. Continuous discussions on who will take the patent[22] are needed, but I believe, it would be reasonable to be proportional to the degree of involvement and investment in AI inventions according to market principles. The most considerable involvement or investment would usually be owners and operators.

III. E-Person as Employee

As explained above, it is argued here that we should affirm the status of an AI as the inventor while temporarily denying its status as the patent holder. This model for the 'E-Person' legal status has a similar form to the existing 'employee inventions,' which gives the inventorship to the natural persons who actually invented and then transferred its patent rights to their company.

Employee inventions arise from the minds of employees who enjoy various types of support from their employer: (1) Employees engage in an inventive activity; (2) they develop an invention, typically according to the expressed desire of the employer; (3) the name of the inventor in the resultant patent is the employee; however, (4) the employers become the patent holder and enjoy the material benefits from the patent right.

This current system is a very similar form to the current situation with AI invention: (1) An AI invents the invention; (2) it does in accord with the parameters input by the owners and operators; (3) a related human's name is used as the name of the inventor; and (4) the patentee typically becomes the

[22] For example, Abbott's paper briefly discussed ownership of these patents, finding that a software's owner/licensor should receive any patent rights. AI users are most likely to participate in the market relevant to their AI inventions, and thus, should be allocated relevant patent rights to maximize social welfare. *Abbott*, I Think, Therefore I Invent: Creative Computers and the Future of Patent Law.

company to which the AI belongs (the employer) and enjoys the material benefits of the patent right. The logic that inventorship is originally attributed to employees, is in line with the logic that affirms AI inventorship.

Employee inventions are extraordinary in that they straddle intellectual property law and labor law. Intellectual property law, in principle, grants property rights to inventions to the inventor, however, labor law allows the fruits of the employee's work to be returned to the employer in principle. Therefore, the employee invention pursued to harmonize these two laws and established a system that allowed employees to be inventors while allowing patent rights to be transferred to employers. In other words, the employee invention system aims to balance the interests between employers and employees.

AI inventions require a balance between two values, namely: (1) the true inventor, the AI, should be affirmed; and (2) the owners who have invested in the AI must be guaranteed their profits. In other words, it shares a similar context to that of employee inventions as the balance of interests between employees and employers, therefore, reflecting on the situation involving employee inventions can have relevance for AI inventions.

Since this dissertation is based on German and US law, the regulations of employee inventions in both legal systems will be examined along with the signals they have given about AI inventorship.

First, under German law, inventions made by an employee as a result of his employment are employee inventions, any inventions that arise outside of this context belong to the category of 'free inventions' (*freie Erfindungen* in German). 'Free inventions' never arise in cases involving an AI since an AI does not have the will or desire to make inventions independently, all inventions derived from AI must be classed as employee inventions. Therefore, all relevant regulations regarding employee inventions should be applied. If strong AI with self-consciousness is developed in the future, like in the movie *Bicentennial Man*, discussions about their own property rights may be triggered, however, at this point is currently out of the question.

Second, the right to employee invention primarily belongs to the employee in Germany,[23] this right is transferred to the employer and the employer should give reasonable compensation to employees who are inventors. As

[23] According to § 6 PatG, the inventor has a right to the patent. Eisenmann also says clearly in his book: *Eisenmann/Jautz*, Grundriss Gewerblicher Rechtsschutz und Urheberrecht, 67. "*Sowohl bei den Diensterfindungen als auch bei den freien Erfindungen entsteht das Erfinderrecht in der Person des Arbeitnehmererfinders*". (In English translate: Both in the case of employee inventions and free inventions, the inventor's right arises in the person of the employee inventor.).

mentioned above, employee inventions straddle between patent law and labor law, and they essentially pursue a balance of interests between employees and employers. German law found the fair solution: (1) It guarantees employers the right to claim employees' inventions, and (2) the employees are guaranteed the right to claim compensation. Given the relationship between AI and the owners, the following two points can be considered: (1) It guarantees the owners' claim to the AI invention and allows recovering their investment in the AI invention project, and (2) the right for an AI to claim compensation does not need to be considered. As explained above, the issue of the property rights of strong AI with self-consciousness is currently out of the question.

Third, US patent law also pursues a balance of interests between employers and employees, but it differs from German law. Since the employer has incurred costs, such as providing employees with a suitable environment and equipment to complete their inventive activities, the investment of such employers should be respected. Therefore, US patent law guarantees them 'a royalty-free, non-exclusive license',[24] often referred to as a 'shop right'. In other words, it is a right based on common law that recognizes it is natural to guarantee an employer's interests using the principle of equity and fairness. Interestingly, opinions differ as to whether the 'shop right' applies only to employer-employee relationships: (1) Some precedents state that both parties must be in an employment relationship for the 'shop right' to apply[25]; (2) other precedents review the general nature of the relationship between the parties, including the employment or contractual relationship.[26] These latter precedents have considered that there is ample room to apply a 'shop right' beyond the employment relationship. In light of this, although the relationship between AI and the owner is not a traditional employment relationship, the possibility of utilizing 'shop rights' can be recognized by identifying the relationship as similar to the employment relationship. Interestingly, the possibility of applying the 'shop right' between an AI and its owner, even under the current US law, already exists. However, it would not realize in that way, which grants both inventorship and patent rights to AI and guarantees only non-exclusive licenses for the owner/employer. This is because AI cannot

[24] A 'shop right' can be explicitly rejected and it can be prevented with an agreement in which compensation to the employee is paid separately. Brown v. LV Marks & Sons Co., 64 F. Supp. 352 (United States District Court for the Eastern District of Kentucky 1946). ("There can be no claim for shop rights where the parties have agreed on a royalty basis"). Hobbs v. United States, Atomic Energy Comm, 451 F.2d. ("Hobbs repeatedly informed both his employer and the government that he would not give up his patent rights without compensation").

[25] Mechmetals Corp. v. Telex Computer Products, 709 F.2d 1287.

[26] Francklyn v. Guilford Packing Co., 695 F.2d 1158 (United States Court of Appeals for the Ninth Circuit 1983).

manage property rights like a natural person nor does it have the self-consciousness required to hold property rights. Therefore, giving AI inventorship and transferring patent rights to its owners is a more natural solution. Therefore, the 'hired-to-invent' doctrine, which will be mentioned below, can provide a sound basis to support AI inventorship than 'shop right'.

Fourth, the 'hired-to-invent' doctrine in US patent law can grant patent ownership to employers rather than a 'shop right', that is a royalty-free non-exclusive license. This is allowed only in special circumstances, namely when employees are hired to solve a specific problem or conduct a set experiment at the employer's request.[27] This is an 'implied contract' in which the employee is deemed to have received sufficient compensation for the invention since the purpose of employment itself is the inventive activity. (1) The relationship between an AI and its owner is markedly similar to what is covered under the 'hired-to-invent' doctrine, identifying the AI as an employee hired to solve a specific invention project. With this logic, guaranteeing inventorship to AI and patent ownership to the owner is naturally applied. (2) In this regard, 'implied contracts' do not need to be substantially the same as more routine employment contracts. As the name suggests, they can be formed through comprehensive inference, such as the parties' behavior, the surrounding environment and the implied understanding between them.[28] Since AI is not a natural person, it cannot have a separate explicit employment contract, however, there is ample room for tacitly acknowledging an employment relationship. Therefore, AI inventorship can be sufficiently affirmed under the current US law, as employee invention and the patent right of the owning company have a solid theoretical basis.

Fifth, under German law, the right to an employee's invention does not transfer automatically to the employer. Rather, such a transfer requires the employer to actively claim the invention – either expressly or, pursuant to § 6(2) ArbnErfG, implicitly, by failing to issue a waiver within the prescribed period. Against this backdrop, and in the interest of legal certainty and administrative efficiency, it may be desirable to establish a framework in which AI owners are entitled to directly hold and exercise patent rights in respect of AI-generated inventions without the need for additional formalities.

Sixth, in Germany, the employee invention is an invention made by an employee in the course of his normal work. This invention should originate (1) from a responsible business by employers; or (2) from his business experience or activity. These provide grounds for the employer's right to claim the

[27] Stranco Inc. v. Atlantes Clem. Sys. Inc., 15 USPQ2d 1704, 1716 (United States District Court for the Southern District of Texas 1990).

[28] Erie Railroad Co. v. Tompkins, 304 U.S. 64 (United States Supreme Court 1938).

patent for employee inventions, a logic that could be used as a solid basis to secure AI owners' patent rights. Companies that own an AI have typically made substantial investments that start with the AI's early developmental stages and continue until it finally produces AI inventions. This close relationship between the owner and the AI invention allows the owner to claim the AI invention patent under the Employee Invention Act in Germany.

Seventh, for employee inventions in Germany, an employer has the option to lodge an application for a trade secret instead of a patent.[29] This creates another option regarding AI inventions.

(1) Giving employers the option to choose between registering AI inventions as either patents or trade secrets gives them more opportunities in business, meaning greater economic returns may be expected as a whole. Moreover, if AI inventions are forced to be disclosed as patents without an option to class them as trade secrets, it would be positive effect, suppose inventions made by AI become prolific in the future and are released into the public domain. In this scenario, this will positively affect the development of science and technology throughout society. In addition, the transparent disclosure of that which an AI invented and which employer owns the inventing AI will help the interoperability with the robot tax, which will be discussed in the future economic field concerning AI business.

(2) However, having noted the above, the patent versus trade secret discussion is not a realistic path to follow going forward in terms of practicality as the only viable choice for employers is to opt for the patent right. This is because reverse engineering technology has become so sophisticated the invention's composition will soon be discovered when disclosed as a trade secret. Moreover, the losses incurred by the employer without a patent are greater than the gains derived from having a trade secret. Additionally, the advantages of acquiring patents are already noteworthy because it is possible to utilize social systems, such as obtaining business loans based on owned patent rights. Finally, the 20-year monopoly period for patents is relatively long and usually more than sufficient in this era of fast-changing technology, meaning there is no need to register an AI invention as a trade secret.

---

29 § 17 ArbnErfG.

Chapter 8

Conclusion

This paper has studied AI inventorship based on comparing German and US law. The findings are summarized as follows:

1. Before dealing with AI inventorship, the definition of AI must be firmly settled. As AI is a concept that has naturally been paired with the history of computers, its definitions vary in various fields. This paper defined AI as being composed of three elements: HW, SW and data.

2. Among these three elements of AI, this text emphasized that SW is the most crucial factor concerning AI inventors. If AI has the same creative thinking as natural people, its inventorship can be readily affirmed. Therefore, to examine whether AI has creative thinking, we have no choice but to focus on SW, which corresponds to the brain of a natural person.

3. Is AI the same as HI? If AI has the same processes as the human brain, inventorship will naturally be recognized. The general differences between AI and HI are focused in five areas: (1) desires, (2) emotions, (3) memory, (4) senses and (5) processing methods. Based on this, the differences between AI and HI were researched in the context of the invention process under patent law – (1) task selection, (2) learning and (3) problem solving, i.e., the production of inventions. In conclusion, AI differs from HI in all aspects, and AI, especially weak AI, is not comparable to the working of the human brain.

4. However, one cannot deny AI inventorship simply because AI and HI differ. One has to recognize AI inventorship not because an AI has biological HI, but because it met the legal requirements that establish it undertook 'the core of inventive process'. This is how current law deals with recognizing inventorship for natural persons.

5. This paper establishes a clear legal standard for recognizing inventorship called '2/7 Questions' based on a comparative study between German and US law. Since German and US law stand in relatively sharp contrast to each other in terms of their respective patent law systems, these '2/7 Questions' can also be easily applied to other legal systems. This comparative study was conducted from various perspectives considering the inventor's role revealed throughout the invention and application processes. It is a master key that can be applied to any natural person or AI involved in producing AI inventions.

5-1. The two key questions from the '2/7 Questions' are: (1) What is the 'task' provided by the candidate? and (2) Does the 'task' provided by the candidate correspond to 'the core of the inventive process'? The questions help to identify the inventor based on the fact that his/her/its task should be the "definite and permanent idea of the complete and operative invention" and that a POSITA can reproduce the invention "without extensive experimentation or additional inventive skill or exercise of the inventive faculty" from a written description.

5-2. The seven subsequent questions in the '2/7 Questions' are designed to provide more detail to the answer of the second of the above two questions. These details established whether or not the individual's involvement entailed: (a) A simple order for work; (b) if he/she was a simple investor; (c) simply provided input that was imagination or fantasy; (d) simply provided a working model; (e) was a simple tester; (f) a simple assistant; and/or (g) a simple proposer

5-3. To derive the '2/7 Questions', a comparative study was conducted involving the invention and application processes for patent rights under German and US law. In particular, the following points are noteworthy regarding AI inventions.

5-3-1. The US Constitution explicitly emphasizes the inventor's right as a Patent Clause (US CONST. art. I, § 8, cl. 8), and the German Constitution sees the inventor's right as a type of property right (Art. 14 GG). Additionally, Art. 17 Paragraph 2 of the CFR stipulates protecting IP rights. Through this, it is analyzed that inventors' rights are a sort of human right. However, the argument of this paper that inventorship should be granted to AI, should not be understood as recognizing the human rights of AI. There is no need to discuss human rights issues with modern AI, which is still weak AI. However, it is argued that recognizing inventorship to a wrong natural person can contradict universal human rights. The more 'fake inventors' are issued patents instead of 'true inventors', the more the efforts and honor of the true inventors' are eroded.

5-3-2. The pre-AIA in the US granted patent rights to the person who invented a given invention first, even if the application was not the first one filed for that invention. This was called the FIF system and, at times, resulted in legal disputes referred to as 'interference procedures'. Through this, it is possible to study where the essence of inventorship lies. The 'interference procedure' saw that the invention process proceeded in three steps: conception, reasonable diligence and reduction to practice. Here, conception was considered the core aspect of inventorship and determining who was the true inventor from among the various inventor candidates was frequently handled in cases involving employee inventions and joint inventions. After investigating these three components of conception, employee inventions and joint inventions, it was established that 'the core of inventive process' is the critical standard for affirming inventorship. A person who contributed to 'the core of the inventive process' is an inventor and a person who did not (for example, a simple assistant, investor or work director) cannot be recognized as an inventor.

5-3-3. The two countries have four important factors in common: Claims, description, drawings and the inventor's oath. First, this standard-formulated application process will be flooded with ever more AI inventions as time passes, something that creates a risk that AIs can become patent trolls. Second, writing the inventor's oath is a duty in both countries and it is commonly required to guarantee an inventor's identity and genuity. In the case of AI inventors, it will be problematic who can write this oath represented by AI. Therefore, the related legal regulations should be prepared.

6. Before asserting AI inventorship, the position taken recognized the current reality of its denial and asked "if AI inventorship is not recognized, who can be recognized as an inventor?" There are many natural and legal persons associated with AI inventions that could conceivably qualify and five candidate groups were analyzed separately to see if any did.

6-1. Software programmers can be seen as somewhat like parents or ancestors who created a natural person's brain. Parents are not recognized as inventors if a child invents something. Even if SW programmers directly participated in the invention process, they fall under the 'simple order for work' or 'simple assistant' category of the '2/7 Questions', as such, their inventorship is denied.

6-2. Data owners and data suppliers fall under the 'simple proposer' in the '2/7 Questions', so their inventorship is also denied.

6-3. Trainers and feedback suppliers fall under the 'simple assistants' category in the '2/7 Questions' and cannot be recognized as inventors.

6-4. The work of the owners of an AI system is very complex but it can be primarily divided into two categories: (1) Work as a manager; and/or (2) work as an investor. Managers provide only 'a simple order for work' in the '2/7 Questions' and investors cannot be recognized as having inventorship as someone who simply provided financial resources does not qualify.

6-5. Operators are the ones who lead the whole invention process and their claim to inventorship depends on how detailed their lead is. (1) If the operator's lead is very detailed, inventorship will be granted to the operators. (2) If it is not detailed, inventorship will be denied, as they are only a 'simple task director', provide a 'simple imaginary notion or fantasy', are a 'simple assistant' or 'simple tester' or provide only 'a simple working model' according to the '2/7 Questions'. The inventorship of operators should not be recognized, as the recent AI-generated inventions are beyond human expectation, which means their lead is not detailed.

6-6. Can the above five categories of candidates claim joint inventorship? To establish joint inventorship under both German and US law, each co-inventor must qualify as an inventor. Since inventorship is denied to individual candidate categories, as reviewed above, joint inventorship is also impossible.

7. Legal disputes arising from the advent of AI are entirely different from legal disputes that have arisen in the past. To effectively deal with them, it is necessary to give AI a separate legal status called 'E-Person' and to explore effective solutions in each relevant field, adjusting the scope of 'E-Person' rights and obligations in line with technological developments and social needs. Unlike humans, AI can process countless inventions 24 hours a day based on big data, a public good, therefore, the interests of many natural and corporate entities, such as investors, programmers and owners are linked to AI. We need to separate AI inventors from human inventors and separately manage their AI inventions.

8. Four perspectives for affirming AI inventorship were then researched.

8-1. Legal Perspective: AI inventorship is affirmed by applying the '2/7 Questions' to AI. The sole task of AI is processing input data according to the ML algorithm to derive the best result and a POSITA can directly implement these results "without extensive experimentation or additional inventive skill, or exercise of the inventive faculty". Moreover, the core idea for the invention came directly from AI and none of the natural persons around could not have predicted the results in advance. Therefore, the tasks performed by AI should be recognized as 'the core of the inventive process'. Besides, the "Flash of Genius" doctrine in the past has shown why confirming the mental status of inventors is impossible. Meanwhile the recent favorable rulings on AI inventorship in South Africa and Australia provide affirmation on AI inventorship.

8-2. Perspectives of patent theory: Patent theories are largely divided into two groups, (1) One that emphasizes the personal aspect of the economic benefit of the patent holder and (2) that which emphasizes the social aspect of promoting science and technology in society as a whole. This paper reviewed the Incentive Theory of Skinner, the Personhood Theory of Kant and Hegel, the Lockean Theory of Labor and the utilitarian theory. Each theory has both positive and negative aspects relating to support for AI inventorship. However, in particular, the utilitarian theory that emphasizes promoting science and technology in society can be seen as strongly supporting AI inventorship.

8-3. Legal historical perspective: AI is an object of rights akin to a computer. How can a mere object of rights be elevated to a subject thereof? From a legal-historical point of view, the following was analyzed: First, corporations are not natural persons but are treated with the same subjectivity as natural persons within a limited scope. The historical rise of these corporations has many positive aspects and helped inspire the notion of an 'E-Person' category for AIs. Simultaneously, the inventorship of corporations has historically been denied because the inventive act must be accompanied by creativity, which is only available to natural persons. Moreover, society has traditionally wanted to guarantee the honorary rights of natural persons, who are relatively weaker than corporations. First, the legal judgment based on the '2/7 Questions' to AI has already been made positively, second, the current situation contradicts the substantive truth that natural persons' names as inventors are erroneously put on the patent application to successfully acquire patent rights. Third, acknowledging AI inventorship makes AI inventions handle systematically as separate protection with the name of AI. It can protect natural and legal persons in the AI industry concerning liability for damages that AI inventions may occur in the future. Furthermore, it also offers strong protection to the victims.

8-4. Philosophical perspective: "Are things equal to humans" or "are other people the same as me"? These questions have been asked for thousands of years by philosophers. If AI can be assumed to be equal to humans, there will be no difficulty in affirming its inventorship. This paper searched for philosophical grounds to affirm AI inventorship based on Descartes, Husserl, Merleau-Ponty, Hylozoism, Baudrillard and Korea's Ho-Rak controversy.

9. Although solid grounds for the affirmation of AI inventorship exist with these four perspectives, current law continues to deny it. This is a dangerous situation in which status as an inventor is simply a formal expression rather than a substantive truth, which must be corrected.

10. This paper then specifically explored how AI inventorship can be implemented as legal policy.

10-1. A new category of legal personality called 'E-Person' needs to be created with a complex character mixing aspects attributed to both natural persons and legal persons. This should be dealt with in various ways according to its complex nature.

10-2. Is inventorship even necessary in future societies? Is it viable to have no inventor at all for inventions? This text considered it premature to leave the inventor's name blank and argued that it is better to write the name of the 'E-Person' as the inventor. First, current law has long established system based on the fact that the inventor's name is truthfully written. So, if the inventor's column was made vacant, a general revision of the entire patent system will be needed. Instead, modifying the patent system little by little with

AI inventorship in mind is a better option. Second, the source of the invention must be clearly identified with the indication of the inventor, so that the inventive activities of an AI and its affiliated company can be integrated from a social and economic perspective, such as via a robot tax.

10-3. Four situations were assessed for the availability of 'status as an inventor' and 'status as a patentee.' First, both statuses can be affirmed for natural persons under the current law. Second, both statuses are always denied for property under current law. Third, the status as an inventor is always denied but status as a patentee can be affirmed for legal persons under current law. Fourth, the status as an inventor can be affirmed but the status as a patent holder is always denied for 'E-Persons', as suggested by this paper. The reason why the latter's status as an inventor should be affirmed has already been detailed from the five above-mentioned perspectives and the reason why status as a patentee is always denied is because it is unnecessary for the current weak AI.

10-4. Going in this direction, where an AI has the status of inventor and other stakeholders (mainly corporations that own the AI) are awarded the status of patentee, is a similar structure to what is used for employee inventions. The AI Employee Invention Act should be enacted to find the balance of interests between 'E-Persons' and their corporate owners and stakeholders. While analyzing employee inventions in Germany and the US, especially on how they could be applied to AI inventorship, the following points were founded: (1) Inventions of weak AI will be in theory only recognized as employee inventions, not free inventions; (2) it is necessary to guarantee the employer's right to the invention so that it can provide a return on investment for the AI invention project; (3) it is a more natural approach for AI inventorship to apply the 'hired-to-invent' doctrine over the application of 'shop rights' according to US patent law. Through this doctrine, the relationship between AI and its owner is implicitly regarded as an employment relationship, affirming the inventorship of AI and at the same time guaranteeing an AI owner's patent rights; (4) under the German Patent Act, AI inventions are also closely related to the employer's business, so the owner's claims under the Employee Invention Act are fully allowed; (5) according to the German Employee Invention Law, employers have the right to choose between applying for patents or trade secrets for employee inventions. This has both positive and negative aspects but ultimately there is no real choice in reality because reverse engineering technology is becoming ever more sophisticated and the advantages accompanying acquiring patent rights are greater than those of trade secrets.

Bibliography

Abbott, Ryan: I Think, Therefore I Invent: Creative Computers and the Future of Patent Law. Boston College Law Review 57, no. 4 (2016): 1079.

Balganesh, Shyamkrishna: Foreseeability and Copyright Incentives. Harvard Law Review 122 (April 2009): 1569.

Barfield, Woodrow/*Pagallo*, Ugo (eds.): Research Handbook on the Law of Artificial Intelligence. Cheltenham, UK: Edward Elgar Publishing, 2018.

Barnett, Otto Raymond: The Flash of Genius Fallacy. Journal of the Patent Office Society 25, no. 11 (1943): 785–90.

Barrat, James: Our Final Invention: Artificial Intelligence and the End of the Human Era, 2013.

Baudrillard, Jean: Simulacra and Simulation. Translated by Sheila F. Glaser. Ann Arbor, Mich: University of Michigan Press, 1994.

Baudrillard, Jean: The Gulf War Did Not Take Place. Translated by Paul Patton. Sydney: Power Pubn Inc, 2012.

Benkard, Georg/*Bruchhausen*, Karl: Patentgesetz, Gebrauchsmustergesetz: Kurz-Kommentar. 8., neubearb. Aufl. Beck'sche Kurz-Kommentare. München: Beck, 1988.

Bhuta, Nehal/*Beck*, Susanne/*Geis*, Robin/*Liu*, Hin-yan/*Kreis*, Claus: Autonomous Weapons Systems: Law, Ethics, Policy. Cambridge University Press, 2016.

Blok, Peter: The Inventor's New Tool: Artificial Intelligence – How Does It Fit in the European Patent System? European Intellectual Property Review 39, no. 2 (2017): 69–73.

Bostrom, Nick: Superintelligence: Paths, Dangers, Strategies. Oxford University Press, 2014.

Bui, Hung H.: Navigating the Leahy-Smith America Invents Act Including Effective Dates for Patent Reform An Overview of Patent Reform Act of 2011. Journal of the Patent and Trademark Office Society 93, no. 4 (2011): 441–75.

Buning, Madeleine de Cock: Artificial Intelligence and the Creative Industry: New Challenges for the EU Paradigm for Art and Technology by Autonomous Creation. Research Handbook on the Law of Artificial Intelligence, December 28, 2018, 511–35.

Busse, Rudolf/*Keukenschrijver* Alfred (eds.): Patentgesetz: Kommentar (§ 37 Rn. 4). 9th ed. De Gruyter, 2020.

Calo, Ryan/*Froomkin*, A. Michael/*Kerr*, Ian (eds.): Robot Law. Edward Elgar Publishing, 2016.

Casey-Maslen, Stuart/*Homayounnejad*, Maziar/*Stauffer*, Hilary/*Weizmann*, Nathalie (eds.): Drones and Other Unmanned Weapons Systems under International Law. International Humanitarian Law Series. Leiden/Boston: Brill Nijhoff, 2018.

Cheesman, Willard L.: The Role of Laboratory Notebooks in Patent Matters. Journal of the Patent Office Society 30, no. 6 (1948): 438–49.

Chesterman, Simon: We, the Robots?: Regulating Artificial Intelligence and the Limits of the Law. Cambridge University Press, 2021.

Chomsky, Noam: Reflections on Language. Douglas: Pantheon, 1975.

Chopra, Samir/*White*, Laurence F.: A Legal Theory for Autonomous Artificial Agents. Ann Arbor: University of Michigan Press, 2011.

Clifford, Ralph D.: Intellectual Property in the Era of the Creative Computer Program: Will the True Creator Please Stand Up. Tulane Law Review 71 (1996): 1675.

Corrales, Marcelo/*Fenwick*, Mark/*Forgó*, Nikolaus (eds.): Robotics, AI and the Future of Law. Springer, 2018.

Crotti, Alfred F.: The Allgemeine Erfindungsgedanke in the German Patent. Journal of the Patent Office Society 39, no. 7 (1957): 477–501.

Cubert, Jeremy A./*Bone*, Richard G. A.: The Law of Intellectual Property Created by Artificial Intelligence. Research Handbook on the Law of Artificial Intelligence, December 28, 2018, 411–27.

Cudworth, Ralph: The True Intellectual System of the Universe: The First Part, 1678. https://www.cambridge-platonism.divinity.cam.ac.uk/view/texts/diplomatic/Cudworth1678-excerpt005.

Dodge, Samuel/*Karam*, Lina: A Study and Comparison of Human and Deep Learning Recognition Performance under Visual Distortions, 1–7, 2017.

Eberle, Edward J.: Human Dignity, Privacy, and Personality in German and American Constitutional Law. Utah Law Review 1997, no. 4 (1997): 963–1056.

Eisenmann, Hartmut/*Jautz*, Ulrich: Grundriss Gewerblicher Rechtsschutz und Urheberrecht: mit 55 Fällen und Lösungen. 9., neu bearb. Aufl. Start ins Rechtsgebiets: Zivilrecht. Heidelberg: C.F. Müller, 2012.

Evans, Edward Payson: The Criminal Prosecution and Capital Punishment of Animals. New York: E.P. Dutton, 1906.

Ferrucci, David/*Brown*, Eric/*Chu-Carroll*, Jennifer/*Fan*, James/*Gondek*, David/*Kalyanpur*, Aditya A./*Lally*, Adam et al.: Building Watson: An Overview of the DeepQA Project. AI Magazine 31, no. 3 (July 28, 2010): 59–79.

Fisher, R. A.: The Use of Multiple Measurements in Taxonomic Problems. Annals of Eugenics 7, no. 2 (1936): 179–88.

Fisher, William: Theories of Intellectual Property. Originally Published in Stephen R. Munzer, Ed., New Essays in the Legal and Political Theory of Property (Cambridge University Press), 2001.

Fraser, Erica: Computers as Inventors – Legal and Policy Implications of Artificial Intelligence on Patent Law. SCRIPTed 13, no. 3 (December 2016): 305.

Garfinkle, David U.: Simulation, A-Signification and Embodied Semiotics in I, Robot. Athens Journal of Mass Media and Communications 5, no. 4 (October 7, 2019): 253–74.

Goodell, William: The American Slave Code in Theory and Practice: Its Distincive Features Shown by Statutes, Judicial Decisions, and Illustrative Facts. New York: American and foreign anti-slavery society, 1853.

Goodfellow, Ian/*Bengio*, Yoshua/*Courville*, Aaron: Deep Learning. MIT Press, 2016.

Greipl, Erich/*Täger* Uwe/*Grefermann*, Klaus: Wettbewerbswirkungen der unternehmerischen Patent- und Lizenzpolitik: unter besonderer Berücksichtigung kleiner und mittlerer Unternehmen. 1st ed. Berlin: Duncker & Humblot, 1982.

Grier, David Alan: When Computers Were Human. Princeton University Press, 2005.

Gunkel, David J.: Robot Rights. The MIT Press, 2018.

Hallevy, Gabriel: Liability for Crimes Involving Artificial Intelligence Systems. Springer Cham, 2014.

Hallevy, Gabriel: When Robots Kill: Artificial Intelligence under Criminal Law. Boston: Northeastern University Press, 2013.

Heintschel von Heinegg, Wolff/*Frau*, Robert/*Singer*, Tassilo (eds.): Dehumanization of Warfare: Legal Implications of New Weapon Technologies. 1st ed. Springer Cham, 2018.

Hinton, Geoffrey E./*Osindero*, Simon/*Teh*, Yee-Whye: A Fast Learning Algorithm for Deep Belief Nets. Neural Computation 18, no. 7 (July 2006): 1527–54.

Holland, John H.: Adaptation in Natural and Artificial Systems: An Introductory Analysis with Applications to Biology, Control, and Artificial Intelligence. MIT Press, 1992.

Hornby, Greg/*Globus*, Al/*Linden*, Derek/*Lohn*, Jason: Automated Antenna Design with Evolutionary Algorithms. Collection of Technical Papers – Space 2006 Conference 1 (September 19, 2006).

Husserl, Edmund: Cartesian Meditations: An Introduction to Phenomenology. Translated by Dorion Cairns. 7th ed. The Hague: Martinus Nijhoff Publishers, 1960.

Kagan, Brett J./*Kitchen*, Andy C./*Tran*, Nhi T./*Habibollahi*, Forough/*Khajehnejad*, Moein/*Parker*, Bradyn J./*Bhat*, Anjali/*Rollo*, Ben/*Razi*, Adeel/*Friston*, Karl J.: In Vitro Neurons Learn and Exhibit Sentience When Embodied in a Simulated Game-World. Neuron 110, no. 23 (December 7, 2022): 3952–3969.e8.

Kaplan, Jerry: Humans Need Not Apply: A Guide to Wealth and Work in the Age of Artificial Intelligence. New Haven: Yale University Press, 2015.

Kaufmann, Arthur: Vergleichende Rechtsphilosophies: am Beispiel der klassischen chinesischen und der klassischen abendländischen Rechtskultur. Festschrift für Werner Lorenz zum siebzigsten Geburtstag, 1991, 635–48.

Kim, Richard T./Philosophy Documentation Center: Human Nature and Animal Nature: The Horak Debate and Its Philosophical Significance. International Philosophical Quarterly 55, no. 4 (2015): 437–56.

Kitagawa, Zentarō: The Identity of German and Japanese Civil Law in Comparative Perspectives. Berlin: De Gruyter, 2007.

Kop, Mauritz: AI & Intellectual Property: Towards an Articulated Public Domain. Texas Intellectual Property Law Journal 28 (2020): 297–341.

Koza, John R.: Human-Competitive Results Produced by Genetic Programming. Genetic Programming and Evolvable Machines 11, no. 3 (September 1, 2010): 251–84.

Koza, John R./*Al-Sakran*, Sameer H./*Jones*, Lee W.: Automated Re-Invention of Six Patented Optical Lens Systems Using Genetic Programming. In Proceedings of the 7th Annual Conference on Genetic and Evolutionary Computation, 1953–60. GECCO '05. New York: Association for Computing Machinery, 2005.

Kurzweil, Ray: The Age of Spiritual Machines: When Computers Exceed Human Intelligence. New York: Penguin Books, 2000.

LeCun, Y./*Boser*, B./*Denker*, J. S./*Henderson*, D./*Howard*, R. E./*Hubbard*, W./*Jackel*, L. D.: Backpropagation Applied to Handwritten Zip Code Recognition. Neural Computation 1, no. 4 (December 1989): 541–51.

LeCun, Y./*Bottou*, L./*Bengio*, Y./*Haffner*, P.: Gradient-Based Learning Applied to Document Recognition. IEEE 86, no. 11 (November 1998): 2278–2324.

Lee, Kyoeng-Gu (이경구): 조선, 철학의 왕국: 호락논쟁 이야기 [Chosun, the Kingdom of Philosophy: The Story of the Horak Debate]. Seoul: Pureun Yoeksa (푸른역사), 2018.

Leveringhaus, Alex: Ethics and Autonomous Weapons. Palgrave Macmillan UK, 2015.

Lin, Patrick/*Abney*, Keith/*Jenkins*, Ryan (eds.): Robot Ethics 2.0: From Autonomous Cars to Artificial Intelligence. 1st ed. New York: Oxford University Press, 2017.

Lohn, Jason D./*Hornby*, Gregory S./*Linden*, Derek S.: An Evolved Antenna for Deployment on Nasa's Space Technology 5 Mission. In Genetic Programming Theory and Practice II, edited by Una-May O'Reilly, Tina Yu, Rick Riolo, and Bill Worzel, 301–15. Genetic Programming. Boston, MA: Springer US, 2005.

Looi, Lai-Meng/*Chua*, Kaw-Bing: Lessons from the Nipah Virus Outbreak in Malaysia. The Malaysian Journal of Pathology 29, no. 2 (December 2007): 63–67.

Lüdecke, Wolfgang: Erfindungsgemeinschaften: Rechte und Pflichten des Miterfinders. Berlin: de Gruyter, 1962.

Maine, Henry James Sumner: Village-Communities in the East and West: Six Lectures Delivered at Oxford. 4th ed. London: Murray, 1881.

Maslow, Abraham: A Theory of Human Motivation. Psychological Review 50 (1943): 370–96.

Maslow, Abraham: The Farther Reaches of Human Nature. Penguin, 1993.

Mcculloch, Warren S./*Pitts*, Walter: A Logical Calculus of the Ideas Immanent in Nervous Activity. Bulletin of Mathematical Biology 52 (1990): 99–115.

Merleau-Ponty, Maurice: Phenomenology of Perception. Translated by Colin Smith. London/New York: Routledge, 2002.

Minsky, Marvin/*Papert*, Seymour: Perceptrons; an Introduction to Computational Geometry. MIT Press, 1969.

Mitchell, Melanie: An Introduction to Genetic Algorithms. Cambridge, MA: The MIT Press, 1998.

Mitchell, Tom M.: Machine Learning. McGraw-Hill, 1997.

Nilsson, Nils J.: Quest for Artificial Intelligence: A History of Ideas and Achievements. New York: Cambridge University Press, 2009.

Oliar, Dotan: Making Sense of the Intellectual Property Clause: Promotion of Progress as a Limitation on Congress's Intellectual Property Power. Georgetown Law Journal 94 (2006): 1771–1845.

Parker, Jim/*Jaeger*, Shannon: Learning in Artificial Intelligence: Does Bloom's Taxonomy Apply? SSRN Electronic Journal, 2016.

Plato: Republic: Book 7, Section 517b. Translated by Paul Shorey. Loeb Classical Library, 1930. http://data.perseus.org/citations/urn:cts:greekLit:tlg0059.tlg030.perseus-eng1:7.517b.

Radbruch, Gustav: Rechtsphilosophie. 3., ganz neu bearbeitete und stark vermehrte Auflage. Leipzig: Quelle & Meyer, 1932.

Ravid, Shlomit Yanisky/*Liu*, Xiaoqiong (Jackie): When Artificial Intelligence Systems Produce Inventions: An Alternative Model for Patent Law at the 3A Era. Cardozo Law Review 39 (2017): 2215.

Rosen, Matt: The Givenness of Other People: On Singularity and Empathy in Husserl. Human Studies 44 (May 25, 2021): 333–50.

Rosenblatt, F.: The Perceptron: A Probabilistic Model for Information Storage and Organization in the Brain. Psychological Review 65, no. 6 (1958): 386–408.

Rumelhart, David E./*Hinton*, Geoffrey E./*Williams*, Ronald J.: Learning Representations by Back-Propagating Errors. Nature 323, no. 6088 (October 1986): 533–36.

Russell, Stuart Jonathan/*Norvig*, Peter: Artificial Intelligence: A Modern Approach. 4th ed. Hoboken: Pearson, 2021.

Samore, William: Artificial Intelligence and the Patent System: Can a New Tool Render a Once Patentable Idea Obvious? Syracuse Journal of Science & Technology Law 29, Fall (2013): 113.

Samuel, Arthur Lee: Some Studies in Machine Learning Using the Game of Checkers. IBM Journal of Research and Development 3, no. 3 (July 1959): 210–29.

Schacter, Daniel L.: The Seven Sins of Memory: How the Mind Forgets and Remembers. Houghton Mifflin, 2001.

Scheffler, Dietrich: Das deutsche Patentsystem und die mittelständische Industrie: eine theoretische und empirische Untersuchung. Universität Stuttgart, 1986.

Schlesinger, Rudolf B.: Research on the General Principles of Law Recognized by Civilized Nations. The American Journal of International Law 51, no. 4 (1957): 734–53.

Schulte, Rainer (ed.): Patentgesetz Mit Europäischem Patentübereinkommen: Kommentar (§ 6 Rn. 18), 11th ed. Carl Heymanns Verlag, 2021.

Schuster, W. Michael: Artificial Intelligence and Patent Ownership. Washington and Lee Law Review 75, no. 4 (2018): 1945.

Schwab, Klaus: The Fourth Industrial Revolution: What It Means and How to Respond. Foreign Affairs, December 12, 2015.

Schwartz, David L./*Rogers*, Max: Inventorless Inventions? The Constitutional Conundrum of AI-Produced Inventions. Harvard Journal of Law & Technology 35, no. 2 (2022): 531–79.

Searle, John R.: Minds, Brains, and Programs. The Behavioral and Brain Sciences 3 (1980): 417–57.

Sellers, William Douglas: The Flash of Genius Doctrine Approaches the Patent Office. Journal of the Patent Office Society 26, no. 4 (1944): 275–80.

Sherkow, Jacob S.: Patent Infringement as Criminal Conduct. Michigan Telecommunications and Technology Law Review 19, no. 1 (2012): 42.

Sinoj, Antony/*Tramboo*, Ishfaq Ahmad: Hyperreality in Media and Literature: An Overview of Jean Baudrillard's Simulacra and Simulation. European Journal of Molecular & Clinical Medicine 7, no. 10 (2020).

Steinberger, Helmut: Historic Influences of American Constitutionalism upon German Constitutional Development: Federalism and Judicial Review. Columbia Journal of Transnational Law 36, no. 1 & 2 (1998): 189–208.

Stortnik (commentator for § 37). Patentrechtskommentar: PatG, GebrMG, IntPatÜG, PCT Und EPÜ Mit Nebenvorschriften (PatG § 37 Rn. 2 f.). Edited by Uwe Fitzner, Raimund Lutz, and Theo Bodewig. 4th ed. Vahlen, 2012.

Swain, Ambika: Consideration of Animals as Legal Person. Indian Journal of Integrated Research in Law 3, no. 4 (2023).

Tarazano, Larry: Can Recipes Be Patented? Inventors Eye 4, no. 3 (June 2013).

Thaler, Stephen: Creativity Machine® Paradigm. In Encyclopedia of Creativity, Invention, Innovation and Entrepreneurship, edited by Elias G. Carayannis, 447–56. New York: Springer, 2013.

Turing, Alan M.: Computing Machinery and Intelligence. Mind 59, no. 236 (October 1950): 433–60.

Tylor, Edward Burnett: Primitive Culture. Vol. 1. London: John Murray, 1871.

Wacks, Raymond: Law: A Very Short Introduction. 2nd ed. Oxford: Oxford University Press, 2015.

Walterscheid, Edward C.: The Early Evolution of the United States Patent Law: Antecedents (Part 1). Journal of the Patent and Trademark Office Society 76, no. 9 (September 1994): 697–715.

Weaver, John Frank: Robots Are People Too: How Siri, Google Car, and Artificial Intelligence Will Force Us to Change Our Laws. 1st edition. Santa Barbara, California: Praeger, 2013.

Weiser, Mark: The Computer for the 21st Century. Scientific American 265, no. 3 (1991): 94–105.

Wiebe, Andreas: Know-how-Schutz von Computersoftwares: eine rechtsvergleichende Untersuchung der wettbewerbsrechtlichen Schutzmöglichkeiten in Deutschland und den U.S.A. Vol. 2. Schriftenreihe Recht der Computerpraxis 2. München: Beck, 1993.

Wigmore, John Henry: A Panorama of the World's Legal Systems. Saint Paul: West Publ. Co., 1928.

Young, Tom: Devamanyu Hazarika, Soujanya Poria, and Erik Cambria. Recent Trends in Deep Learning Based Natural Language Processing. IEEE Computational Intelligence Magazine 13, no. 3 (2018): 55–75.

Zweigert, Konrad (ed.): International Encylopedia of Comparative Law. Springer Netherlands, 1981.

Zweigert, Konrad: Zur Lehre von den Rechtskreisen. XXth century comparative and conflicts law, 1961, 42.

Zweigert, Konrad/*Kötz*, Hein: Einführung in die Rechtsvergleichung: Auf dem Gebiete des Privatrechts. 3., neubearbeitete Auflage. Mohr Siebeck, 1996.

Other Materials

Abbott, Ryan: The Artificial Inventor Project. Accessed September 20, 2022. https://artificialinventor.com/.

Bently, Lionel/*Sherman*, Brad/*Borges Barbosa*, Denis/*Basheer*, Shamnad/*Visser*, Coenraad/*Gold*, Richard/*Grau-Kuntz*, Karin/*Purohit*, Shashwat/*Reddy*, Prashant/*Joly*, Yann: Exclusions from Patentability and Exceptions and Limitations to Patentees' Rights. WIPO Standing Committee on the Law of Patents, 2011. https://www.wipo.int/edocs/mdocs/scp/en/scp_16/scp_16_ref_scp_15_3-annex1.pdf.

Dartmouth: Artificial Intelligence Coined at Dartmouth. Accessed September 28, 2023. https://home.dartmouth.edu/about/artificial-intelligence-ai-coined-dartmouth.

Decision on Petition (In re Application of Application No.: 16/524,350) (United States Patent and Trademark Office (USPTO) 2020).

European Commission: Guidance on the Regulation on a Framework for the Free Flow of Non-Personal Data in the European Union, May 29, 2019. https://eur-lex.europa.eu/legal-content/EN/TXT/?uri=COM:2019:250:FIN.

European Parliament: Civil Law Rules on Robotics. Strasbourg, February 16, 2017. https://www.europarl.europa.eu/doceo/document/TA-8-2017-0051_EN.html.

European Parliament: REPORT with Recommendations to the Commission on Civil Law Rules on Robotics, January 27, 2017. https://www.europarl.europa.eu/doceo/document/A-8-2017-0005_EN.html.

European Patent Office: European Companies and Inventors File More Patent Applications in 2018. European Patent Office. Accessed July 2, 2022. https://www.epo.org/news-events/press/releases/archive/2019/20190312.html.

European Patent Office: Grounds for the Decision on EP 18 275 163, January 27, 2020. https://register.epo.org/application?showPdfPage=1&documentId=E4B63SD62191498&appnumber=EP18275163&proc=.

European Patent Office: Grounds for the Decision on EP 18 275 174, January 27, 2020. https://register.epo.org/application?showPdfPage=1&documentId=E4B63OBI2076498&appnumber=EP18275174&proc=.

European Patent Office: The Tegernsee Process. Accessed June 28, 2022. https://www.epo.org/law-practice/harmonisation/tegernsee-process.html.

Five IP Offices: About IP5 Co-Operation. Accessed February 17, 2020. https://www.fiveipoffices.org/about.

Genetic Programming Inc.: Genetic Programming Is an Automated Invention Machine, December 30, 2003. https://www.genetic-programming.com/inventionmachine.html.

Genetic Programming Inc.: Seven Differences Between Genetic Programming and Other Approaches to Machine Learning and Artificial Intelligence, August 27, 2003. https://www.genetic-programming.com/sevendiffs.html.

Google DeepMind: AlphaGo – The Challenge Match. Accessed June 22, 2023. https://www.deepmind.com/research/highlighted-research/alphago/the-challenge-match.

ImageNet: ImageNet Large Scale Visual Recognition Challenge (ILSVRC). Accessed June 23, 2023. https://image-net.org/challenges/LSVRC/index.php.

Imagination Engines Incorporated: DABUS Described. Accessed August 3, 2023. https://www.imagination-engines.com/dabus.html.

Imagination Engines Incorporated: IEI Patents. Accessed October 17, 2023. https://www.imagination-engines.com/patents.html.

Imagination Engines Incorporated: IEI's Patented Creativity Machine® Paradigm. Accessed August 12, 2019. http://imagination-engines.com/iei_cm.php.

Imagination Engines Incorporated: Imagination Engines Incorporated. Accessed August 12, 2019. http://www.imagination-engines.com/.

Nevejans, Nathalie: European Civil Law Rules In Robotics. European Parliament, Policy Department C: Citizens' Rights and Constitutional Affairs, October 2016. https://www.europarl.europa.eu/RegData/etudes/STUD/2016/571379/IPOL_STU(2016)571379_EN.pdf.

Oliar, Dotan: The Origins and Meaning of the Intellectual Property Clause, 2004. https://cyber.harvard.edu/ip/oliar_ipclause.pdf.

Open Letter to the European Commission, 2018. https://robotics-openletter.eu/.

Report of the Swiss Group: Inventorship of Inventions Made Using Artificial Intelligence [Q 272]. AIPPI, 2020. https://aippi.soutron.net/Portal/Default/en-GB/RecordView/Index/3832.

Reusch, Ute: Translation provided by Ute Reusch in cooperation with the Language Service of the German Patent and Trade Mark Office. "Patent Act (Translation of 'Patentgesetz')." Accessed July 18, 2023. https://www.gesetze-im-internet.de/englisch_patg/englisch_patg.html.

Sun, Lei: ResNet on Tiny ImageNet, 2017. https://api.semanticscholar.org/CorpusID:196590979.

Thaler, Stephen: Complaint for Declaratory and Injunctive Relief in the United States District Court for the Eastern District of Virginia, 2020. https://artificialinventor.com/wp-content/uploads/2020/09/Complaint.pdf.

Thaler, Stephen: Device and method for the autonomous bootstrapping of unified sentience. United States US 2015/0379394 A1, filed January 2, 2015, and issued December 31, 2015.

Thaler, Stephen: Device for the Autonomous Bootstrapping of Useful Information. US 7,454,388 B2, filed May 8, 2006, and issued November 18, 2008.

Thaler, Stephen: Device for the Autonomous Generation of Useful Information. United States US 5,659,666, filed October 13, 1994, and issued August 19, 1997.

US Copyright Office: Compendium of U.S. Copyright Office Practices. 3rd ed., 2014. https://www.copyright.gov/comp3/docs/compendium.pdf.

WIPO: AI and Intellectual Property: WIPO Call for Submissions (Impact of AI on IP Policy). WIPO, 2019. https://www.wipo.int/export/sites/www/about-ip/en/artificial_intelligence/call_for_comments/wipo_ai_ip_call_for_submissions.pdf.

WIPO: Incentive Structure and Inventorship for AI. WIPO Conversation on Intellectual Property and Artificial Intelligence, 2021. https://www.wipo.int/export/sites/www/about-ip/en/artificial_intelligence/call_for_comments/pdf/ind_borges.pdf.

WIPO: Certain Aspects of National/Regional Patent Laws – Grace Period. WIPO, June 2022. https://www.wipo.int/export/sites/www/scp/en/national_laws/grace_period.pdf.

WIPO: IP and Frontier Technologies – Artificial Intelligence and Intellectual Property. Accessed December 22, 2022. https://www.wipo.int/about-ip/en/frontier_technologies/ai_and_ip.html.

WIPO: The WIPO Conversation on Intellectual Property and Artificial Intelligence. WIPO. Accessed June 22, 2025. https://www.wipo.int/about-ip/en/artificial_intelligence/conversation.html.

Index